KU-163-576

NATIONS OF THE MODERN WORLD

ARGENTINA   H. S. Ferns
Professor of Political Science,
University of Birmingham

AUSTRALIA   O. H. K. Spate
Director, Research School of Pacific Studies,
Australian National University, Canberra

AUSTRIA   Karl R. Stadler
Professor of Modern and Contemporary History,
University of Linz

BELGIUM   Vernon Mallinson
Professor of Comparative Education,
University of Reading

BURMA   F. S. V. Donnison
Formerly Chief Secretary to the Government of Burma
Historian, Cabinet Office, Historical Section, 1949–66

CEYLON   S. A. Pakeman
Formerly Professor of Modern History,
Ceylon University College

CYPRUS   H. D. Purcell
Professor of English
University of Libya, Benghazi

DENMARK   W. Glyn Jones
Reader in Danish, University College London

MODERN EGYPT   Tom Little
Managing Director and General Manager of
Regional News Services (Middle East), Ltd, London

ENGLAND   John Bowle
A Portrait   *Professor of Political Theory, Collège d'Europe,*
Bruges

FINLAND   W. R. Mead
Professor of Geography, University College London

EAST GERMANY	David Childs *Lecturer in Politics, University of Nottingham*
WEST GERMANY	Michael Balfour *Reader in European History, University of East Anglia*
MODERN GREECE	John Campbell *Fellow of St Antony's College, Oxford* Philip Sherrard *Lecturer in the History of the Orthodox Church, King's College, London*
MODERN INDIA	Sir Percival Griffiths *President India, Pakistan and Burma Association*
MODERN IRAN	Peter Avery *Lecturer in Persian and Fellow of King's College, Cambridge*
ITALY	Muriel Grindrod *Formerly Editor of* International Affairs *and* The World Today *Assistant Editor* The Annual Register
KENYA	A. Marshall MacPhee *Formerly Managing Editor with the* East African Standard *Group*
LIBYA	John Wright *Formerly of the* Sunday Ghibli, *Tripoli*
MALAYSIA	J. M. Gullick *Formerly of the Malayan Civil Service*
MOROCCO	Mark I. Cohen *Director of Taxation, American Express* Lorna Hahn *Professor of African Studies, American University*
NEW ZEALAND	James W. Rowe *Director of New Zealand Institute of Economic Research* Margaret A. Rowe *Tutor in English at Victoria University, Wellington*

NIGERIA	Sir Rex Niven
	Administrative Service of Nigeria, 1921–54 *Member, President and Speaker of Northern House of Assembly, 1947–59*
PAKISTAN	Ian Stephens
	Formerly Editor of The Statesman *Calcutta and Delhi, 1942–51* *Fellow, King's College, Cambridge, 1952–58*
PERU	Sir Robert Marett
	H.M. Ambassador in Lima, 1963–67
POLAND	Václav L. Beneš
	Professor of Political Science, Indiana University
	Norman J. G. Pounds
	Professor of History and Geography, Indiana University
SOUTH AFRICA	John Cope
	Formerly Editor-in-Chief of The Forum *and South Africa Correspondent of* The Guardian
THE SOVIET UNION	Elisabeth Koutaissoff
	Professor of Russian, Victoria University, Wellington
SPAIN	George Hills
	Formerly Correspondent and Spanish Programme Organiser, British Broadcasting Corporation
SUDAN REPUBLIC	K. D. D. Henderson
	Formerly of the Sudan Political Service and Governor of Darfur Province, 1949–53
TURKEY	Geoffrey Lewis
	Senior Lecturer in Islamic Studies, Oxford
YUGOSLAVIA	Stevan K. Pavlowitch
	Lecturer in Balkan History, University of Southampton

NATIONS OF THE MODERN WORLD

EAST GERMANY

EAST GERMANY

By

DAVID CHILDS

PRAEGER PUBLISHERS

New York · Washington

BOOKS THAT MATTER
Published in the United States of America in 1969
by Praeger Publishers, Inc.
111 Fourth Avenue, New York, N.Y. 10003

Second printing 1971

© 1969 by David Childs

All rights reserved

Library of Congress Catalog Card Number: 73-76976

Printed in Great Britain

Preface

ANY BOOK on East Germany is something of a hot potato for Germans. I will therefore refrain from naming the many Germans in both parts of the country who have given me the benefit of their views or provided materials for this manuscript. I thank them all and hope they will not be too disappointed with the result.

Dr Alfred Zauberman of the London School of Economics and Political Science gave me his valuable and expert comments on Chapter 6 for which I am very grateful. Mrs Margaret Cornell, editor of *The World Today*, and Mr Thomas Barman, formerly BBC Diplomatic Correspondent, made many helpful and constructive comments on Chapter 12. They have my sincere thanks. My thanks are also due to the Rev. Paul Oestreicher of the British Council of Churches, who did not read any part of this manuscript, but who, at very short notice, agreed to discuss the position of the Churches in East Germany.

Of my colleagues at Nottingham University I particularly want to thank Colonel Robert L. Frazier (U.S. Army retired) of the History Department who read Chapter 11 and gave me the benefits of his years of experience in Germany and elsewhere. I am also indebted to John W. Morley of the Department of Industrial Economics, who saved me from certain pitfalls with Chapter 7. Professor Richard Pear, my boss, head of the Department of Politics, also earns my gratitude. Although he has had no direct influence on this work, his friendly and kindly manner help to create the kind of atmosphere conducive to writing and research. I am equally grateful to Mr R. Innes of the Derby and District Colleges of Art and Technology, formerly of Berlin, and a frequent visitor to Eastern Europe, who gave me his views on the manuscript as a whole. Finally, I must thank my wife, Monir, for putting up with many evenings of loneliness punctuated only by the noise of my typewriter.

Let me emphasize the obvious—that none of these kind people is responsible for any of the errors great or small which doubtless appear, or indeed for any of the opinions expressed.

Nottingham   DAVID CHILDS
February 1969

Contents

List of Illustrations

Map

Acknowledgements

ACKNOWLEDGEMENT for kind permission to reproduce illustrations is made to the following to whom the copyright of the illustrations belongs :

Associated Press Ltd : 2
Camera Press Ltd : 18
Lex Hornsby and Partners London : 15a, 15b, 16
Heinz Kruger, Berlin : 3, 23
Zentralbild, Berlin : 1, 4, 5, 7, 8, 9, 10, 11, 12, 13, 14, 17, 19, 20, 21, 22

Acknowledgement is also made to George Allen and Unwin Ltd for permission to quote extracts from *The East German Army* by Thomas M. Forster.

Abbreviations

CDU	*Christlich-Demokratische Union*
DBD	*Demokratische Bauernpartei Deutschlands*
DDR	*Deutsche Demokratische Republik*
DFD	*Demokratischer Frauenbund Deutschlands*
FDGB	*Freier Deutscher Gewerkschaftsbund*
FDJ	*Freie Deutsche Jugend*
GST	*Gesellschaft für Sport und Technik*
KB	*Kulturbund*
KVP	*Kasernierte Volkspolizei*
LDPD	*Liberaldemokratische Partei Deutschlands*
LPG	*Landwirtschaftliche Produktionsgenossenschaft*
MTS	*Maschinen-Traktoren-Station*
NDPD	*Nationaldemokratische Partei Deutschlands*
NöS	*Neues ökonomisches System*
NVA	*Nationale Volksarmee*
PB	*Politbüro*
SED	*Sozialistische Einheitspartei Deutschlands*
SSD	*Staatssicherheitsdienst*
VdgB	*Vereinigung der gegenseitigen Bauernhilfe*
VEB	*Volkseigener Betrieb*
VVB	*Vereinigung volkseigener Betriebe*
ZK	*Zentralkomitee*
TKO	*Technische Kontrollorganisation*

Other Abbreviations:

CPSU	*Communist Party of Soviet Union*
FDP	*Freie Demokratische Partei*
NSDAP	*Nationalsozialistische Deutsche Arbeiterpartei* (Nazis)
SAP	*Sozialistische Arbeiterpartei*
SPD	*Sozialdemokratische Partei Deutschlands*
KgU	*Kampfgruppe gegen die Unmenschlichkeit*

Introduction

THIS BOOK attempts to outline for the English-speaking reader the main aspects of life and politics in a little-known part of Europe, the German Democratic Republic (DDR) or, as we commonly call it, East Germany. Some of it is based on articles written for specialist journals between 1965 and 1968. Most of it, however, was put on paper during the Czech crisis of May–December 1968. That crisis brought home to the writer once again the need for such a volume. The East German leaders were rightly said to be even more concerned than most Communist leaders about developments in Prague. This prompted discussions on conditions in the DDR and an otherwise serious television programme managed only a few halting sentences over some tired, stock film of the Berlin Wall. The import of these sentences was that the East German leaders were still unashamed Stalinists and that life beyond the Wall was still pretty grim. Yet on 11 March 1968 Chancellor Kiesinger of West Germany told his people that the East Germans

> Had to contend with more difficult conditions than we did in building up their economy, and that they are therefore quite rightly proud of this achievement as well as of the success which they have had in the field of science and technology, culture and sport.
>
> We are glad that the economic situation in the other part of Germany continued to improve last year. Commodity production increased by nearly 7 per cent; exports rose by 8 per cent; and the turnover in the retail trade rose by 4 per cent.
>
> As a result, the standard of living has continued to grow.

Herr Willy Brandt, leader of the German Social Democratic Party and later Foreign Minister of the Federal Republic, told his party's congress in 1966 that East Germany could 'be called a colonial territory of the Soviet Union [but] its progress from the status of a satellite towards that of a partner is unmistakable'.

If this book has a 'thesis' it is neither that the rulers of East

15

2 * *

Germany are misunderstood, kindly, 'liberals', nor is it that they are hard-hearted, orthodox, Stalinists. It is that the DDR, its politics, and society, are a good deal more complicated than most people in the West imagine. For instance, for all its alleged Stalinism the East German revolution has devoured few of its children, far fewer than the other East European régimes did during the purges of 1948–53. Again, the DDR, like Czechoslovakia, initiated economic reforms considerably wider in scope than those attempted in the Soviet Union. As the *Wall Street Journal* (4 October 1965) recorded : 'East Germany leads the way in Red scramble for reform'. On the other hand, it is perfectly true that unlike Yugoslav institutions, the massive, formally democratic, popular bodies of the German Democratic Republic, still operate as though the age of the human robot had arrived. Yet in this land of unnational and wholly artificial unanimity, the people get a far from Stalinist view of, for example, Britain. In fact, the average East German is likely to have a better and more realistic picture of the United Kingdom than Britons have of the DDR. And as far as freedom of religion is concerned, Christians in East Germany are probably better off than any others in Eastern Europe. The middle classes too, in recent years, have been better placed than their colleagues were in Czechoslovakia under the 'conservative' régime of President Novotny. In social welfare, and levels of personal consumption, though standards are high, East Germany's progress has not been all that remarkable considering German traditions. The DDR's performance in housing, which may surprise some Anglo-Saxons who have been on conducted tours of the country, has been poor. In education, though not in intellectual life, on the other hand, remarkable developments have taken place. This is equally true of sport.

More than most 'People's Democracies' the DDR reflects the pattern of the Soviet Union in recent years—faltering steps towards greater material well-being and towards a more relaxed society, coupled with dread lest the brakes be taken off too quickly. In East Germany there was a general 'thawing out' starting in 1962, gaining momentum at the VI SED Congress in 1963, and drawing to a close at the eleventh plenum of the Central Committee of the SED at the end of 1965. Since then there has been a tightening-up especially in intellectual life following a similar trend in the Soviet Union.

But East Germany is not the USSR. It has its own 'personality' and peculiar problems. It was born of foreign occupation rather than domestic revolution and many of its citizens still feel the pull of the

other German state, not just because relatives live there but because
it is the rich and powerful relation enjoying greater international
prestige. Things are changing. By the time this volume is in print the
German Democratic Republic will be just about celebrating its
20th anniversary which falls in October 1969. It has lasted longer
than either the Weimar republic or Hitler's Reich. By 1970 East
Germans will be bound by a common experience of twenty-five
years—a period as long as the two earlier régimes combined! This
common experience must affect the consciousness of the East Germans and their attitudes to the DDR and the Federal Republic
alike. A noted American observer of the East German scene,
Professor Jean Edward Smith, described the progress in the following way:

> As years pass, the bonds of friendship fade; the ties of family
> ebb, and the links of common experience recede. Science and
> technology begin to diverge; language and literature grow apart;
> trades and professions separate. Patterns of education, of eco-
> nomic growth, of trade and transportation develop independently.
> These trends are well advanced. And unless urgent efforts are
> made to resume contact, the trends will accelerate.

Who dare doubt that acceleration did take place during the Olympic Games in Mexico as East Germans watched the brilliant successes of their sportsmen and women competing for the first time
as an East German team?

In the past many discussions took place about the non-recognition
of the German Democratic Republic. It was argued that it should
not be recognized because it was not free from Moscow, because
being Soviet-imposed, it was not capable of development, because,
in the long run, a deal over its liquidation could possibly be
arranged with the USSR. Events in 1956, 1961, and again in 1968
have proved how illusory these views are. The Czech crisis, as the
earlier crises, proved the utter determination of the Soviet Union
to maintain governments satisfactory to it in areas which it regards
as vital to its security. In this sense East Germany is no more and
no less independent than any of the other Warsaw Pact states
(Romania being the possible exception). The non-recognition of the
DDR serves no useful purpose. On the contrary it provides the
'conservatives' in that state with an additional weapon. By under-
writing the régime through recognition the West would be promoting
the flexibility and progress most East Germans, both outside and inside the SED, want. In the long run such progress must mean in
East Germany, as surely as in the Soviet Union, a democracy which

is worthy of the economic, social, and educational progress the DDR has recently been making—the kind of democracy people with refrigerators, TV sets and washing machines, a five-day week, security of employment, and an expensive education will demand even more than their down-trodden fathers and grandfathers. For a start this must mean free discussion, for, in the words of Rosa Luxemburg, a revolutionary honoured in East Germany, 'Freedom is only really freedom when it is freedom for those who think differently.'

It is difficult to cover all aspects of the life of a nation in one volume with equal emphasis, accuracy, and completeness. The writer therefore asks the indulgence of the reader in this matter. If the book conveys to the reader something of the achievements of the East German people—Communists, anti-Communists, and non-Communists, as well as the better known shadows, scars, and contradictions of East German society, he will feel satisfied.

Chapter 1

The SED: Where the Power Lies

The Road to Unity

IT IS APPROPRIATE to start any study of the German Democratic Republic with an examination of the Socialist Unity Party (SED) and this for two reasons. First, notwithstanding the formal text of the East German constitution—dealt with separately —the real power centres of the DDR are the highest echelons of the Unity Party. Secondly, even the broadest outline of the history of the East German state—and not being an historical survey this volume aims to give no more than a broad outline—cannot be disentangled from the history of the SED. In fact the history of the SED is almost the history of the DDR.

As the word 'Unity' in its title implies, the setting-up of the Socialist Unity Party of Germany represented the coming together of socialists of different directions. Officially it represented the uniting of the German Communist Party and the German Social Democratic Party. In practice it meant the fusion of these two parties in the Soviet Zone of Germany in April 1946. We are never likely to know the full story of the merger but it is fair to say that it was due to a mixture of conviction and coercion.

The conviction that a party which united all socialists was necessary was born, in the first place, of the belief that it was the divisions in the working-class movement before 1933 which in large measure contributed to the victory of Nazism. The German people did not vote a majority for the Nazis at a free election. At the last free election in November 1932 the Nazis got 'only' 11.7 million votes. The Social Democrats gained 7.3 million and the Communists 5.9 million. The Catholic Centre Party won 4.2 million and the right-wing German Nationalists 3 million. In other words, the working-class parties, the 'Marxists', the Social Democrats and Communists combined, received more votes than the Nazis. These parties and the Catholics were stronger than the Nazis and Nationalists, later in coalition, together. Even after Hitler became Chancellor and used terror against his opponents he failed, in March

1933, to persuade a majority of Germans to vote National Socialist. Armed with these facts and with twelve years of enforced inactivity or exile those on the left who survived started to play the game of 'If only . . .'. If only Social Democrats and Communists had been united they could have prevented the rise of Nazism. Obviously, the truth or otherwise of such speculation is impossible to establish. What is important for this discussion is that socialists of all directions believed it.

A second factor helping to create a mood favourable to a united working-class party was shared experiences either in Nazi prisons and concentration camps or in the emigration. Remnants of the pre-1933 SPD executive in the USA, for example, supported the idea of such a party.[1] These two factors were there in 1945 before political activity was resumed. Soon another stumbling block appeared to have been removed. The first Communist appeal to the German people was not only remarkably moderate, it, and later appeals, seemed to put the Communists four-square behind a Western-type democracy. They further came out in favour of a 'German' rather than a 'Soviet' road to socialism and, as the Communist International had been disbanded during the war, could claim to be independent of Moscow. The Communists had not yet faced the agonizing problem of the new eastern frontier, a frontier which represented a considerable loss of German land, wealth, and homes, and which was very hard to reconcile with traditional Marxist principles.[2] Finally, both parties stressed their continued adherence to Marxism and to the traditions of pre-1914 social democracy, and admitted they had made mistakes before 1933.

Among the rank and file of the Social Democratic and Communist parties then there existed, in the early days after the fall of the Third Reich, a widespread feeling that a united party could not, and must not, be long delayed. It appears that it was the Social Democrats in Berlin who made the first proposal of a fusion of all socialist forces.[3] In the West too, notably in Hamburg, Social Democrats were the first to raise the unity issue but due to the British military authorities and the Communists a unity party was not set up.[4] The fears of the British were obvious. They were worried lest such a united body would soon fall under Communist influence and

[1] Albrecht Kaden, *Einheit oder Freiheit. Die Wiedergründung der SPD 1945/46,* Verlag J. H. W. Dietz, Hanover, 1964. p. 36.
[2] Communists' position, *Die Welt* (1 March 1947) (Max Reimann); *Neues Deutschland* (14 September 1946) (Pieck and Fechner).
[3] Carola Stern, *Porträt einer bolschewistischen Partei,* Verlag für Politik und Wirtschaft, Cologne, 1957, p. 16.
[4] Kaden, op. cit., p. 68.

aid a Communist take-over in Germany. But why did the Communists hesitate? Certainly not because they opposed such a party in principle. They probably greatly overestimated the appeal of communism in post-Hitler Germany. As we have seen, communism in Weimar Germany had been a mass movement which appeared to be in the ascendant until it was smashed by Nazi terror. The Communists could claim, as they had not been in office, that they were not responsible for the failures of the Weimar republic—unlike the Social Democrats—and that they had warned that Hitler would lead the German people into a new war. This had happened. Surely then, they must have argued, they had a right to expect not only to retain their old support but also to get a great boost in recognition of their correct prediction about Hitler, their suffering at the hands of the Nazis, and their association with the power which had done most to bring about the downfall of Nazism. They might also have been expected to have gained from their lack of association with the powers which had caused so many German civilian casualties by aerial bombardment. They were to be disappointed. Many Germans were too shocked by the fate of their country or too preoccupied with their immediate survival to care about politics. Many of those who might have persuaded them had perished in the concentration camps. Thirdly, although all the allies had agreed to the expulsion of the Germans from the territories beyond the Oder-Neisse Line, it was the Soviets and the Poles who were actually carrying it out. Naturally enough they attracted hostility for this; so did those who were associated with them. The influence of the German Communists was also weakened by the conduct of many Soviet troops and by the extreme dismantling measures they carried through. Few Germans, especially the women, understood the even harder fate of the East European peoples under the Nazis. Many of the male working class, who would be more likely to support the Communists than their sisters or their grandparents, were scattered around the world in prisoner-of-war camps. The Communist leadership no doubt sought to build up a well-disciplined, mass party, which would then be able to dominate any left-wing alliance or merger. They received a shock at the Austrian elections of November 1945. In Austria many of the same factors were at work as in Germany, the positive as well as the negative. The Austrian Communists had not been in the strong position of the German Communists in the twenties and early thirties, but they expected to pick up about the same number of votes as their socialist rivals. In fact the Communists received a mere 174,257 votes as against 1,434,898 for the socialists and 1,602,227 for the (Catholic) People's

Party.[5] It was after these results became known that the German Communist leadership started to press for the immediate fusion of the two parties.[6]

Personal rivalries seem to have played a part in the events which followed. Erich Gniffke, himself a pro-Unity Party Social Democrat who later went to West Germany, has claimed that the West German Social Democratic leader Kurt Schumacher in effect pushed the leader of the East Zone Social Democrats, Otto Grotewohl, into the arms of the Communists by his aloof and mistrusting attitude on the few occasions that they met. Gniffke believed Schumacher feared Grotewohl as a rival in a Social Democratic Party covering all four zones of Germany.[7] Gniffke also emphasized the good impression made on the Social Democrats by the veteran Communist leader Wilhelm Pieck and the oratorical skill of Grotewohl to convince a mass audience of the rightness of any policy he was advocating. It is generally believed in the West that Grotewohl wavered on the unity issue but that he believed the Social Democrats could dominate any such alliance and that he had been given assurances by the Soviets that they would, within very broad limits, give the party freedom to develop its own German road to socialism.

Originally, after the fall of Nazism, a group of Social Democrats who had had some authority in the pre-1933 SPD set up a new Social Democratic organization in Berlin. Grotewohl, who had been a member of parliament in the Weimar republic, was among them. As they had set up their organization in the old Reich capital they expected they could gradually extend their influence to all parts of Germany. The Social Democrats in the Soviet Zone accepted their leadership. Kurt Schumacher, also a former member of parliament, operating from the British Zone, did not. Grotewohl, who soon became leader of the Social Democrats centred on Berlin, and Schumacher, who emerged as leader in the British Zone, agreed to respect each other's authority in their separate zones until an all-German conference should have the chance to settle the leadership issue. The Social Democrats and Communists of the Soviet Zone and Berlin were united in a unity of action pact from June 1945 on. In February 1946 a conference of thirty leading Social Democrats and thirty leading Communists agreed on a timetable for unity. Both leaderships were to call conferences of their respective

[5] Ludwig Reichhold, *Zwanzig Jahre Zweite Republik*, Verlag Herder, Vienna, 1965, p. 31.

[6] Wolfgang Leonhard, *Die Revolution Entlässt Ihre Kinder*, Kiepenheuer & Witsch, Cologne, 1955, p. 425.

[7] Erich Gniffke, *Jahre Mit Ulbricht*, Verlag Wissenschaft und Politik, Cologne, 1966.

parties to agree the proposal. The protagonists of unity now became
very active. In some places in the Soviet Zone rank-and-filers of
both parties kicked over the traces and merged their local organizations. In those places where there was reluctance the local Soviet
commandant invited the officials to talk it over with him as chairman. Western sources claim, and no doubt rightly in view of the
Stalinist 'administrative measures' favoured at the time, that where
argument failed threats and bribes succeeded.[8] Gniffke maintains
that the Russians, the Americans, and the British generally used
presents, often food packets, to gain friends and influence people.

In Berlin, under Four-Power control, the establishment of the
Unity Party faced the open and determined opposition of some
Social Democratic officials.

Led by Franz Neumann, who later became prominent in the
Western-orientated Social Democratic Party, the opponents of im-
mediate unity demanded that a party referendum be carried
through to give all members a chance to have their say on the issue.
The leadership, collectively known as the *Zentralausschuss* or Central Committee, rejected this, saying they would put it to a full
SPD conference made up of duly elected delegates from all local
SPD organizations. This, they claimed, was the traditional Social
Democratic way of doing things. However, with the help of the
Western powers a vote was carried through in the three Western
sectors of Berlin. Both Western and Eastern writers very largely
agree on the results of this vote. In all 32,547 members voted. Of
these only 2,937 voted for the immediate fusion of the Social
Democratic and Communist parties. But 14,763 voted for an alli-
ance of the two parties which would eliminate inter-party strife.
Only 5,559 were against any fusion and any alliance.[9] Obviously
these results could give some comfort to both sides. The pro-
Schumacher 'Westerners' could stress that they had only been
allowed to carry out the vote in the Western sectors and there the
great majority had voted against immediate fusion. The pro-
Grotewohl 'Easterners' could claim that there were some 66,000
Social Democrats in the whole of Berlin, that many who supported
them had heeded the leadership's call not to vote, that in any case,
of those who had voted very few had rejected all co-operation with
the Communists. The *Zentralausschuss* pushed ahead with their
plans for unity, their opponents set up a separate organization in
all four sectors of Berlin after holding a conference on 7 April 1946
in Zehlendorf. All things considered it seems likely that there were

[8] Stern, op. cit., p. 33; Gniffke, op. cit., p. 60.
[9] Leonhard, op. cit., p. 433.

considerable numbers of Social Democrats in the Soviet Zone, as
well as the Soviet sector of Berlin, who had their doubts about the
issue. Conversely, many Social Democrats in the West would have
readily agreed to such a move. The Americans carried through a
survey on the issue in their zone, an area where the Social Democrats were traditionally more to the right than most of their comrades. Commenting on this survey a Western scholar has written,
'Just how strong the desire to unity was among Social Democrats,
outside the Soviet Zone as well, is often overlooked. In March,
1946, after months of struggle against co-operation with the Communists, every third SPD member in the American Zone was prepared to support Grotewohl's "unity party" if this would in fact
replace the Social Democratic and the Communist parties.'[10]

The *Zentralausschuss* organized a party conference to decide on
unity. Delegates came from all parts of the Soviet Zone and from
Berlin. There were also delegates from a number of places in West
Germany. East German historians claim there would have been
many more from the Western zones had not the Occupation Authorities there held up travel documents for potential delegates and
had not pro-Schumacher officials threatened them with expulsion.[11]
The German Communist Party also held a conference in Berlin to
discuss the unity issue and of course reached the same decision as
the Grotewohl Social Democrats. Two days later on 21 April 1946
the Socialist Unity Party held its first congress or *Parteitag* in what
is now East Berlin's Metropol theatre. After listening to the overture
from Beethoven's *Fidelio* the delegates watched Wilhelm Pieck, the
veteran Communist, and Otto Grotewohl come on to the stage
from left and right respectively and shake hands. One need not
doubt the official commentary which refers to the tremendous
enthusiasm of the delegates for, as one Western antagonist of the
SED has put it, 'There were many old SPD officials for whom . . .
the unification with the Communists was nothing more than a reunification, the ending of long years of fratricidal strife'.[12]

A Party of a 'New Type'

Parity was the rule at all levels of the new Party. Accordingly,
Pieck and Grotewohl were elected joint chairmen, Walter Ulbricht
and Max Fechner vice-chairmen, and the eighty-member executive
(*Vorstand*), elected by the congress, was drawn equally from both

[10] Lewis J. Edinger, *Kurt Schumacher*, Westdeutscher Verlag, Cologne,
1967, p. 148.
[11] *Geschichte Der Deutschen Arbeiter Bewegung*, Dietz Verlag, (East)
Berlin, 1966. Vol. 6, p. 143 (henceforth *GDAB*).
[12] Stern, op. cit., p. 33.

parties. The executive, again according to the rule of parity, elected from its midst a fourteen-member *Zentralsekretariat*. Of its original members in 1946, five were still active at the Central Committee (*ZK*) level; the latter later replaced the *Vorstand*, at the SED *Parteitag* in 1963. Three of these veterans were re-elected to the *Politbüro*, the organ which superseded the *Zentralsekretariat* in 1949. Three of the original fourteen had died by 1963, one had retired, one defected to the West, four had been removed for alleged political failings (one of these is once again in the *ZK*), and two, one a member of the *ZK*, are serving the Party at lower levels. Since 1963 one more veteran, Otto Grotewohl, has died.

At this first party congress there were 548 Social Democratic delegates, 103 from West Germany, and 507 Communists, 127 from the West. The Soviet Zone delegates represented 680,000 Social Democrats and 620,000 Communists.[13] The congress passed, without dissent, a whole series of resolutions on principles, aims, and policies. Twenty-one comrades decided, however, to vote against the party constitution, four abstained.[14] The policy demands were based on earlier Communist and Social Democratic statements and the Potsdam Agreement: everything from punishment of war criminals and reparations to the smashing of capitalist monopolies, democratic educational reform, and the development of social insurance. These policies were very similar to the ones advocated a short time later at the Hanover congress of the West German SPD. East German historians today admit that the congress resolutions represented a compromise. They did not recognize Leninism as such nor did they recognize the 'leading role' of the Soviet Communist Party in the world movement.[15]

Although Walter Ulbricht said at the second *Parteitag* that the SED was already on the way to becoming a 'Party of a new Type', in other words a Leninist party,[16] the resolution approved by the delegates did not seem to indicate this. True, it mentioned the Unity Party as a party of a new type, but it then defined this as simply, 'a party which in its principles and aims, as well as in its political work, takes into consideration the lessons of the past'. The resolution also spoke of Marxism rather than Marxism-Leninism.[17] Individual speakers who used this classic term, such as Max

[13] *GDAB*, Vol. 6, p. 145.
[14] Ibid., p. 146.
[15] Ibid., p. 150.
[16] *Protokoll Des II Parteitages Der Sozialistischen Einheitspartei Deutschlands*, Dietz Verlag, (East) Berlin, 1947, p. 479 (henceforth *Protokoll*).
[17] *Protokoll*, pp. 534, 545.

Fechner[18] and Erich Gniffke,[19] did not seem to be using it in the original, exact sense. The decision to transform the SED into a Leninist party seems to have been finally taken by the Party *Vorstand* in September 1948.[20] This decision meant the throwing out of the theory of the 'German Way' put forward by Erich Gniffke, Anton Ackermann, and Ernst Thape, recognition of Leninism, recognition of the leading role of the CPSU, and certain important organizational changes. Today historians make a distinction between the views of the protagonists of the 'German Way' and statements made by Pieck and Grotewohl to the effect that they recognized the example of the Soviet Union but also took into consideration certain special features of the German situation.[21]

The organizational transformation of the Socialist Unity Party into a Leninist party was the result of decisions taken at the twelfth session of the *Vorstand* in July 1948 and the first *Parteikonferenz*, a kind of minor *Parteitag*, in January 1949. What did these decisions mean for the Party? First of all, the *Zentralsekretariat* was abolished and, following the Soviet pattern, replaced by a *Politbüro*. The latter was given its own secretariat, a powerful team of top party civil servants, and at each level the elected bodies were 'supported' by similar teams. The importance of these teams cannot be overstressed : they became an important instrument in the hands of the secretary of the SED, Walter Ulbricht, who has admitted that these bodies have overridden their formal, elected, superiors (see below, p. 54). The parity principle was also abolished to facilitate the transformation of the SED. It was said that it tended to divide the Party along the old, pre-Unity Party lines, and that it held back the most able, especially those who had not belonged to either of the old parties. The method of recruitment of new members was also changed. No longer were members to be recruited at public meetings or by the other methods normal in Western socialist or Communist parties. In future would-be members had to receive recommendations from two existing members and the favourable decision of an appropriate party meeting. From then on such potential members had to complete satisfactorily a period of probationary or candidate membership. Finally, in selecting its new members, the SED decided to pay due regard to its existing social structure and social class needs. For instance, if the decision were taken to expand

[18] *Protokoll,* p. 49.
[19] Ibid., p. 165.
[20] *GDAB,* Vol. 6, p. 269.
[21] Ibid., p. 270; *20 Jahre Sozialistische Einheitspartei Deutschlands 1946–66,* Dietz Verlag, (East) Berlin, 1966, pp. 124–5 (henceforth *20 Jahre*).

a particular part of the economy and the Unity Party were weak in that sector efforts would be made to recruit the appropriate people.[22]

Quite apart from any reasons connected with the Cold War, going through a bitter phase at this time, the SED claimed it had to examine its membership and recruitment methods because its structure was not developing evenly. Who were the SED members at this time? At the second *Parteitag* in 1947 Gniffke gave the following picture: 860,000 industrial workers (46 per cent); 323,000 white-collar employees (17 per cent); 115,000 craftsmen and small traders (6 per cent); 104,000 farmers and 65,000 agricultural workers (8 per cent); 80,000 technicians, 30,000 teachers, and 33,000 doctors, lawyers, and artists (7 per cent); housewives, pensioners, and others 246,000 (13 per cent).[23] He was proud of the SED's proletarian connections, pointing out that many of the housewives and pensioners were of the working class. He might also have added that so were many of the white-collar workers and, no doubt, the teachers and lawyers (many of whom were emergency trained to replace Nazis). The delegates were somewhat less proletarian than the Party as a whole, but they could be proud that between them they had served 1,512 years in Nazi jails and concentration camps. Most of them appear to have been veterans in that 1,043 claimed to have been politically involved before 1933. They were not as old as this might seem to suggest: 115 were under 31, 259 were between 31 and 40, 459 between 41 and 50, and 280 over 50.

By the middle of 1948 there were 1,800,000 SED members of whom 57 per cent were workers, 20 per cent white-collar employees, 17 per cent 'working farmers', and 5 per cent traders. As for age, 14 per cent were under 25. Women also made up about 14 per cent[24] of the members. It is now said that this structure left much to be desired in that there were too few young people, women, white-collar workers, scientists, teachers, and engineers.[25] Measures were taken to correct this and at the same time the Party 'cleansed its ranks of careerist, corrupt, class alien, and party hostile forces. Above all there were such elements who advocated bourgeois, nationalist, anti-Soviet views and in many cases under the cover of SED membership carried out activities for imperialist spy agencies, especially the Eastern Bureau of the SPD'.[26]

The whole period from 1948 to 1953 was one of spy hysteria and

[22] *20 Jahre*, pp. 128–34.
[23] *Protokoll*, p. 123.
[24] *20 Jahre*, p. 131.
[25] Ibid., p. 131.
[26] Ibid., p. 128.

mutual suspicion. Of course, this was the height of the Cold War
and it is as well to remember that other East European countries,
such as Hungary and Czechoslovakia, had excesses far greater than
those in East Germany, and that America had its McCarthy era. In
1949 the Soviet authorities in Germany issued an order that anyone
who had been in Western or Yugoslav emigration or who had been
a prisoner-of-war in any of these countries was no longer eligible
to hold important office.[27] The party watch-dogs were, at the same
time, on the look-out for, in Communist parlance, left sectarians,
those who had concealed their Nazi pasts, and, of particular importance at this time, Tito-Trotskyites. A whole group of veteran Communists fell from favour. Paul Merker, a *Politbüro* member, Lex
Ende, editor-in-chief of the party newspaper, *Neues Deutschland,*
and a number of others were arrested. Apparently they had all
known Noel H. Field, the American convicted in Hungary as a spy
but released as innocent in 1954, and this was enough to get them
incarcerated. Franz Dahlem, likewise a member of the *Politbüro,*
suffered a similar fate though he is once again in the Central Committee. The official SED history is now prepared to concede that,
'Under the influence of J. V. Stalin' and 'L. P. Beria and his accom-
plices groundless charges were raised against the leaders of the
Yugoslav party. This incorrect procedure affected the international
workers' movement to the extent that it produced an atmosphere of
intolerance and mistrust, which exceeded the necessary amount of
vigilance.'[28] The history also concedes that account was not taken
of the specific national conditions in the various countries of socialism and that comrades were unjustly imprisoned.[29]

The years between 1948 and 1953 were years of rapid political
and economic development in both parts of Germany, and years of
crisis. The most dramatic and the most momentous of these crises
was undoubtedly the Berlin blockade of 1948–9. Briefly, the Four
Powers could not agree on a currency reform to replace the old
currency made worthless by inflation, so the Western Allies decided
to introduce their own reform in their zones. They later extended
this to their sectors of Berlin. This could have been a danger to the
Soviet Zone economy. The Russians therefore sought to seal off
West Berlin from the West zones in the expectation that the Western
powers would get out of a city they could not provision. The Allies
responded with the 'Air Lift' which lasted nearly a year. It was a
great organizational and technological achievement that neither the

[27] Stern, op. cit., p. 118; *GDAB*, Vol. 7, p. 113.
[28] *GDAB*, Vol. 6, p. 274.
[29] *GDAB*, Vol. 7, p. 113.

Soviets nor most in the West had believed possible. By May 1949 Stalin finally agreed to call off the blockade. The result of this crisis was a stiffening of Western attitudes towards the USSR which helped to produce NATO in 1949, a more generous treat- ment of the West Germans by the Western powers, and a feeling, rightly or wrongly, that the Soviets were interested solely in cutting off their zone from the rest of Germany. The Federal Republic of (West) Germany was proclaimed in 1949, and shortly after, on 7 October of that year, the Soviet Zone became the German Democratic Republic. Already in September 1948 Berlin had been divided politically by the decision of the non-SED majority on the Berlin city council to move to the Western sectors because they had been subject to harassment in the Soviet sector. In East Berlin the SED and its supporters then decided to set up a separate administra- tion.

In economic affairs both parts of Germany were once again recovering. In the west owing to the currency reform, American aid, and, in 1950, the Korean war boom, the 'economic miracle' began. In East Germany the economy was also expanding but at a slower rate. In 1948 a two-year plan was embarked upon. This was designed not only to raise production levels but also to ensure the dominant position of the public sector in the economy. At the third Unity Party *Parteitag* in July 1950 the emphasis was still, on the one hand, on 'measures that encourage the reunification of the German People under the banner of the democratic and peace- loving Germany'.[30] Nevertheless, on the other hand, 'the draft of the first Five-Year Plan was the most important document of the third *Parteitag* of the SED' and 'with the carrying through of the pro- posed Five-Year Plan for 1951–55 the building of the basis of socialism was started.'[31]

In February and March 1952 the DDR and Soviet governments put out notes proposing a united, neutral, Germany with its own defence forces. This represented, according to one Western com- mentator, 'a clear if dignified and partial offer of retreat', which met with a 'haughty and intransigent' Western reaction.[32] And another Western expert has argued: 'These notes, which certainly arrived at a rather late stage, cannot be said to have been seriously considered. Instead they were regarded as a sign that the policy of negotiating from strength was beginning to yield results and, if

[30] Stefan Doernberg, *Kurze Geschichte der DDR*, Dietz Verlag (East) Berlin, 1964, p. 166.
[31] Ibid., p. 169.
[32] Sebastian Haffner in *Survey* (London) (October 1962), p. 44.

pursued, would result in still more conciliatory offers'.[33] Dr Adenauer, the West German Chancellor, believed that by massive rearmament, by negotiating from military strength, the West could force the Soviets to abandon their interests in Germany and the DDR could thus be incorporated into the Federal Republic. He failed to realize how rapidly the USSR was catching up to the USA in armaments. Just how serious the Soviets were we shall never know. The Western powers were not prepared to halt the rearmament of West Germany to test the sincerity of the offer. In July of the same year, following the signing of the European Defence Community by West Germany, the SED responded to the Western rejection of the notes by proclaiming the building of socialism at its second *Parteikonferenz*. Thus a new stage was embarked upon in the DDR. The 'anti-fascist democratic order' of 1945–52 was giving way to a more definitely 'socialistic' order. This phase was to last until 1958, when the period of the consolidation and victory of socialist production relations began.

This new phase led immediately to more nationalization and, in accordance with Stalin's theory, the intensification of the class struggle. This included measures to eliminate private businesses, measures to curb the influence of the Churches, discrimination against would-be students from bourgeois families, and the confiscation of the ration cards of the middle classes.[34]

Economic difficulties started to develop and the numbers leaving the republic rose correspondingly.[35] This in turn caused further difficulties. In addition, the second *Parteikonferenz* had also proclaimed the decision to set up armed forces in the DDR.[36] This meant increased pressure on sparse resources. Only by getting the workers to produce more for the same wage, only by cutting social welfare measures, could this pressure be relieved. East German historians now admit that the authorities failed to convince the workers of the need to do this but simply used 'administrative measures' to ease the tensions which were inevitably created. They further admit that the organs of justice did not always distinguish between enemies of the republic and workers who, owing to various pressures, broke the law.[37] Finally, they admit that the deliberate sharpening of the class struggle was wrong.[38] The result of all this

[33] Michael Balfour, *West Germany*, Benn, London; Praeger, New York, 1968, p. 213.
[34] Martin Jänicke, *Der Dritte Weg*, Neuer Deutscher Verlag, Cologne, 1964, p. 23.
[35] *GDAB*, Vol. 7, p. 230; Doernberg, op. cit., pp. 218, 220.
[36] *GDAB*, Vol. 7. p. 176.
[37] Doernberg, op. cit., p. 220.   [38] *GDAB*, Vol. 7, p. 230.

was 'a loosening of the ties between the Party and the state and the workers.'[39]

Another factor making for general alienation of the masses from the régime was the prominence given to everything Soviet or Russian, and the adoption of everything Soviet from Stalinist architecture and organizational forms right down to the habit of speakers applauding themselves at meetings. Everything Soviet was the best whether it really was or not. This was a very bitter pill to swallow for a people which was, on the one hand, a *Kulturvolk* and a nation of skilled people, and, on the other, a nation indoctrinated before 1945 to believe that the Russians and the Slavs in general were inferior to the 'Nordic' people. This Soviet-SED cultural line no doubt made it more difficult for the masses to understand the need for reparations and to understand the extent of Nazi crimes in the USSR.

Even after the death of Stalin, in March 1953, the SED leadership continued to pursue measures brought in under his influence. On 28 May the East German government ordered the raising of the output norms of the industrial workers without any corresponding increase in pay. Less than a month later, on 9 June, they tried to undo some of the damage done over the past year or so. This amounted to what the *Manchester Guardian* correspondent called, in his report of 11 June, '180 deg. change of course'. But these new measures were mainly concerned with placating the middle classes and the Churches; they could be compared with Lenin's New Economic Policy of the early twenties. The fatal mistake of the East German leadership was to leave the issue of the increased output norms in a state of confusion. A strike broke out among the building workers on the prestige project at the Stalinallee in East Berlin. This was on 16 June. The following day the strike movement spread to various parts of East Berlin and the surrounding republic. Demonstrations also took place, in some cases turning into riots. As the most authoritative Western account of these events points out, it is impossible to be certain about the exact nature, development, and extent of the outbreaks of 17 June.[40] The popular Western conception which interprets them as a people's or a workers' revolution which ended in a blood-bath, is certainly a myth. Happily, Western and Eastern sources now largely agree on the extent of the strikes. Communist writers concede that strikes involving roughly 300,000 took place in 272 localities. Western

[39] Doernberg, op. cit., p. 221.
[40] Arnulf Baring, *Der 17. Juni 1953*, Deutscher Bundes-Verlag, Bonn, 1958, p. 37.

3 * *

researchers claim strikes involving 372,000 in 274 places.[41] There
were about 5½ million East Germans employed as industrial workers
at that time so that only between 4.5 and 5.5 per cent of them went
on strike. A study carried out for the West German Ministry for
All-German Affairs writes of twenty-one fatalities, which means for
instance fewer deaths in this 'revolt' than occurred in one night of
political disturbances in Mexico in 1968.[42] The West German study
admits that had it not been for the extreme moderation of Soviet
troops and East German police the casualties would have been
much higher. The *Manchester Guardian* (22 June 1953) agreed.

'The Red Army troops evidently were given the strictest instructions
to behave with restraint. There are few cases reported of their having opened fire on demonstrators—even though they were stoned
and insulted and their tanks and armoured cars physically attacked
by the demonstrators'.

What had the East German leaders to say about these outbreaks?
They had enough sense to admit that the workers had 'genuine
grievances' but at the same time they tried, and still try, to blame
West German intelligence agencies for the disturbances. Naturally
it is impossible to test the strength of these assertions. Certain known
facts which lend plausibility to them must in fairness be mentioned.
Firstly, Western sources freely admit that anti-East German intelligence services of all kinds operate from West Berlin. The *Sunday
Times* correspondent in Berlin reported on 10 January 1954 about
a 'Spy War in Berlin' and called the former German capital 'a city
where spying has become almost an industry. Apart from the two
main contestants in the spy war across the Iron Curtain, there are
at least three dozen lesser espionage groups owned or backed by
pressure groups or political parties and owing their existence to
the frantic concern for secrecy in a city obsessed by the cold war'.
On 2 July 1958 the independent West German weekly *Der Spiegel*
dealt with one such organization, the KgU. According to this
Western magazine, the KgU, which for a time received funds from
the United States, which was for some years led by a SPD member,
which counted among its personnel former SS men, gave out fake
ration cards to create shortages, sent false information to the
DDR's trading partners purporting to come from East Germany,
interfered with post, made food unusable, sabotaged industrial
undertakings, attempted to blow up bridges, and tried to intimidate
families of SED officials. Secondly, and also lending some plausi-

[41] Baring, op. cit., p. 38. See also his article in *Der Spiegel* (16 June 1965).
[42] Ibid., p. 58. For Mexico see *The Economist* (2 October 1968) which says
30 deaths. *Observer* (6 October) implied more.

bility to the East German charges, anyone could walk unmolested between the two parts of Berlin and it was extremely easy to go from Berlin into the republic. The West German study for the Bonn Ministry for All-German Affairs, referred to above, says that one would not be wrong to suppose that West Berliners were involved in the incidents in East Berlin. The *Manchester Guardian* (18 June 1953) also agreed at the time that 'in the case of East Berlin it may be true that the riots have been partly spurred on from the Western sectors'. Heinz Brandt, then still on the other side of the barricades, has written from the vantage point of West Germany, that 'numerous West Berliners' and 'political adventurers with dark aims and dark employers' joined in the mêlée.[43] The *Sunday Times* report quoted above mentioned that 'several hundred' West German agents had been arrested in East Germany 'following their betrayal' by a Western agent 'who absconded to the Communists'. Some years later evidence before the US Congress revealed something of the activities of the Central Intelligence Agency in organizing revolts and overthrowing governments, deeds which were denied at the time of their execution.[44] Finally, one interesting point about the strike leaderships revealed by official West German research is that they contained a relatively large number of former professional soldiers, mainly former NCOs. According to their research, this was probably due to two factors. German professional servicemen tend to be right-wing orientated and would therefore have been in principle hostile to the régime. Secondly, they were strategically placed due to the fact that they had had to take up factory work, their old profession being no longer open to them. They were also used to taking the initiative and exercising authority. This West German research does not, however, go quite so far as to agree with East German claims made at the time that such elements were mainly responsible for the events of 17 June 1953.[45] This writer believes that, whatever the numbers of outside or undercover elements, the strikes were largely spontaneous. Most working-class people, whether they be in East or West Germany, Britain or elsewhere, feel they cannot afford to strike. They do not strike lightly, though 'agitators' may sometimes exploit their dissatisfaction.

With or without Western agents large numbers of East Germans had shown their deep dissatisfaction with the existing situation. Many of them were the very people in whose name the SED

[43] Heinz Brandt, *Ein Traum der nicht entführbar ist*, Paul List Verlag, Munich, 1967, p. 242.
[44] See, for instance, reports in *Daily Telegraph* (27 April 1966); *The Times* (28 April 1966); *Die Zeit* (29 April 1966).
[45] Baring, op. cit., pp. 52–3.

exercised power—the workers. This fact was a bitter blow to SED loyalists as the writer found out at the time. Young men with little experience of life or politics, who had been armed, so they believed, to defend the workers' rights, found themselves in the streets with orders to disperse hostile workers. Veteran Communists, themselves workers by origin, experience, and emotional ties, watched from their office windows as Soviet troops secured the large factories and other strategic buildings. As one National Prize winner of the DDR sorrowfully told the writer in July 1953, 'We have not got 10 per cent of the people with us'. Whatever the percentage for or against the régime the SED had to act to restore confidence. The measures adopted to put things right were known as the New Course or *Neuer Kurs*. They included not only the above-mentioned modifications to help the middle classes but a revision of the piece rates of the workers as well. The authorities were careful not to cause more discontent by excessive witch-hunting of rebels. Western sources say seven death sentences were handed out and another eight accused were sentenced to life imprisonment. About another thousand received an average sentence of four years.[46]

The events of 16 and 17 June had shaken the Socialist Unity Party from top to bottom and the leadership carried through a *post-mortem* investigation to determine why they had happened and how the Party had stood up to this test. The party leaders toured the factories and, for a time at least, the discussions were pretty frank and open. There was also a whole series of discussions at all levels of the Unity Party itself. Remarkably perhaps, when the day of reckoning came it was not Party Secretary Ulbricht or Prime Minister Grotewohl who were shown the door but some of their colleagues who before, during, and after the catastrophe had demanded a more fundamental change of party policy than the one envisaged. Many of those now purged were veteran Communists, some of them former emigrants in the Soviet Union who had been regarded as safely entrenched. Others were 'opportunists' or 'Schumacher men'. Among the top men removed were Wilhelm Zaisser, *Politbüro* member and Minister for State Security, and Rudolf Herrnstadt, editor-in-chief of *Neues Deutschland*, the SED newspaper, and a candidate member of the *Politbüro*. They were old Communists and were charged with having formed an 'anti-party faction' with a defeatist line.[47] One former Social Democrat to fall from office was Max Fechner, Minister of Justice, who like the others was accused of defeatism.

[46] Ibid., p. 68.
[47] *20 Jahre*, p. 188.

During the period between June 1953 and the SED fourth *Parteitag* in April 1954 both the stick and the carrot were used to restore morale, order, and discipline. Much was done to raise living standards. But in the ideological sphere there was a renewed struggle against 'Social Democratism' and a number of trials were held. These trials involved some alleged to have taken part in the events of 17 June and many others said to be guilty of economic sabotage, 'slandering the DDR', or 'spreading rumours'. At the fourth *Parteitag* the leaders admitted that 'bureaucracy' was holding back production, expressed fear about the spread of 'imperialist ideology' among the youth, and regretted that food rationing would have to continue. A new party statute was adopted, similar to that of the Soviet party, one important aspect of which was a strengthening of SED control over industrial management.

Stalin Dethroned and the Harich Affair

The New Course was continued with varying emphasis, though by 1955 there was a partial turning away and an intensification of military propaganda and preparations. In 1955 West Germany regained its sovereignty and was admitted to NATO; and the first *Bundeswehr* generals were appointed. The Warsaw Pact was set up in the same year. However, 1955 marked a partial thaw in East–West relations. Dr Adenauer headed a West German delegation to Moscow and the USSR and the Federal Republic established diplomatic relations. In the same year the Austrian State Treaty was signed which meant the end of the occupation of that country. The Soviet leaders further showed a conciliatory attitude in international relations by going, cap in hand, to seek a *rapprochement* with Tito. Despite such moves the outlook for German reunification looked bleaker than ever. Both the West and the Soviets made proposals on the issue starting at the Berlin conference of February 1954 and repeating them through to the Foreign Ministers' meeting at Geneva in October 1955. But they were unable to agree on the issues of free elections or the future status of Germany. The USSR wanted to neutralize the country but the USA and Britain insisted that, after reunification, Germany must be free to choose her own alliance—in practice to be free to join NATO. Perhaps Soviet recognition of Bonn meant that they now thought German reunification was out of the question.

In internal affairs too the Soviets were slowly reversing some of the worst features of Stalin's rule. In the DDR this had been happening, partly because of the New Course. But the virtual demolition of Stalin at the 20th Congress of the Soviet Communist Party

in 1956 came as a shock to the SED leadership. Only a few days
before the congress *Einheit*, the SED theoretical journal, published
a long article praising the *Short History of the CPSU (B)* and
claiming this was a 'must' for all party members. It was this very
book which was so utterly condemned at the Moscow congress by
Mikoyan as a distortion of history. Remarkably, a publication of
the party school 'Karl Marx', which appeared in 1966, still praised
the decision of 1948 to make it the duty of all party members to
study this textbook.[48] The official history of the movement put out
by the *Institut für Marxismus–Leninismus* of the SED would seem
to contradict this. It claims that under Stalin's influence there had
been too much study of his work and not enough of the work of
Marx, Engels, and Lenin.[49] The result was, according to this source,
'dogmatism' in the social sciences, the arts, education, and the
economy.

On 4 March, about a week after the end of the 20th Congress,
Neues Deutschland published a statement from Ulbricht which
largely repeated what by this time most party members had no
doubt heard from other sources. About a fortnight later Ulbricht
felt obliged to deal with the matter more fully. In *Neues Deutschland* on 18 March he went further in his criticisms than even a good
many foreign Communist leaders had done. Naturally the smashing
of the Stalin cult was a bitter blow to many party members, particularly those younger ones who had learned their politics in the
last phases of the Stalin era. Educated within the framework of
Stalinist dogma and obedience, their ability to think independently
had been lamed. Now Ulbricht was telling them that they had the
responsibility and the duty to think for themselves. They were
assured of a fair hearing even if their views were wrong. Those
who started to question the leadership about overcoming the 'cult
of personality' in the DDR were told that there was in fact much
less to overcome than in the other socialist states because the
Socialist Unity Party had early embarked upon such corrective
measures and, in any case, there had not been as many 'distortions'.[50]

A meeting of the Central Committee of the SED in July 1956
continued the work of drawing the right conclusions from the
Soviet congress. The report of this meeting which appeared in
Neues Deutschland (31 July 1956) confessed that the cult had led
'to a crippling of initiative, to the hindering of independent study
of new social problems', and faulty propaganda work. The propa-

---

[48] Ibid., pp. 110–11.
[49] *GDAB*, Vol. 8., p. 41.
[50] Ibid., pp. 16–18, 38–42.

ganda of the SED had, it said, led to sectarian exaggerations and had 'coarsely wounded the feelings of Christian workers'. Further members who sought honest discussion to find the truth must not in future be abused or defamed. On the other hand, the Party must not assume that 'under the flag of freedom, criticism, and scientific conflict of opinion the fundamental principles of Marxism and Leninism are being abandoned'. Another important—at least for the individuals concerned—result of this meeting was the rehabilitation of many of the party officials earlier condemned. These included Franz Dahlem, Anton Ackermann, Hans Jendretzky, Frau Elli Schmidt, and Paul Merker. Rudolf Herrnstadt and Wilhelm Zaisser were not mentioned in the communiqué of the meeting.

The troubles in Poland and Hungary in October of the same year also caused a great deal of discussion and heart-searching among party members and especially among the students. The press and the other official organs, as expected, took the view that in Hungary supporters of the pre-war dictator, Admiral Horthy, and clerical fascists had staged a *coup* in the hope of exploiting the 'severe transgressions' committed by the former Communist leaders against Leninist norms, and the 'earlier error in the relations between the socialist states'.[51] In Poland also 'counter-revolutionary forces were trying to exploit errors in the political and economic fields' which were allied with 'offences against socialist legality'. In Poland 'the Party's ties with the masses had been loosened'. Many students were not satisfied with these explanations and had specific grievances of their own. They felt over-burdened with compulsory 'political' subjects such as Russian and 'Marxist' social science (still compulsory today together with sport, maths, and a second foreign language) which often had nothing to do with their future professional activities. Some also objected to the style and operations of the official youth organization, the Free German Youth or FDJ.

The activities of Dr Wolfgang Harich, brilliant 36-year-old SED academic of the Humboldt University, and his group were part and parcel of the same phenomenon. Harich claimed to have learned from the resolutions of the 20th Congress and 'from contacts with comrades abroad. Personal discussions with Polish, Hungarian and Yugoslav comrades have confirmed us in our conclusions'. He also identified his group with the Hungarian revisionist philosopher Gyorgy Lukačs who had given succour to the Hungarian revolutionaries. For years Lukačs had enjoyed a high reputation in East Germany as a literary historian. Dr Harich further

[51] Ibid., pp. 56–7.

claimed to have had the sympathetic ear of Bertolt Brecht until the latter's death. What did the Harich group seek to achieve? Firstly to reform the SED from inside, make it more democratic in its organization and in its ideology, whilst keeping to Marxism–Leninism, take account of the contributions of Trotsky, Bukharin, Luxemburg, Kautsky, Fritz Sternberg, the Social Democratic theorist, the Poles, Yugoslavs, and the Chinese. Secondly, to put the emphasis in economic policy on raising living standards. Thirdly, to raise the status of the workers by profit-sharing, giving them the same pension rights as intellectuals and functionaries, and by setting up workers' councils on the Yugoslav model. Fourthly, to end land collectivization, inappropriate to East Germany, and give equality of treatment to big nationalized and small private industries. Fifthly, restoration of freedom of thought, including making peace with the Churches and giving universities autonomy. The Harich group also advocated the complete abolition of the state security service and of secret trials. Parliament should have supreme power though the 'block system' of party alliances could be maintained. At elections there should once again be more candidates than seats, at the same time retaining the single-list principle. In foreign policy the DDR's existing alliances and pledges should be honoured but there should be real independence and equality in the 'socialist camp'. The Harich group claimed it wanted to achieve its aims by open and legal opposition if possible though the method of faction and conspiracy would be used if necessary. Harich took up contacts with West German journalists and publishers and the Eastern Bureau of the SPD. He was also hoping to get into contact with Polish opposition elements.[52]

Harich and two others were arrested towards the end of 1956 and brought to trial in March 1957. They were charged with offences against Article 6 of the East German constitution : incitement to murder democratic politicians, spreading religious and racial hatred and militarist propaganda, etc. Harich was sentenced to ten years, his two companions to four and two years respectively. The prosecution claimed they were not punishing Harich for his views but for his conspiratorial methods, aimed at bringing about a fundamental change of the socialist order of the DDR by threat or force.[53]

Was Harich guilty? He was certainly guilty of wanting reforms. In court he confessed to more than this. He admitted that had he

[52] *Observer* (17 March 1957) published what it said was the full text of Harich's political platform. See also *Der Spiegel* (19 December 1956).
[53] *Neues Deutschland* (9 & 10 March 1957).

not succeeded in persuading his colleagues in the Party to remove Ulbricht and his allies and to introduce the desired reforms he would have been prepared to seek assistance from West Germany. This accords with his 'manifesto' published in full in the *Observer* (17 March 1957) in which he stated, 'we intend to conduct an open and legal opposition. But we are ready also to use the method of faction and conspiracy if forced to it'. But in this account he clearly said he was working to avoid a rising in East Germany. In the East German version he was working to foment one.

More important than his doubtful 'guilt', however, were his ideas. How realistic were they in October 1956? According to the *Observer* Harich wanted to achieve German reunification and the unification of the reformed SED with the West German SPD. Before reunification could take place a Social Democratic majority in the Bonn parliament would have to carry out the following policies: reversal of remilitarization; withdrawal from NATO; removal of fascists and militarists from administrative positions in the Federal Republic; nationalization of key industries; agricultural reform—parcelling out of large estates wherever this was economically and politically appropriate; education reform—higher education must not remain a privilege of the rich. As for the SED, 'since in West Germany the unity of the German working class has been realized inside the Social Democratic Party, a future united workers' movement would inevitably, through the greater weight of the Social Democratic Party, bear more likeness to the latter than to the reformed Socialist Unity Party'.

To many East Germans who shared some of Harich's views about democratization of the DDR, his ideas for the creation of a neutral, united, Social Democratic Germany seemed, no doubt, out of date and unrealistic. It was in September 1956 that the Communist Party was banned in West Germany. In July 1956 the West German parliament had agreed to the reintroduction of conscription (introduced in the DDR in 1962). The SPD, most of whose parliamentarians had voted for conscription at its Munich conference, showed every sign of abandoning its remaining socialistic proposals and was in any case defeated once again at the Federal elections of 1957. These events, and Hungary and Suez, gave the Ulbricht group all the evidence they needed to convince their colleagues in the *Politbüro* that Wolfgang Harich was—well-intended or not—dangerous.

Although many of Harich's views were unrealistic he represented the genuine desire of many members of the SED intelligentsia—a desire still prevalent today—for free intellectual discussion within the framework of socialism and the Warsaw Pact, for a parliament which is more than a rubber-stamp body, and for parliamentarians chosen by competing for votes even if this is done within the framework of the single-list system.

In its report of the trial of Wolfgang Harich on 10 March 1957 *Neues Deutschland* mentioned that apart from Ulbricht, Grotewohl, and Matern, Harich wanted to have Karl Schwirdewan removed from the leadership of the Unity Party. Schwirdewan was removed just less than one year later but by his colleagues, not by Harich. This happened at the meeting of the Central Committee in February 1958. With him went Ernst Wollweber, formerly security chief, and Fred Oelssner. Both the latter-named were members of the Central Committee and Schwirdewan was in the *Politbüro*. These three were accused of having misinterpreted the Soviet 20th Party Congress, misunderstood the policy of international relaxation as one of internal toleration for the class enemy, protected the 'counter-revolutionary Harich group', and wanted German reunification at any price. The differences between these three and their colleagues first arose in the autumn of 1956, when Schwirdewan, it was said, wanted to open 'safety valves' in the DDR along the lines of those in Poland and Hungary. Schwirdewan, it was further claimed, was over-tolerant of Harich and his group. Worst of all, however, he and the other two formed a faction against the Party.[54] The group were also in conflict with their colleagues about economic policy. Ulbricht wanted to carry through economic reforms which in certain respects could be labelled 'tough' but in other respects spelt decentralization. Briefly, the industrial Ministries were to be abolished in favour of VVBs or federations of nationalized industries. In future, economic policy would be worked out jointly by them and by a central planning commission. There was also to be tighter labour discipline, greater attempts to increase productivity, and some speeding-up of nationalization of remaining private enterprises.[55] Some feared this meant a return to the policy pursued in 1952–3 which caused so much discontent at that time. Wollweber, as head of security, probably thought he was in a better position to judge public opinion than most of his comrades. Zaisser had been in a similar position in 1953. In addition to the three accused Gerhart Ziller, a member of the Central Committee's all-important secretariat, had supported them. He committed suicide. The changes and dismissals meant promotion for Dr Erich Apel, who became head of the planning commission and later became known

[54] *Der Spiegel* (19 February 1958).
[55] Jänicke, op. cit., pp. 90–1; *20 Jahre*, pp. 240–60.

as a kind of East German Liberman (see below, p. 126), Alfred Neumann, who, already a member of the secretariat, became with Ulbricht the only person to be a member of that and the *Politbüro*, Gerhard Grüneberg, Erich Honecker, Paul Fröhlich, and Paul Verner. All four joined the secretariat. The last three named later were elected to the *Politbüro*. Grüneberg, Honecker, and Fröhlich are still in the secretariat of the Central Committee. As we shall see, this reformed party management had a fair degree of success for the next two years or so, but, on the economic front, their reforms did not go far enough and with full employment and high wages in West Germany the problem of bringing wages into line with what was economically desirable was not solved.

From the 'Great Leap Forward' to the Berlin Wall

In the field of economic policy there were a good many experts who went on demanding reforms of various kinds, demands which could be summed up as a re-evaluation of the role of heavy industry, greater decentralization of economic decision making, and a radical overhaul of the method of fixing prices. These demands were not new. Already in 1954 Professor Fritz Behrens, a leading economist, had been making a searching reappraisal of the Party's economic theory and at a key conference of economic specialists in March 1955 similar views were heard. Fritz Selbmann, the then Minister of Heavy Industry, claimed, 'that for years we have tolerated certain decisive mistakes in our practical economic laws ... For years, almost systematically, we have been breaking certain economic laws ...' These views were partly the result of the DDR's economic development from a lop-sided—in certain respects underdeveloped—economy, to a more complex one. They were also an attempt to promote the de-Stalinization of economic thought, and more important, economic policy. The 'cult of personality' had had a deadening effect on the work of so many brilliant economic experts at the disposal of the SED, with the consequence that theories, which in many cases were the results of the improvisation of the Soviet Communists managing a backward economy, were taken over lock, stock, and barrel, and put into effect in the DDR. There was little attempt to examine the *besondere Bedingungen*, the special conditions, the peculiar characteristics of East Germany. Autarky, or something approaching it, became the aim not only in the DDR but in the other Communist countries as well.[56] Of course, it must be admitted that East Germany, like the other

[56] Heinz Köhler, *Economic Integration in the Soviet Bloc*, Praeger, New York, 1965, p. 80.

Soviet bloc states, had to face the Western trade embargo and had for allies mainly underdeveloped countries. Both Behrens and Selbmann had difficulties over their views on economic affairs though both enjoy the Party's favours today.[57] In the economic field it was to be 1963 before the reformers were to get their way completely.

At the fifth *Parteitag* in July 1958 a beginning of a reform was included in the Party's new economic proposals. It was decided that in future the DDR should concentrate on those branches of the economy which it could do best, particularly those requiring few imported raw materials but a high degree of skill. These were defined as the chemical industry, engineering, and energy.[58] Another aim agreed was that the economy should be developed to such a degree that 'in a few years'—at one point Ulbricht actually mentioned 1961[59]—*per capita* consumption of food and consumer goods would be higher than in West Germany. Thus the congress agreed to follow the Soviet Union, in proclaiming an unrealistic policy goal, for the Soviets had just set their sights on overtaking the USA within a few years. The Chinese likewise had decided, perhaps more modestly, to overtake Britain only in gross industrial production. Following the style developed by Khrushchev, Ulbricht had some critical remarks to make about certain East German products, comparing them unfavourably with similar products produced in capitalist countries.[60] Again echoing his Soviet senior colleague, he had some critical remarks to make about the League of Communists of Yugoslavia and some praise for Mao Tse-tung.[61] The whole economic policy of the *Parteitag* was embodied in the Seven-Year Plan agreed by the East German parliament, the *Volkskammer*, in October 1959. This plan was the result of the earlier discussions among the countries of the Council for Mutual Economic Aid, to intensify co-operation among member states and to go over to seven-year planning.

Although in the new official history N. S. Khrushchev barely gets a mention, he was, according to the official conference report, given several minutes of excited applause by the 1,648 delegates and their guests after delivering a message of greetings from the CPSU.[62] Most of his speech was taken up in condemning the Yugoslavs but he did find time to say something about the German problem. The main point of this was that the two German states should

[57] Jänicke, op. cit., p. 91; *Der Spiegel* (19 February 1958).
[58] *Protokoll Des V Parteitages*, Vol. I, pp. 73–5.
[59] Ibid., p. 23.
[60] Ibid., p. 91.
[61] Ibid., pp. 48–9, 43.
[62] Ibid., p. 304.

negotiate directly, in the way proposed by the DDR government, on the building of a German Confederation. 'No one can deny', he continued, 'that West Germany's entry into NATO, the introduction of conscription and now the decision to equip the *Bundeswehr* with atomic and rocket weapons further aggravates the international situation and especially the relations between the two German states. The Bonn government itself erected, stone by stone, the wall between the two parts of Germany.'[63] Ulbricht's proposals on Germany were West German withdrawal from NATO and East German withdrawal from the Warsaw Pact, the recognition of Germany's post-war frontiers, the guaranteeing of all fundamental democratic freedoms, and the overcoming of revanchism. He also endorsed the idea of a confederation.[64] A reunited Germany would be allowed its own armed forces for defensive purposes.

Finally, the fifth *Parteitag* proposed certain educational reforms, dealt with elsewhere, aimed at bringing students closer to the lives of the workers, and adopted its own version of the Ten Commandments.[65] The educational reforms were in part the result of similar changes in the Soviet Union and in part the result of difficulties in the universities.

Ulbricht and his closest associates could afford to feel much more confident in 1958. The DDR had made a good deal of progress since 1953 and, using the falling number of refugees as their barometer, they could feel they were gaining the trust of the citizens of the DDR. They were also in high spirits because of Soviet space achievements beginning in late 1957. In 1959 things were even better. The number of those leaving the republic fell to below that of any other year since 1949. Things were soon to change, for between then and the sixth *Parteitag* in 1963 events were turbulent, as turbulent as those of the earlier years. In 1960 further measures of socialization were implemented in industry and, more important, the total collectivization of agriculture was carried through. This affected over 500,000 farmers and agricultural workers. It brought with it its own problems. Some farmers who opposed the measure picked up their bags and went West. Others worked in the new co-operatives without enthusiasm.[66] In any case, the enthusiasm of the others did not make up for their lack of management experience. The result of this hasty measure was a worsening of the food situation which in turn reacted on industry. Once again the number of

---

[63] Ibid., p. 279.
[64] Ibid., p. 33.
[65] Ibid., pp. 176, 160.
[66] Doernberg, op. cit., pp. 357–9.

people going West increased. Khrushchev's famous ultimatum—
which amounted to an attempt to force the West to recognize the
DDR or suffer interference with its position in West Berlin—in
May 1961 after the failure of the Paris Summit meetings was possibly also responsible for causing some people to leave the DDR
through fear of worse to come. Rumours of various kinds, perhaps
inspired by the West German secret service,[67] caused something like
a panic, increasing the flow of refugees still further. One influential
British journalist writing at the time claimed to know that West
German firms were also responsible for the refugees: 'some local
firms have undoubtedly been actively recruiting in East Berlin.'[68]
The number of those leaving the DDR reached the highest level
since 1953—207,026. The result was the Berlin Wall in August
1961. Even those who agreed with the necessity for the new frontier
consolidation were saddened by the event. Spirits were low. In the
events leading up to the Wall one must not forget the germ of truth
in the East German justifications for it. These were the continuing
activities of all kinds of agents from West Berlin, the illegal export
of quality goods, Western recruitment of East German labour, and
the fact that East German proposals for solving the German problem had been rejected out of hand. The Wall also came after the
U–2 incident and after the abortive Bay of Pigs invasion—both of
which figure in East German justifications as signs of Western
aggressive intent and 'part and parcel of the global strategy of world
imperialism'. From the East German point of view the situation
seemed to be getting worse. The SPD, which had in 1959 brought
out its 'German Plan', a plan containing the basis for genuine discussion on reunification, a plan quickly shelved, identified itself with
the unflexible, negative CDU approach to national and defence
issues.

All these developments might have caused the SED leadership
to steer an extreme course but, the Wall apart, this did not happen.
Any exponents of such an extreme line would certainly have found
themselves in an embarrassing position in Moscow. In October
1961 the 22nd Congress of the CPSU took place and there the
emphasis was on continued peaceful co-existence, 'liberalization',
and de-Stalinization. In an interview in *Neues Deutschland* on
1 January 1962 Ulbricht confirmed the policy of internal relaxation. The crux of his message was that in future the Party would
try to convince, rather than force, people and that honest differ-

[67] Willi Frischauer, *Evening Standard* (23 October 1963).
[68] Industrial Editor, *Financial Times* (25 July 1961).

ences of opinion would be tolerated. In fact a thaw of sorts was beginning which was to last at least until the end of 1965.

The only controversy at the sixth *Parteitag* in 1963 was caused by a guest—the representative of the Chinese Communist Party. He bitterly attacked the Yugoslavs but, in contrast to 1958, he was met with boos and feet-stamping. Ulbricht condemned Chinese activities on the Indian frontier.[69] Khrushchev caused a few polite laughs by being his usual effervescent self.

The *Parteitag* announced that the DDR was entering a new phase of development, that of the 'complete and comprehensive building of Socialism'. Part and parcel of this, the delegates were told, was the introduction of 'the New Economic System of Planning and Managing the Economy'. This system is based very largely on Liberman's model and adapted for East Germany by the late Erich Apel and Dr Günter Mittag. Needless to say, it followed similar moves in the USSR. The details are given in Chapter 5 and all that need be said here is that the main points are that *Gewinn* (profit) is reinstated as a legitimate, even desirable, measure of economic utility, that there is supposed to be far greater decentralized decision-making, that the quality of production is at least as important as the quantity, and that, where possible, there will be specialization on 'intelligent intensive' products needing limited raw materials. The SED claimed that, in the main, it was not undoing past mistakes but simply assuring that economic management kept pace with a highly complex economy.

This congress also promised that there would be great strides forward in freedom of the individual. The party leaders claimed they did not want power for its own sake but to develop the socialist base of society which alone could, in the long run, make freedom of the individual a reality. Now that the socialist economic system and state in the DDR were secure they could start extending personal freedom for all citizens irrespective of their social background.

These sentiments found expression in the first fundamental programme of the SED which was adopted by the congress.[70] For this first programme the Unity Party is heavily indebted to the CPSU which had itself adopted a new programme at its 22nd Congress in 1962. In fact, considering the Soviet Union is supposed to be building communism, a higher stage of social development than socialism, and the DDR is still only completing the construction of

[69] *Protokoll Des VI Parteitages,* Vol. I, pp. 67–8.
[70] *Protokoll,* Vol. IV, pp. 297–405. The Soviet Programme was published by the Foreign Languages Publishing House, Moscow.

socialism, there is a remarkable similarity between the two. The
SED programme starts with an introduction, 'A New Age Has
Begun', which actually makes reference to the Soviet document,
comparing it with the 1848 Communist Manifesto of Marx and
Engels, 'the Communist Manifesto of the 20th Century'. There
follows Part I, 'Means and Ends', which sets out the SED's version
of events since 1945 and its proposals for solving the German problem. Part II is closely modelled on Part II of the Soviet programme
in form but its content is of course concerned with the SED's task
in the comprehensive building of socialism in the DDR. This section sets out the broad outlines of the New Economic Policy, the
details of which are dealt with in a separate chapter. There is a
section dealing with the raising of living standards which, very
sensibly in view of the Party's past experience, does not commit it
to specific pledges. As mentioned above, this section also contains
certain general promises about an improvement in the work of the
legal organs, the further development of socialist democracy, and
wider personal freedom. Like their Soviet comrades, the Germans
pledged themselves to intensify their struggle against the remnants
of the capitalist past in the thinking and way of life of the working
people, against backward attitudes, manifestations of egoism, indi-
vidualism, and superstition. The programme also incorporates the
ten principles of socialist morality adopted at the 1958 congress.
Part II contains a section promising further educational progress
and another on the world socialist system once again emphasizing
the Soviet Union as 'the centre of the world working-class movement' and promising that the increasing co-operation between the
socialist states is leading to a 'united world commonwealth' which
Lenin had already mentioned in 1919. The last part of the programme deals with 'Communism—The Future Of Mankind'. It
sets out the SED's belief that world communism would triumph
through peaceful competition with capitalism. In Germany the
building of socialism in the DDR would help the peace-loving
forces in West Germany to bring a change there. The programme
then ends with the rather heroic words, 'Socialism is the result of
countless good deeds by millions of people. It is the conscious and
planned realization of all ideals of freedom and of the progressive
efforts of the German working people. It is the transition into the
kingdom of true humanity, equality and fraternity, of peace and
freedom'.[71]

What kind of party had the Socialist Unity Party become by the
time of the sixth *Parteitag*? According to its official statistics it

[71] *Protokoll,* p. 405.

had certainly become a less proletarian party since 1946–7. Now only 33.8 per cent of its members were classed as workers, only 6.2 per cent as farmers. There had been little change since the fifth *Parteitag*. Like other left-wing parties, the SED was weak among the female population, who comprised only 24 per cent of membership in a country where 47 per cent of the labour force were women. But this was an improvement on 1948. The number of comrades under 25 was 9.8 per cent—fewer than in 1948! In the latter year there had been 14 per cent under 25 and this had been dismissed as too low a figure. As for veterans, there were 145,000 or about 10 per cent who had been in the working-class movement before 1933.[72] At the end of 1960 it had been found necessary to expel 13,029 members as hostile or careerist elements—not many in a party of 1,610,679 which regards itself as an élite.[73]

Among the delegates to the sixth *Parteitag* were 613 listed as workers, 445 functionaries, 285 farmers, 308 intellectuals, 219 white-collar workers, and 36 students, housewives, or pensioners.[74]

Looking through the biographies of the Unity Party's representatives in the 1963 *Volkskammer* the writer found that roughly 56 out of 125 had started life as workers, a further 12 or so seemed to be currently engaged as workers and, in all, roughly 100 claimed to be from working-class families (excluding working farmers). Nearly half of the SED's parliamentarians had been in a working-class party or youth organization before 1933 (KPD 47, SPD 10, SAP 2), 34 had suffered imprisonment, 46 had served in the *Wehrmacht*, 17 had been emigrants, and nine of these had fought in Spain. At this level then the SED's members were largely out of a working-class or lower middle-class milieu, but few, very few, were actually getting their hands dirty. A significant number had shared the war experience of their generation and an almost significant number could claim to be part of the élite of suffering created by Hitler.

Both among the SED parliamentary members and among its Central Committee members one notices the large number who, though they may have started in humble surroundings, have gone on to get academic or technical training. It was the Party which gave many of them their chance. A Western investigation of the ZK in 1964 showed that of its 181 members and candidate members about 93 fitted into this category, only 60 were workers.[75]

[72] Ibid., p. 292.
[73] Ibid., p. 255.
[74] *Protokoll*, Vol. II, p. 119.
[75] *Documents: Revue des Questions Allemandes*, Strasbourg, March–April 1965, p. 89.

Obviously, the SED faces the danger of bourgeoisification. It may also be on the road to becoming a party of experts and managers. Sixteen of the 121 full members of the *ZK* elected in 1963 were members of the old 80-member *Vorstand* of 1947. Of the 106 full members elected in 1958 60 remained in 1963, a relatively large turnover. Also of interest is the fact that a Western source claimed that of the 1963 Central Committee, 12 had belonged to the NSDAP though it did not accuse them of being more than purely nominal members of that body.[76] Only seven members of the *ZK* in 1963 were pre-war Social Democrats.

In the highest organ of the Unity Party, the *Politbüro*, all the members elected in 1963 were pre-1933 Communists (11 of them) or Social Democrats (three). Ten were of working-class origin and two were sons whose fathers had been full-time officials in the movement before the Third Reich. Eight had been imprisoned by the Nazis, seven had been emigrants, three had fought in Spain.

Herr Ulbricht must have mounted the rostrum at the VII Party Congress in April 1967 with more confidence than ever before. He could rightly claim that the Wall and the New Economic System based on 'the exploitation of economic levers especially price, profit, credit, and interest as well as wage and bonus',[77] had produced successes. As Jean Edward Smith, a former officer attached to the US garrison in West Berlin, told the American Political Science Association in 1966, 'the Wall ... inaugurated one of Europe's most far-reaching economic miracles—and paved the way for an equally profound shift in popular attitudes'.[78] Both these points were confirmed by his colleague, Professor Hans Apel, in the Hamburg weekly *Die Zeit* (16 and 23 June 1967). The result of the economic upsurge is, according to *Newsweek* (13 March 1967), that 'Display windows are crammed with consumer goods'. Equally important, so the *Daily Telegraph* (19 April 1966), 'If East Germany is a police State, it is a remarkably liberal one by Himmler–Beria standards.' In its own glossy way *Life* (10 July 1967) was forced to agree, telling its readers, 'Even the most vehement dissenting East Germans we met admitted that they enjoyed considerable freedom of expression'. Internationally too, apart from this belated and grudging recognition by the Western press, the

[76] *Ehemalige Nationalsozialisten in Pankows Diensten,* July 1965, Unter-suchungsausschuss Freiheitlicher Juristen, (West) Berlin, p. 5.

[77] Erich Apel and Günter Mittag, *Neues Okonomisches System und Investitionspolitik*, Dietz Verlag, (East) Berlin, 1965, p. 190.

[78] Prof. Jean Edward Smith, *International Journal* (Toronto), Spring 1967. See also his article in *Political Science Quarterly* (Columbia University), September 1967.

DDR had gained much since the VI Congress of 1963. In June 1964 the Soviet Union signed a Treaty of Friendship with the DDR, guaranteeing its frontiers for twenty years. Much to the anger of the West German government the International Olympic Committee decided to allow the DDR to field its own team at future international events, thus recognizing its separate status. In Tanzania the DDR gained some diplomatic recognition despite the protests of Bonn. More serious still, President Tito, who had recognized the DDR in 1957, thus forfeiting relations with Bonn, drew closer to Ulbricht by paying a state visit to East Germany. Walter Ulbricht also went to far-away places. He staged a highly publicized visit to Cairo which led to West Germany's recognition of Israel. This in turn caused the Arab states to break off relations with the Federal Republic. Looking westward, Ulbricht must have got some satisfaction from his victory over Adenauer in their office-holding marathon, and from the difficulties which followed his rival's departure : the Bonn defence row over the disastrous safety record of the 'Starfighters'; the 'revolt of the generals'; the whole question of defence strategy; the failure of the government to solve the problem of the slump in the Ruhr coalfields; the continuing tensions between the warring factions of the Christian Democratic camp, and between the Establishment Christians and their coalition partners, the Free Democrats; the argument about the significance of the relative success of the nationalistic National Democratic Party and what to do about it; the tensions in the Social Democratic Party after its defeat in the 1965 elections and the controversy around the person of Herr Wehner; the heartsearching about the proposed emergency powers legislation; the final crisis leading up to the resignation of Chancellor Erhard and the formation of the 'Grand Coalition'; and, finally, the discussion both in West Germany and abroad, about the suitability of the new Chancellor, Dr Kiesinger, to lead the Federal Republic because of his past membership of the NSDAP.

Even so, despite all this, Walter Ulbricht went to the VII Congress of his party knowing that he faced many problems. On the domestic front, as the writer has found out, there is discontent over restrictions on travel, the high prices of certain goods, and the lack of private transport. And, as official East German reports make clear, house-building lags woefully behind demand. Then there is the still thorny question of the SED's relations with its intellectuals. The régime has done much to ensure the material well-being of this group. They are not only well paid but able to travel abroad much more often than most of their fellow citizens. They are provided

with clubs and, not least, with honours. Yet the SED has not
managed to work out a sensible relationship with its cultural élite.
All too often it has been clumsy and brutish in its handling of them.
Because of this the DDR lost some of its best cultural ambassadors
to the West who went more in sorrow than in anger. At the eleventh
session of the Central Committee in December 1965 Erich
Honecker,[79] said by many to be Ulbricht's heir apparent, attacked
three kinds of tendency in the cultural life of the DDR. The first
was the tolerance, and even encouragement, of Western 'pop' music
owing, he claimed, to a faulty estimate by the FDJ of such music.
Those responsible in the youth movement had interpreted it as the
musical expression of the age of the technical revolution, failing to
see that this music was exploited by their Western opponents to
work up the young people into a frenzy. In the months before the
ZK meeting there had been certain minor youth riots of the type
experienced in Britain, West Germany, and other places. Honecker
also criticized the emphasis on sex and violence in the mass media.
One's judgement of the SED's stand on this will depend mainly
on whether one considers too much sex and violence, too much 'pop
culture', makes young people more likely to go off the rails or not.
Honecker's second attack was on the emphasis in so much of the
DDR's literary output on the shortcomings of the Stalinist past;
he was not, it should be stated, trying to rehabilitate that past. He
named Stefan Heym's unpublished book about the events of 17
June 1953 in this connection, claiming it painted a completely false
picture. Thirdly, he attacked the continued expression of works of
scepticism whose thesis was 'doubt everything, doubt all authority'.
Wolf Biermann, the poet, was put into this category. The effect of
all this, he said, was that young people did not know where to turn
for ideals and examples and that these tendencies would interfere
with the resolve of the people to increase production and therefore
living standards. Culture will remain a problem for the leaders of
the SED, for East Germany is fully exposed to Western influence
through radio and television and the re-examination of the past
must inevitably continue to raise awkward questions. In addition,
because the DDR, like all other states, is not perfect, Marxist
ideology itself will continue to furnish the young with food for
thought about the state of things at any given time.

One of the most recent of the Marxist critics of the régime who,
the Party thought, was embarrassing them, was Professor Robert

[79] This account is taken from 'Bericht des Politbüros an die 11. Tagung
des Zentralkomitees der SED 15–18 Dezember 1965', *Berichterstatter*
Genosse Erich *Honecker*, Dietz Verlag, (East) Berlin, 1966.

Havemann of the Humboldt University. Havemann, imprisoned by the Nazis and a highly thought-of scientist, had in effect called for more freedom of thought in the DDR and, like Biermann, had published his views in the West. He was expelled from the SED and removed from his university post in 1964. Another well-known East German intellectual, Christa Wolf, was rewarded for championing Biermann by being removed from the Party's Central Committee.

The December 1965 session of the Central Committee marked a turning point in the politics of the DDR away from the relative 'thaw' which started in 1962 to a 'hard' line.

Another embarrassment for Ulbricht and his colleagues before the VII Congress was the suicide in December 1965 of Erich Apel, East Germany's top planner and a candidate member of the *PB*. Whatever the circumstances of his death it could not help feeding rumours about the allegedly unfavourable terms of the new trade treaty with the Soviet Union.

Nor had the SED been entirely successful in the propaganda duel which it had sought with the SPD. Briefly, the SED had suggested an exchange of speakers between the two parties. Surprisingly, in view of past form, the SPD agreed in principle. Negotiations followed. Difficulties arose over the form the meetings were to take and about guaranteeing the safety of the East German speakers—East German journalists and politicians invited to West Germany have on occasion been arrested. The SPD, partly no doubt out of fear of censure from the West German press and government, wanted to avoid any manifestations of friendship, even tolerance : there were to be no handshakes, for instance. Secondly, the ruling CDU/CSU-FDP coalition in Bonn hesitated at first about guaranteeing the SED speakers' safety—they no doubt were afraid the SPD would gain popularity by its all-German manoeuvres. They finally passed legislation granting safe-conduct for the period of the proposed visit only. The SED then turned awkward and rejected these concessions. From the East German point of view the proposed exchange was part of their battle for recognition. They would have liked pictures of the SPD leaders, especially Brandt, shaking hands with some leading SED official. This they were not going to get. They would have also been going to West Germany like representatives of a beleaguered fortress under a flag of truce guaranteed by their opponents. Why should they accept such indignities for their top leadership? However, the manner in which they ended the encounter made it easy for Western propagandists to claim they were afraid. This the writer doubts. The East German population get the message of Willy Brandt and Herbert Wehner any time they like on television or radio. Two or three addresses before hand-picked audiences would not change much.

The régime's biggest single liability in terms of its 'image' both at home and beyond its frontiers continued to be the Berlin Wall. Official West German sources say that between August 1961 and the end of November 1968 at least 63 people died while trying to escape from the East to West Berlin. Most of these were killed at the Wall. Altogether, at least 137 people were killed during the same period attempting to cross the frontier between East and West Germany. Apart from deaths on the Wall there were the dramatic escapes which brought renewed attention to it, exposing the Ulbricht régime to ridicule as well as contempt. Among some of the more unusual escapes of 1961–5 were : a group who successfully posed as a party of Soviet officers; a painter and a bus conductor who escaped, Harry-Lime-style, through a public drainage system; a group who got away on a pleasure boat; a truck-driver who got his family out by hiding them in his refrigerator van—he was on a routine trip taking meat to West Berlin; holders of phoney diplomatic passports; a 32-year-old East German teacher who was saluted by DDR police as he passed from East to West in a home-made imitation of an American officer's uniform.[80]

The West Germans managed to cast a shadow over the VII Congress by their diplomatic offensive in Eastern Europe which led to the exchange of ambassadors between Bonn and Bucharest on terms unfavourable to the DDR. This is discussed elsewhere (see below pp. 261–2).

Always afraid of isolation, the SED leadership were particularly gratified in view of Bonn's offensive to see so many fraternal guests at the congress representing Marxist and workers' parties from all continents, from the mighty CPSU to such mini-parties as the Northern Ireland CP. Only the Chinese, who were once again under fire, the Albanians, and the Cubans did not send delegations. Castro's party did send a telegram of best wishes. The foreign delegates included some of communism's top brass such as Leonid Brezhnev, secretary of the CPSU, and Wladislaw Gomulka of Poland. Grateful though the delegates were for such manifestations of solidarity, they were mainly concerned with domestic issues, above all with living standards. The leaders showed how important they regard this by an ostentatious visit to a special exhibition of consumer goods organized in honour of the congress. They also made clear to the congress that, in addition to material incentives, pro-

[80] *Der Spiegel* (11 August 1965).

duction and thus living standards would be boosted by even more application of science to industry than ever before. A massive delegation of the DDR's scientists pledged their support and one of their number, Dr Klaus Fuchs, of the 'Manhattan Project', Harwell, and Wormwood Scrubs, was given the unusual honour of being elected a full member of the *ZK* without any probationary period.

The congress made a number of realistic pledges to the East German people, technically suggestions to the DDR government, including a five-day working week to be introduced in September 1967, increased minimum wages, a minimum annual holiday of 15 working days (many already had 18 days or over), higher family allowances, higher retirement pensions and disability pensions in 1968, and wage-related pensions at a future date.

What changes had taken place in the SED between the VI and VII Congresses? The main features were steady expansion of membership and stability of leadership. Starting at the bottom the Party numbered, according to *Neues Deutschland* (17 April 1967), 1,769,912 members on 31 December 1966. This was an increase of roughly 160,000. Thus it comprised about 10 per cent of the population of 17 million and well over 15 per cent of those over 18. In somewhat different circumstances it had more members than all three West German parties taken together. Some 41.2 per cent of members had been in the Party for over 15 years, 6.9 per cent or 122,285 were in the movement before 1945. The proportion of women members had increased and now stood at 26.5 per cent. But the proportion of under-25s had declined to 8.2 per cent. The SED had tried to halt the bourgeoisification process and claimed that 62.4 per cent of the new members were workers. In all, 45.6 per cent of the membership were said to be currently employed as workers and 6.4 per cent as co-operative farmers. The SED also had its capitalists! The report mentioned that 12,218 comrades were entrepreneurs of mixed private-state enterprises.

The Central Committee showed remarkable stability between the last two congresses. Of the 121 members elected in 1963 only 20 were no longer members.[81] Probably half of these had been removed by natural causes. Some of the others had moved on to other important work. The trend towards professionalism in the *ZK* is continuing. Now at least 100 of its 131 full members have had some formal university or professional training. This does not mean that the younger generation of technocrats had completely taken over the Committee by 1967: 56 of its full members belonged to the pre-1945 generation of Marxists. The SED's effective

[81] *Neues Deutschland* (23 April 1967) gives the full list of the new *ZK*.

decision-making body, the *Politbüro*, had lost two of its full members since 1963. Both died of old age and long illnesses. Their places were taken by Günter Mittag and Gerhard Grüneberg, both of the post-war generation. The congress saw the election of another new member, Horst Sindermann, who, although only 51, spent 11 years in jail under Hitler.

The Great Monolith

It is impossible for the outsider, even one who has met a number of the leading, and many ordinary, members, to get a clear picture of the working of the SED. At the *Parteitag* in 1963, however, it was admitted that a number of functionaries were still riding roughshod over their nominal superiors, the elected committees.[82] It was also admitted that there had been apathy and indifference in carrying out party decisions. The *Parteitag*, which is officially the highest organ of the SED, is a massive, stage-managed jamboree where the faithful are summoned to hear, acclaim, and perhaps mingle with, the mighty. Officially the *Parteitag* elects the *ZK* or Central Committee but this appears to be a rubber-stamp decision on the basis of the list proposed to the congress by the leaders. In addition to the seven party congresses between 1946 and 1967 there have been three *Parteikonferenzen*. The latter were held in 1949, 1952, and 1956. These conferences were in practice similar to the congresses though in theory they do not have as much formal power. Many lesser conferences have been held during these years to discuss specific areas of policy. To some extent they compensate for the fact that congresses are now only called once every four years—originally, under the 1946 SED constitution, they were to be held annually. The congress elects the Central Committee which meets about four times a year. Its deliberations are not published in full so that it is difficult to appraise its work accurately. But it is doubtful that it is a really effective body of the best activists who propose and amend party policy. Its size and the relative infrequency of its meetings, and the fact that its members see little or nothing of each other between sessions, must greatly reduce its effective role and it is unlikely to be in a position to oppose the leadership for these reasons alone. In addition, the full-time officials of the secretariat inevitably are better prepared for most of the discussions, having a wide range of material at their disposal. Apart from these senior party functionaries a good many Central Committee members are full-time party officials at slightly lower levels and it seems likely that they will be just a little more dependent on their senior party

[82] *Protokoll Des VI Parteitages,* Vol. IV, p. 282.

colleagues than other *ZK* members whose main work lies outside the Party. Thus they may represent a powerful prop to the highest party functionaries. As we have seen, the Central Committee is becoming increasingly a body of technically qualified people and one wonders whether this will increase its stature and promote free discussion. It is also a representative body in that its members are drawn from all the various categories of party members—party and state officials, officials of the mass organizations, economists, co-operative farmers, intelligentsia, women, and so on. This enables the top leadership to exchange ideas with members from the various sectors of national life. This inevitably leads to modifications of policy, especially on technical, if not very often on political, problems. The *ZK* has a number of commissions, *Kommissionen* and *Büros*, which are organized to supervise work, and help to solve problems, in particular fields—science, industry, agriculture, defence. Those who take part in the deliberations of these bodies are not always members of the SED. They may be drawn from other parties or be non-party specialists. The only way the Central Committee could conceivably play a decisive part in changing policies or leaders would be in concert with a member or members of the *Politbüro*. Even this would be difficult as meetings of groups outside official sessions could be classed as 'building a faction' which is forbidden by the party constitution.

The *Politbüro*, which is elected by the Central Committee, meets about once a week and is the nearest thing to a Western cabinet in the DDR. It is the decisive power centre of the republic. Its members are either in charge of important state affairs—for instance, Willi Stoph, Prime Minister; Friedrich Ebert, Lord Mayor of East Berlin until 1967; Herbert Warnke, Chairman of the Free Trade Union Federation; Walter Halbritter, Director of the Office for Prices; or full-time SED officials, such as Paul Fröhlich, first secretary of the Leipzig SED; Professor Albert Norden, secretary in charge of agitation and propaganda; etc. Some of the members are secretaries of the *ZK,* that is members of the *Sekretariat* of the *ZK*, the powerful headquarters organization. The *Politbüro* had 15 full members in 1968, seven of them secretaries. Thus the secretaries of the *ZK*, usually regarded by Western experts as Ulbricht's closest associates, were in a very strong, though not completely dominant, position. Of the six candidate members two were secretaries. There were nine secretaries, apart from Ulbricht himself. The secretaries of the *ZK* are in charge of departments or *Abteilungen* which either 'shadow' important Ministries or deal with particular areas of party policy—agitation and propaganda, security, ideology, agriculture. The secretaries of the *ZK* effectively run the Party, each having an army of officials under him.

The members of the SED are divided among over 50,000 basic organizations, either where they work or where they live. These elect and are subject to *Stadt–*or *Ortsleitungen,* which cover mainly relatively small towns or villages. Next come the *Kreisleitungen,* covering larger towns and large factories. They have their own secretariats. Higher still are the 15 *Bezirksleitungen,* corresponding to the administrative districts of the DDR. There is a separate *Leitung* for the uranium mining company, Wismut A. G. Like all Communist parties to date the SED is run on the principle of 'Democratic Centralism' which means in theory that all organs are elected by members but that all lower organs are subject to the decisions of higher ones. Given the 'Communist' system of party elections with various conferences receiving a proposed list of candidates from above, the leadership and full-time officials have enormous power. As one can see from this limited account of the SED's organization, the ordinary members have little power. It might well be significant that the 1963 constitution accords members eleven duties and five rights. They probably enjoy a little more influence than they did a few years ago for, as we shall see in the following chapters, East Germany, in common with most of the Communist world, has made some progress in recent years towards at least starting a dialogue between the rulers and the ruled.

The Socialist Unity Party was born of the desire of the Soviet Union for an effective political instrument in Germany to advocate and if possible execute a policy favourable to it, and of the hopes and dreams of thousands of ordinary, honest, Germans, who wanted to put aside that which has divided Germany from the country of nations and build a new society based on equality, freedom, and social progress. After it found itself in the ghetto of the Soviet Zone it too on the herculean task of making an unviable economy and state work. It also declared its aim, an even greater one, of building a socialist society in its part of Germany. Here and there in this book the writer compares the reality of East German life with some of the ideas expressed by the classic thinkers of Marxian socialism. The reader will inevitably conclude that the SED still is a very long way away from realizing its high ambitions. Nevertheless, it has brought considerable economic, social, and educational progress to East Germany. In the following chapters we shall be looking in greater detail at this progress as well as the failures and shortcomings and shadows which are still part of the German Democratic Republic today.

Chapter 2

The East German Elite: the Red Jesuits and the Others

THE LATE Arnold Zweig, for many years doyen of German Communist literature, once said, 'Humanism and strict organization have always been in contradiction. Even the Jesuits, who left us great spiritual power, were not so strict in their organization as we are in building the DDR'.[1] The strict organization of East German life and administration is discussed elsewhere in this book. Here the aim is to dissect the East German élite and separate the Red Jesuits from the others. But are the top men of the other German state really Red Jesuits as Arnold Zweig would seem to have been implying? Of course, what they think and what they do in private is their secret and though the writer has met some of them he would not presume to know anything about their innermost conflicts, thoughts, desires, and aspirations. And Robert Conquest, in discussing the problem of assessing revolutionary élites, has rightly reminded us : 'In practice these are not joined by Simon Pure idealists, but consist of a hodge-podge of members in which the idealist component is accompanied by all sorts of motivations—vanity, power-seeking and mere freakishness'. This judgement could equally well apply to the Jesuits. The top members of the East German élite, the members of the SED *Politbüro,* like the Jesuits, have devoted their lives to a cause, claiming to be interested only in the betterment of man, a cause which took on the strengths and weaknesses of religion. As a prominent Jesuit has written : 'Without whittling away the vital differences . . . I hope to show that Christianity and Communism do propose comparable answers to many questions . . . The Christian equally with the Marxist has a passion for the redemption of his fellow men—and, what is more, he is confident that he has in his religion the wherewithal to bring

---

[1] Martin Jänicke, *Der Dritte Weg,* Neuer Deutscher Verlag, Cologne, 1964, p. 58.

it about again'.[2] Again, like the Jesuits of old, the top members of the SED believe they must give their wards what is good for them, what they ought to want, rather than what they may actually want at a given moment. Some of them, somewhat arrogantly, assume they have mastered a complex science, Marxism, which few others can grasp.

Who are the Red Jesuits of the *Politbüro*? Most of the full members elected by the seventh *Parteitag* in 1967 are veterans of the movement. Hermann Matern, aged 75 in 1968, has the longest membership stretching back to 1911. He is followed by Walter Ulbricht who joined the Social Democratic Party in 1912. Friedrich Ebert, 74 in 1968, the son of the first President of the Weimar republic, is the only other to join before the First World War. He joined in 1913. All three served in this war, but, when it was over, Ulbricht and Matern decided for the newly founded German Communist Party while Ebert stayed in the Social Democratic Party. All three became full-time political workers during the Weimar republic. Ulbricht and Ebert became members of the German parliament, the *Reichstag*, as did one other SED *PB* member, Herbert Warnke. Out of the 15 full members of the *Politbüro* all but three were active in the working-class movement before 1933. Of these pre-1933 Marxists, only one, Willi Stoph, was not either in the emigration or imprisoned by the Nazis. Stoph was 18 when the Nazis seized power in 1933 and was not important enough to gain the Gestapo's attention. Some of these thirteen, Erich Honecker, Bruno Leuschner, and Erich Mückenberger, spent virtually the whole 12 years of the Third Reich in the hell of Nazi jails and concentration camps, a fact which should never be forgotten when judging the post-war activities of these men. Ebert and Fröhlich, by comparison, got off lightly, spending just enough time in jail and camp to know what they were like. Ulbricht, Hager, Neumann, Norden, Verner, and Warnke escaped abroad. As is well known, Ulbricht spent almost the entire period in Moscow. Professor Kurt Hager, Alfred Neumann, and Paul Verner fought in Spain, but whereas Hager and Verner got out of Spain to England and Sweden respectively, their comrade fell into the hands of the Gestapo. Paul Verner and Herbert Warnke were later imprisoned for anti-Nazi activities in wartime Sweden. Professor Albert Norden was lucky; he managed to get to the USA where he worked as a journalist. His father, however, a rabbi, died in a concentration

[2] Fr Martin D'Arcy, SJ, *Communism and Christianity*, Penguin Books, London, 1956, p. 8; Robert Conquest, *The Great Terror*, Macmillan, London, 1968, p. 508.

camp. The three *PB* members who were not in either the SPD or
the KPD before 1933 are Horst Sindermann, Günter Mittag, and
Gerhard Grüneberg. Sindermann, now 51, spent most of the Nazi
period in prisons or camps. Mittag was only 18 when the Third
Reich collapsed and joined the SED in 1946. Grüneberg was 23 in
1945. He had joined the Communist children's movement, the Red
Pioneers, in 1928 and remained a member until it was banned. He
served in the forces during the war and joined the SED in 1946.

Obviously the members of the *PB* are tough—they had to become
so to survive those years of physical and mental torture during
which their side seemed to be losing : the years of the Nazi take-
over, Hitler's annexation of the Saar, the *Anschluss* of Austria and
the destruction of Czechoslovakia, the defeat of Republican Spain,
Stalin's purges, the Non-Aggression Pact, the fall of Poland and
the collapse of France, Hitler's early successes in the Soviet Union.
Those who were not hounded from one European tragedy to another were nearly all in the camps wondering whether each day
would be their last. How different, it may be said, were the lives
of most of Bonn's leading politicians.

Walter Ulbricht

The top man of the East German élite, First Secretary of the
SED and Chairman of the Council of State, Walter Ulbricht, must
be a remarkable man. He has held his *de facto* position of power
for longer than Hitler, Adenauer, Erhard, Hindenburg and the
other leaders of the Weimar republic, Lenin, Khrushchev, and the
post-war generation of British Prime Ministers or American Presidents. In the European Communist world his only rivals in experience of office are Tito and Enver Hoxha of Albania. In non-
Communist Europe the only leaders who have held office longer
are General Franco and Dr Salazar. However, Ulbricht's feat is so
much more remarkable because East Germany has been a kind
of hothouse of economic, social, educational, and political revolution for over twenty years, and has been dependent on a mighty
neighbour undergoing equally momentous changes. Ulbricht's
durability is also remarkable because he is said to be a glutton for
work. Who is this man Ulbricht?

In terms of hard facts not all that much is known about him
apart from the details of his life which can easily be verified in
East and West. Other than these biographical details, which are
set out below, most opinions we get about him are those of either
the official writers in East Germany, who treat him like a saintly
monarch, or of embittered ex-Communists whose views are coloured

by past struggles against him and the present political climate. Indeed, because, as one Western writer put it, our view of the DDR, and therefore its leader, 'tends to be filtered through the hostile lens of the Cold War at its coldest',[3] even a normally reasonable Westerner sub consciously thinks of Ulbricht as the Ogre of the Wall, the man who never was, the rubber dummy blown up each morning by a Soviet colonel and then deflated again each night. When one meets him one cannot entirely shake off this indoctrination. For what it is worth, his handshake is reasonably, though not anxiously, firm; he gesticulates, smiles, answers questions in a homely, astonishingly croaky, Saxon voice. Ulbricht's appearance is remarkable for its oddity. His neat sober clothes are those of a bank official, his beard and belly would not, according to one Middle Eastern visitor of the writer's acquaintance, make him feel out of place among the holy *Haji* of the bazaars, the prosperous shopkeepers who have made the pilgrimage to Mecca. Some years ago a Western journalist described his appearance in the following way : 'Personally, Ulbricht has, even today, something decidedly humdrum to him; but, together with it, the bounce and cockiness of the little man who has had success. In appearance he is what can only be called dapper. Under middle height, he carries himself very erect; his little Lenin beard is carefully trimmed, his slightly sagging frame covered with very well-tailored double-breasted suits, usually pastel coloured'.[4] In his private life he is believed to live quietly in a modest apartment with his wife Lotte. A non-smoker, who drinks little alcohol, he still has a fondness for sport that he has retained from his youth. He has the reputation of finding it difficult to communicate with people on a personal basis but, certainly in recent years, he has tried to overcome this. On one social occasion : 'He even danced with some of the young girls and matrons, proposed a game of forfeits, and gave one of the girls a friendly kiss on the cheek'.[5] This was from a Western account, though now the 'kiss on the cheek' is part and parcel of Ulbricht's official image. Even so, in the early post-war period, when Ulbricht's image in the West was about at its lowest, and when he had a reputation, even more than now, for being a wooden, menacing, dictator, his colleagues did not seem to have been afraid of him. We have this

[3] Jean Edward Smith, *International Journal* (Toronto), Spring 1967, p. 235.
[4] *Observer* profile (7 December 1958).
[5] Carola Stern, *Ulbricht A Political Biography,* Praeger, New York; Pall Mall Press, London, 1965, p. 133.

from Erich Gniffke[6] in his account of the (entirely innocent) fun and games which went on when the party leaders went together for a weekend in the country. Ulbricht did not join in much but his comrades had their games all the same. Later on, during the Stalinist purges of the late forties and early fifties, and in his own struggles for survival, he avoided turning the ruling circles of the SED into a kind of imitation Borgia court. As one Western academic put it:

> he is certainly not the ogre Stalin was, and his drive for personal power has never burst out in murderous vendettas. Indeed, Ulbricht has survived for almost forty years as one of the leading figures of German Communism and his longevity doubtless attests his basic acceptability to all factions, reformist as well as reactionary. There is also the question of competence. Here too Ulbricht has been grossly underrated. Of all the European Communist heads of state, only Ulbricht must contend with a divided nation longing to be reunited—and his portion of that nation is scarcely the largest, the richest, or the most productive.[7]

Rumours have circulated since Ulbricht became prominent that he was responsible in the 1930s for turning his comrades over to the Stalinist secret police and to the Gestapo. He is also accused of preventing the escape of the leader of the KPD, Ernst Thälmann, who was held in a Nazi jail and finally liquidated. His main West German biographer, a former SED member and for many years a staunch opponent of communism, has written:

> On the basis of the materials available to me, I have remained unconvinced that Ulbricht bears the guilt for Thälmann's imprisonment or that he blocked Thälmann's transfer to the Soviet Union during the time of the German-Soviet Nonaggression Pact. Nor am I of the opinion that Ulbricht primarily is to blame for the fate of those German Communists who died during the Soviet purges of 1936–38. We must be careful not to fall into the trap of a reverse 'personality cult'.[8]

What about the 'personality cult'? Ulbricht, like all the other European Communist leaders of his generation, took part in the eulogizing of Stalin. His excuse could be that he was in a more precarious position than most. The German Communist emigrants

[6] Erich W. Gniffke, *Jahre Mit Ulbricht*, Verlag Wissenschaft und Politik, Cologne, 1966, pp. 182–4.
[7] Smith, op. cit., pp. 232–3; Prof. H. R. Külz, of the West German Federal Administrative Court, *Die Zeit* (23 June 1967).
[8] Stern, op. cit., Preface, p. vi.

in Moscow were entirely dependent on their Soviet hosts and in 1945 they returned to Germany because the Red Army had been successful, not because the German masses had risen to overthrow Nazism. Even before 1933 the KPD was dependent on Moscow. As E. H. Carr put it, 'A weak opposition party, often persecuted in its own country, is clearly no match for a party which has a victorious revolution behind it, and controls the affairs of a great nation ... The weak, unsuccessful foreign party inevitably tends to take its cue from the strong, successful, Russian party . . .'[9] Ulbricht, the son of a worker, himself originally a worker, brought up to expect a revolution of the German proletariat, for so long the pride of the international working-class movement, must have been deeply disappointed by what happened in 1933. It would have been entirely human to have come to hate and despise his own people. Although Ulbricht saw some terrible things in the Soviet Union, for someone brought up in a closed system to admit that the Soviet Union might be wrong in some fundamental sense would have been tantamount to spiritual suicide. At the height of Stalin's purges it would very probably have been physical suicide as well. It is likely that Ulbricht from early on developed a personal devotion to the Soviet Union. Apart from finding refuge there after the rise of Hitler he had been helped out by the Soviet party in 1924 when he was wanted by the police in Germany. His devotion to Stalin was no doubt an extension of his devotion to the Soviet Union and, in any case, the European socialist movement had treated its leaders as larger than life before Stalin. With Stalin the cult of the God-like, charismatic leader reached its climax. When one considers that those cool, empiricist Fabians, the Webbs, after a lifetime of experience in the highest circles, were completely taken in by Stalin, one ought to be able to understand that Ulbricht, ex-cabinet-maker, provincial, functionary of a secular religion, had no chance.

Much more reprehensible has been Ulbricht's own 'personality cult', which is of course a complete negation of Marxism. In a famous letter to Wilhelm Blos, written in November 1877, Marx clearly indicated his 'aversion to any personality cult...' The Ulbricht cult has taken the usual forms, the naming of institutions of all kinds after him, undue deference, etc. One particularly regrettable form of this cult is the tendency of writers on virtually all subjects to over-quote him in a way which would give a Martian visitor the impression that he is a combination of Marx, Henry Ford, Jesus Christ, Thomas Mann, and others besides, with the

[9] E. H. Carr, *Studies In Revolution*, London, 1950, pp. 196–7.

wisdom of Job and the knowledge of an encyclopaedia. For instance, in a book[10] on the New Economic System, originally the product of the minds of Soviet academics such as Liberman and Nemchinov as modified for the DDR by Apel, Mittag, and others, Ulbricht gets 40 mentions as against one each for the authors of the new system. Others mentioned are Marx (10 mentions), Lenin (6), Engels (one), the late Oskar Lange, the Polish economist (2), Stalin, in a negative way (2), etc. All these quotations are a way of emphasizing one's complete orthodoxy and loyalty to the leader. The Ulbricht cult reached a new high in June and July 1968 when the most lavish and servile adulation was heaped on the DDR Head of State. 'Walter Ulbricht honoured by millions', was the headline in the Liberal Democratic organ *Der Morgen* on 2 July 1968, and, according to this paper, for days on end there were queues of people waiting at Ulbricht's official residence to record their tributes in specially prepared books and leave their presents. Clearly for any unit of any organization in any part of East Germany not to conform to this ritual would have been regarded as disloyal. The 30 June edition of *Der Morgen* was devoted largely to prominent East Germans' eulogies of Herr Ulbricht. The director of the Dresden *Staatstheater*, Hans Dieter Mäde, said that Ulbricht was 'one of the most active, information-hungry, knowledgeable theatre-goers in the DDR'. Professor Lea Grundig thanked him for his tips on painting, and scientists, university teachers, and the writer Arnold Zweig also contributed their hosannas. A manufacturer of ladies' underwear, Herr Flaig of Plauen, recalled an 'unforgettable spring day' when he met Ulbricht at a reception; but Otto Krauss, a prominent member of the DDR parliament, hinted, in *Der Morgen* on 29 June 1968, at the scepticism of many ordinary East Germans when he admitted, 'Often I am asked, does the Chairman of the State Council, Walter Ulbricht, really know what it's like "below" [among the people]?' It all recalled the celebrations in honour of Stalin's birthdays.[11]

Ulbricht served Stalin faithfully like most other Communist leaders of the day and still promotes a Stalin-style personality cult. Is he still a Stalinist? Certainly not in the sense of applauding Stalin's theories and actions. In view of Ulbricht's dependence on Soviet goodwill this would be impossible. Certainly not in the sense of bashing out the brains of anyone whom he considers his rival or who opposes him. The deaths on the Wall and the West frontier apart, there have been few political killings in East Germany either before or after 1953. Certainly not in the emphasis given since 1963 to economic, managerial, and sociological techniques. But Ulbricht, like his friends in Moscow, remains Stalinist in two ways, the one following from the other. Firstly, there is the complete party control of the Arts and the information media. This is discussed later in this chapter and is the result of a much more fundamental similarity with Stalinism. The late Isaac Deutscher, in seeking to explain the differences between Stalin and Trotsky, exposed the essential characteristics of Stalinism are still with us:

> What underlay Trotsky's attitude was a cautious and yet very real revolutionary optimism, a belief that, if only the rulers pursued the right Socialist policy, the working classes would support them. This belief had indeed been implicit in Marxist thinking; and Stalin never openly contradicted it. But between the lines of his policies there is always present a deep disbelief in the popularity of socialism, and even more than that: an essentially pessimistic approach to man and society. In the last instance the revolutionary optimist sets his hope on his frank appeal to the people, even when he may seem to hope against hope. The pessimist in power distrusts those whom he rules. The Communist pessimist treats his own doctrine as a piece of esoteric knowledge. He does not believe that the working classes are really capable of accepting it, unless it is, brutally speaking, pushed down their throats.[12]

This lack of trust of the people is just as profound an aspect of the Ulbricht régime today as it is of the USSR now and under Stalin. It was probably the most important reason for the invasion of Czechoslovakia—the fact that Dubček wished to trust the people—though there may have been secondary military reasons as well.[13]

Was Ulbricht's influence of decisive importance in persuading Soviet intervention in Czechoslovakia? Some Western papers seemed to think it was. Vladimir Dedijer, the unorthodox Yugoslav Communist historian, told *Der Spiegel* (13 January 1969) that he thought Ulbricht had advocated intervention though he admitted he had no firm evidence. Ulbricht could claim to be the most experienced pro-Moscow Communist leader, heading the most stable and the most powerful of the pro-Soviet Communist states. Thus it could be argued that he would have great influence in Moscow, influence

---

[12] Isaac Deutscher, op. cit., p. 264.
[13] L. L. Whetten, 'Military Aspects of the Soviet Occupation of Czechoslovakia', *The World Today* (February 1969).

for intervention. It could also be argued that, being himself afraid, he could have frightened the Russians by spelling out what would happen in the DDR if the rot in Prague was not stopped. Against all this, given Ulbricht was for intervention, it is difficult to believe that the Soviet leaders would have allowed themselves to be lectured and swayed by a *German* and they are likely to treat with caution the views of the older, Stalin, generation of leaders even though they themselves still use many of the old methods. Some of them may have argued that in view of certain weaknesses of the Ulbricht system he is not the man to advise them. On balance, lacking any firm evidence either way, this writer believes we must assume the decision was made by Moscow and only by Moscow.

The main facts[14] about Ulbricht are that he was born in 1893 in Leipzig, the son of a poor tailor. He was the eldest of three children; his sister went to live in Hamburg and his brother emigrated to the USA. After completing the normal eight years schooling he became an apprentice cabinet-maker. He also tried to continue his education in the workers' education movement. The son of a loyal Social Democrat, he joined the socialist youth movement in 1908 and the SPD in 1912. In 1914, at the outbreak of the war, when Social Democrats had to choose between Kaiser and war or international working-class solidarity, he chose the latter, unpopular, somewhat risky, course. He was called up for military service and twice attempted to desert, ending the final period of the war in a military prison. He was a foundation member of the German Communist Party and by 1923 a member of its Central Committee. He soon lost this position due to the internal party struggles of the time but was back on the Central Committee by 1927, and has held that membership ever since. He took part in the armed struggles of the early 1920s, at the same time becoming a full-time KPD official. In 1929 in the Communist International he was backing the pro-Moscow 'Left' faction in the British Communist Party against most of that party's leaders.[15] From 1928 to 1933 Walter Ulbricht served in the Reichstag. After the seizure of power by the Nazis he had to leave Germany because he, like all other Communist officials, was on the Nazis' black list. Until the outbreak of the 1939–45 war he did various jobs for the Communist International, the Comintern. From 1941 onwards he did propaganda work among German prisoners-of-war and also at the front, a task which involved some

[14] The details of Ulbricht's life were taken largely from Stern and *Die Volkskammer Der Deutschen Demokratischen Republik 4 Wahlperiode,* Staatsverlag, (East) Berlin, 1964, pp. 567–9.

[15] L. J. MacFarlane, *The British Communist Party*, MacGibbon and Kee, London, 1966, p. 232.

risks. In 1945 he was entrusted by the Soviets to head a group of German Communists who were given the job of starting up municipal services in the Soviet Zone, selecting suitable anti-fascists to take over administrative and political posts in the municipalities, organizing essential supplies and carrying on liaison work between the newly formed German organs and the Soviet military government. Later, when political parties were allowed, the 'Ulbricht group' came to dominate the German Communist Party which fused with the SPD in the Soviet Zone in 1946. Officially the former Communist leader Pieck and the former Social Democratic leader Grotewohl were Ulbricht's superiors in the new Party but from the start he seems to have been the most important single member. He had the ear of the Russians, Pieck was already well past his prime, and Grotewohl's health steadily got worse. Walter Ulbricht and Max Fechner were official vice-chairmen but Ulbricht seems to have emerged stronger than Fechner. After 1948 the SED was gradually transformed into a 'Party of a new type' and Ulbricht's influence increased until, in 1950, he was elected the Party's general secretary. He was also first deputy Prime Minister. He gave up this post when, after the death of President Pieck in 1960, he became Chairman of the newly created Council of State.

Walter Ulbricht has been married twice. His first marriage broke up after he left Germany for the Soviet Union though his divorce only became official some years after the war. His daughter by his first wife is married and lives in West Germany. He has no children by his second wife, Lotte, who is ten years his junior, and a life-long Communist. The couple have, however, an adopted daughter. Frau Ulbricht was also an emigrant in the Soviet Union and it was there that she met her husband.

It is generally acknowledged that the First Secretary of the SED is a first-class organizer; much of his success has been due to this. He has also been opportunist in the sense that many politicians are opportunist, in the sense that he had made, at least publicly, some astonishing and startling changes of course in line with changes in Moscow. It would be wrong though to conclude from this that he is a man without principles, or beliefs. Certainly in his younger days he stuck his neck out in support of unpopular policies. Apart from a lasting belief in his interpretation of Marxism, he has also had a lasting loyalty to the Soviet Union. Now in his seventies, he wants to ensure the continued existence of the DDR as a socialist, prosperous state before his exit. This is probably in part due to a revived feeling for his *Heimat,* Saxony, poor when he was a young man and now a very important part of East Germany.

Old Communists and Young Technocrats

The Red Jesuits are to be found not only in the *Politbüro* but at all levels of the SED. In 1963 there were 145,000 pre-war members of the working-class movement in the ranks of the Unity Party.[16] Many of these were no doubt members of the élite of suffering created by the Nazis. Most of the SED do not belong to this category and even at the highest levels of the Party the pattern is changing. This is particularly so among the candidates of the *Politbüro*. First of all they are younger than the full members. The average age of the full member, when they were elected in 1967, was just over 57, that of the candidates was 40. The youngest of the six candidate members was Guenter Kleiberthen, aged 35. He is an electrical engineer and computer expert and joined the SED in 1949. The fact that he has studied is also significant. Of the candidates four were university graduates, whereas only two of the 15 full members could be so classed. Only one of the candidates, Hermann Axen, who had been in concentration camps, was in the pre-1933 movement. As is pointed out in the chapter on the SED, this tendency towards a party élite made up increasingly of academically trained experts is clear at the Central Committee level. Who are the members of East Germany's other leading organs?

The *Staatsrat* or Council of State, in theory the highest organ of the state, consists of 23 members with an average age of 48. At least fifteen of the 1965 members had studied and this is further evidence of the trend towards professionalism in the higher organs of the East German state. Of course the *Staatsrat* is meant to represent all the classes in East German society and the traditional middle class would expect to have some representatives there; and they help to swell the ranks of the graduates. Among the members of the old middle class in the *Staatsrat* are Dr Homann, Professor Dr Lieselott Herforth, Professor Dr Erich Correns, and Hans Rodenberg. About nine members of this body were born into the middle class, 12 into the industrial working class, and two into farming families. No one could be classed as a worker by current occupation. At least 14 of the 24 members were members of the SED in 1965 though not all of these were actually elected into the *Staatsrat* as Unity Party representatives. Other East German parties had two representatives each in the Council. One member, Erich Correns, is not a member of any party. Of the 1965 members six were members of the KPD before 1933, one was a Social Democrat, one

[16] *Protokoll Des VI Parteitages Der SED*, Vol. IV, p. 292. See for example Deutscher, op. cit., p. 318.

was a member of the small Democratic People's Party (DVP), and one, Dr Homann, was in the Nazi Party. Seven of these members had been persecuted in the Third Reich and 12 of the 20 male members had served in the German armed forces, four in the First World War.

Of the bourgeois members of the Council of State Professor Dieckmann, who died in February 1969, was the most distinguished. Johannes Dieckmann was born near Bremen, the son of a parson. He served in the First World War after studying economics. In the Weimar republic he worked as a journalist for the DVP and is said to have been an intimate associate of Gustav Stresemann, the conservative politician and protégé of the business interest who worked for Germany's fulfilment of the Versailles Treaty. During the Nazi régime Dieckmann found a berth with the coal industry but immediately became politically active again in 1945 when he took part in setting up the Liberal Democratic Party (LDPD) which in West Germany later became the Free Democratic Party. He readily accepted all the political changes which took place in East Germany and soon became prominent there. He was often given the task of putting the régime's case to Western and neutral politicians. Heinrich Homann, a deputy chairman of the National Democratic Party (NDPD), is the son of a Bremerhaven shipping magnate and became a professional soldier, reaching the rank of major, and a member of the Nazi Party. He was taken prisoner by the Soviets in 1943 and immediately became associated with the 'National Committee for a Free Germany'. After the war he studied law and rapidly advanced through the system. Since 1960 he has been a deputy chairman of the Council of State. Dr Homann was sentenced to death *in absentia* by the Nazis.[17] Little is known about Frau Herforth but according to biographical details given in the handbook of the East German parliament[18] she was born in 1916, the daughter of a writer. In 1936 she took up physics at the Technical University of Berlin. She must be something of an individualist for she graduated with a degree in engineering in 1940—more remarkable in view of the Nazis' opposition to higher education for women —and gained her doctorate in the same subject in 1948. She has since pursued an academic career, becoming a professor in 1957, and must now be regarded as one of the DDR's top academics and technical experts. Surprisingly, she is in the Council of State as one of the East German TUC's representatives. She became a member of the SED in 1963. Professor Correns is also a technical expert

[17] *Democratic German Report* (11 June 1965).
[18] *Die Volkskammer,* p. 300.

rather than a politician. He was born in West Germany in 1896, the son of a scientist. After service in the First World War he studied chemistry, physics, and botany in Berlin and Tübingen. He worked in industry between 1925 and 1945 and though apparently non-political throughout this period, he immediately took up service under the Soviets in 1946. Since then he has risen through the ranks of East Germany's managers and technical experts. Rodenberg is one of the SED's bourgeois members of the *Staatsrat* and was born in Lübbecke in 1895. He just managed to serve in the 1914–18 war. He worked as an actor and director before 1933 and was an emigrant in the Soviet Union. Since then he has carried on a successful film and political career. He joined the Council of State in 1960.

The German Democratic Republic's other leading state organ is the *Ministerrat,* or Council of Ministers, headed by Willi Stoph. In 1967 it had 39 members. Like the members of the Council of State the Ministers come from a wide variety of social and political backgrounds. However, roughly speaking, as in the *Staatsrat,* three socio-political groups can be discerned—the veterans of the working-class movement, who are mainly of working-class background, the remnants of the old middle class, and the members of the new intelligentsia. At this time about ten Ministers were veterans of the working-class movement and over 30 were from working-class families. Roughly about the same number had completed a course of some kind of higher education, and this is part and parcel of the trend to replace the older type of functionary with the younger specialist. For instance, with the average age hovering around the mid-forties, this is, to a considerable extent, a government of men and women who began their political careers in their twenties just after the war. The Council of Ministers is almost wholely a SED affair. In 1966 only five Ministers of the Council were not Unity Party members.

Few members of the three top organs mentioned—*Politbüro, Staatsrat,* and *Ministerrat*—are members of more than one of them. Willi Stoph, the East German Prime Minister, is a member of all three but he is the only one thus placed. Ulbricht is First Secretary of the SED and Head of State, that is, Chairman of the Council of State. Friedrich Ebert is also in the *Staatsrat* and the *Politbüro.* Alfred Neumann is a member of the *PB* and the Council of Ministers and so is Günter Mittag. Correns has the distinction of being a member of both state organs.

Apart from Ulbricht, Stoph is, on the face of it, in the most powerful position. He must have unrivalled experience in the different branches of Party and state. He also appears to have a good image, among ordinary East Germans. In 1968 he was a member of the SED delegations to Bratislava and to Karlovy Vary. Erich Honecker was another member of both delegations. He is Ulbricht's deputy in the SED and is usually regarded as his most likely successor in that position. Both Honecker and Stoph are relatively young, being 58 and 56 respectively in 1969. Günter Mittag was also a delegate to both Czech conferences. He became a full member of the *Politbüro* in 1966 when he was 40. He must be regarded as a strong contender, and perhaps increasingly so, for Walter Ulbricht's job. Friedrich Ebert, now in his seventies, is gradually retiring from political life.

It seems likely that when Ulbricht finally goes no one man will occupy more than one top post.

The East German parliament, or *Volkskammer,* although by no means as important as its British counterpart, is also one of the élite institutions of the German Democratic Republic. It is meant to mirror the social structure of the population, to emphasize the direction the régime wants its citizens to go, and to honour worthy contributors to the building of socialism. According to official figures in 1963 245 deputies were working-class by birth, 48 were from the working peasantry, 52 the sons or daughters of craftsmen and small shopkeepers, 57 from white-collar homes, six whose fathers were higher civil servants, 21 from the professional classes, two from church families, and three the offspring of capitalists or rich farmers. Many of the deputies were people who had obviously 'got on', for the figures show a deviation between social origin and the profession members had actually learned. None were listed as unskilled workers, 172 were described as skilled industrial workers. There were 21 engineers (meaning university-level and technicians), 89 skilled agricultural workers, 14 qualified personnel from the retail trade, 22 craftsmen and shopkeepers, 39 white-collar workers, ten journalists and editors, 38 scientists and medical practitioners, 19 educationalists, six from the Arts, and four others. There is a further deviation between the profession learned by the *Volkskammer* deputies and the one they were actually engaged in when elected in 1963. Most of the intelligentsia were in fact still carrying on the profession they had qualified in, but this was not true of the skilled workers. A closer look at the latter's biographies revealed that only between 40 and 50 were actually working in industrial enterprises—many as foremen. Many of those classed as skilled agricultural workers were actually the chairmen of co-operative farms, some of the white-collar workers or *Angestellte* were actually leading officials of state or Party. For instance, Alexander Abusch is listed as an *Angestellter* though in fact he is a deputy Prime Minister. Gerhard Bläsing is recorded as an agricultural worker though he was in 1963 deputy works-manager of the heavy machinery-making plant 'Ernst Thälmann' at Magdeburg. Among those listed as workers are Ulbricht, Ebert, Rolf Berger, deputy chairman of the FDGB, and Alois Bräutigam, first secretary of the Erfurt SED, among many others. The chamber elected in 1967 is little different from the earlier one.

The members of the *Volkskammer* are just a small part of East Germany's élite. The *Deutscher Kultur Bund,* another élitist organization, contains within its ranks about 65,000 members of the professions and nearly 50,000 persons listed as *Angestellte,* most of them probably at the higher levels of the administration. Behind the members of the *Bund* are roughly 600,000 East Germans who had completed university or *Fachschulen* courses by the mid-1960s. Less than 100,000 of these belonged to the pre-war intelligentsia. The German Democratic Republic has then created a new and fairly wide élite which is continuing to expand at a steady rate. This mass of well-educated and mainly younger people is inevitably different from the 'Jesuits' of the *Politbüro*. Most of them must be somewhat mellower than their leaders if only because they have not lived through the same trials and persecution. Most of them have learned their Marxism as a school subject rather than as a faith which represented both comradeship and danger for those who followed it. On the other hand, a great many of the new intelligentsia are people who owe their success to the SED. Were it not for the reforms carried through under its leadership very many of them would not have the chance to study. And had it not been for the removal of so many Nazis and the emigration of middle-class people (as well of course as the demands of the 'second industrial revolution'), promotion prospects would not have been so rosy for the members of the post-war intelligentsia. East Germany is very much a land of opportunity for these young people in a way that few others, including the Federal Republic, are or can be. Although it would be naïve to suppose that the bulk of this mass élite are fervently enthusiastic about the régime, a great many of them are likely to have a basic, if critical, loyalty to the state.[19]

[19] Peter Christian Ludz, *Parteielite im Wandel,* Westdeutscher Verlag, Cologne, 1968, p. 325. This is broadly the conclusion of Herr Ludz of the Free University of West Berlin in this systematic analysis of the SED élite.

Nazis and 'Westerners'

Two other groups in the East German élite are worth discussing : the ex-Nazis and those who know the non-Communist world. One can fairly state that the Soviets and the East German SED cleaned out former Nazis much more thoroughly than did those in control of West Germany. The figures relating to graduates mentioned above show the relative unimportance of anyone, Nazi or Communist, liberal or socialist, trained before 1945.

In 1966 the DDR had 128,877 fully qualified schoolteachers; 93 per cent of them trained since the end of the war.[20] And if one looks at the *PB,* the officer corps of the NVA, the legal profession, the police, and the Council of State, one has to come to the conclusion that the old ruling class has been broken. This old ruling class included the Nazis, in the strict sense, as well as the more traditionalist-minded. This does not mean—and the East German leaders have never sought to hide this—that there are not former Nazi Party members in responsible positions in the DDR. It would be strange if it were otherwise. Marxist members of the old intelligentsia were relatively rare and the Nazis killed off many of them, so that the new régime had fewer experts among its veterans than it would otherwise have had. It had therefore to 'salvage' some former Nazis who had skills which were in great demand. Secondly, Ulbricht and his colleagues could claim that it was part and parcel of socialist humanism to give former Nazis, that is those who were not war criminals or important exponents of National Socialism and were prepared to be 're-educated', a second chance. Thirdly, it might have been dangerous to condemn for the rest of their lives a considerable section of the community.

Who are East Germany's ex-Nazis and how much influence do they have? A Western anti-Communist organization[21] does regular research into this question and from its findings many of East Germany's former Nazis are in the technical and medical professions. Let us look at a few examples, as stated in a report of 1965. There is Professor Dr Franz Amon who has the chair of industrial hygiene at the University of Greifswald. He joined the NSDAP in 1933 and later the SA, working as a doctor for the Nazi labour organization. Dr Karl Heinrich Barthel is also a medical practitioner and was for a time a member of the *Volkskammer*. Barthel, now a member of the NDPD, joined the Nazis in 1932, became a medical

---

[20] *Democratic German Report* (24 June 1966).
[21] *Ehemalige Nationalsozialisten in Pankows Diensten,* Untersuchungsausschuss Freiheitlicher Juristen, (West) Berlin, 1965.

officer in the SA, and held certain local offices in the Nazi Party. Three other professors are Ulrich Bogs (Pharmacy), Heinrich Borriss (Botany), and Wilhelm Brekenfeld (Epidemiology). Apart from the fact that they joined the Nazi Party nothing more is known against the first two. As for Brekenfeld, he was also active in the German Red Cross and wrote a 'patriotic' article about his work. All three have received medals from the East German state for services rendered. Then there are scientists like Professor Herbert Dallmann. Now a member of the SED and professor of chemistry, he joined the Nazi Party in 1933. Professor Heinrich Dathe, director of the East Berlin Zoo, is also said to have joined the Nazi Party. Another group of ex-Nazis in East Germany are those who campaigned against the Nazis *before* 1945 after being taken prisoner by, or going over to, the Soviets. One of the most prominent of these is Dr Egbert von Frankenberg und Proschlitz, now a fairly prominent journalist and a member of the NDPD. He joined the NSDAP in 1931 and the SS in 1932 and was something of a 'hero' as a major of the *Luftwaffe*. He fell into Soviet hands early on in the campaign and some time after that became well-known as an anti-Nazi propagandist. Another prominent member of this group is Dr Homann whose background is given above. Colonel Hans Gossens of the NVA joined the Nazi Party in 1939 but was already undertaking dangerous propaganda work for the National Committee for a Free Germany by 1943. Another area where there are a fair number of ex-National Socialist Party members is in the press, particularly the provincial 'bourgeois' press, that is the press of the East German CDU, NDPD, and LDPD. Here again most of the cases listed by the anti-Communist source referred to are of journalists who were purely nominal members of the NSDAP. The same source tells us that in 1963 there were 53 former Nazis in the East German parliament. However, it is only able to list 29 of these who merely joined the NSDAP, 21 of them under the age of 21 at the time, and four others, three of whom were officers in the *Wehrmacht* and who took part in anti-Nazi propaganda. The odd man out was a local student leader under the Nazis. Most of these *Volkskammer* members were working-class, many still pursuing working-class occupations. One person listed by the Western source does not appear to be a member of the *Volkskammer*.

Our anti-Communist survey of 1965 gives details of five members and three candidates of the Central Committee of the SED at that time who were listed as former members of the Nazi Party. All eight are listed as purely nominal members and, as far as is known, all joined as teenagers during the war. Heinz Matthes joined in 1944

at the age of 18, as did Manfred Ewald. Dr Herbert Weiz joined in
1942, then aged 18. In any case, they form a very small part of the
ZK, which is a body comprising 121 members and 60 candidates.

The nearest East Germany has got to a scandal of the kinds that
have been relatively common in the Federal Republic involving a
political figure and his past was the case of Ernst Grossmann. Grossmann advanced, as the chairman of a co-operative farm, to the
Central Committee. Unknown to the SED, he had been a member
of the SS and, for a time, a guard at Sachsenhausen concentration
camp. After his past was revealed by Western sources he was
removed from the ZK.

East Germany is a 'totalitarian' society in the sense that, the
Soviet influence apart, there is only one source of effective power
and authority, the top élite of the Socialist Unity Party which
subjects all bodies within its domain to a system of control. Even
if, therefore, the DDR's ex-Nazis had any inclination to influence
their fellows in the direction of racialism, reclaiming the lost territories, refusal to recognize the Nazis' crimes, and the other hall-
marks of the ideology of militant German nationalism, they would
have no power to do so. In this sense they do not pose the potential
threat which the National Democrats and other far right organizations and individuals pose in 'pluralistic' West Germany.

Something which is not generally known in the West is the fact
that there are a number of former 'Western' emigrants in important
positions. It has already been noted that four members of the 1968
Politbüro—Hager, Norden, Verner, and Warnke—belong to this
category. In the Council of Ministers one deputy Prime Minister,
Alexander Abusch, was in exclusively Western emigration. The
Minister of Culture, Klaus Gysi, was an emigrant in France and
Britain and studied at Cambridge. Erwin Kramer, for many years
Minister of Transport, spent some time in France. Among the other
prominent 'Westerners' are Horst Brasch, Hermann Axen, the
editor of the paper Neues Deutschland, who was in France
before Auschwitz and Buchenwald, Professor Walter Friedeberger,
Deputy Minister of Health (France), and writers Arnold Zweig,
Anna Seghers, and Stefan Heym (among others). The importance
of this 'group' has been increasing. The number of the ex-Soviet
emigrants in the Central Committee of the SED has declined
slightly over the years. There were 21 full and candidate members
in this category in 1954, 22 in 1958, and 19 in 1963. The number
of West emigrants in 1963 was 17 as against about half that number
in 1954.[22] This is not to say that these 'Westerners' as a group would

[22] Ludz, op. cit., p. 174.

oppose the 'Easterners'; some may be 'harder' and more 'dogmatic' than some of the ex-Soviet emigrants, and vice versa. It is merely to suggest that there is a broader experience of the world available in the top echelons of the SED than is generally supposed.

A New Class?

Before leaving the élite, one problem must be briefly discussed, that of its relationship to the régime. As already mentioned above, it seems likely that the majority of the élite have some kind of loyalty to the DDR and to their leaders. Many of them have been given their chance by the SED; they enjoy, in varying degrees, the privileges of East German society; they would be less than human if they did not feel a sense of pride at the schemes they have worked so hard to realize; and years of political education must have had some effect on them. Yet there are many who either remain sceptical or have become disillusioned. Here one must distinguish between the 'technical intelligentsia', the engineers, technicians, statisticians and the like, and those engaged in literary and artistic activities. The mass of the technical intelligentsia are likely to judge the régime on its ability, or otherwise, to give them Western living standards; its general competence in science and industry; whether or not it gives them the opportunity to get on, without too much bureaucratic interference, with the jobs they have been trained to do; and its general prestige, not only in international political terms but also in terms of its technical and scientific, sporting and cultural, achievements. (From the writer's talks with East Germans even Soviet space achievements helped to boost the DDR.) Only when the régime does something to outrage these people in its general behaviour (such as participation in the occupation of Czechoslovakia?) is its prestige likely to slump.

By the nature of their calling, those in the Arts have somewhat different problems. They too—most of them anyway—want high living standards. They too want to get on with their jobs. But they, especially the serious Marxists among them, are also concerned about the quality of life. Yet they are more closely watched than their fellows. In part this is due to the fact that Marxist movements have always taken the Arts seriously, have believed that Art is not something divorced from the political struggle. It is also the result of Russian and Stalin's influence in East Germany, as well as the régime's feeling of insecurity and its genuine attempt to wipe out the vestiges of Nazi ideology. For all these reasons the Arts are firmly under SED control. It is worth mentioning that the SED's view is in marked contrast to that of certain other Communist movements. For instance, in 1963 Palmiro Togliatti, then leader of the Italian Communists, was reported in *Le Monde* (19 April) as saying that he felt it was entirely consistent with Marxism-Leninism to disagree with 'the attitude adopted by the Soviet Union on the subject of artistic problems. We are of the opinion that tolerance is necessary when one speaks of artistic expression'. And 'An artist belonging to an ideological current judged erroneous by some can frequently produce an authentic masterpiece'. The results of this excessive control are pointed out in Chapter 1 : that the SED has never really solved the problem of its relations with its cultural élite. This is shown by four things. Firstly, by the conflicts between the Unity Party leadership and some of its outstanding intellectual exponents. Secondly, by the emigration of some of the cream of the East German cultural élite. Thirdly, by the scanty output of many of these people. Finally, by the themes of East German books, plays, and films.

In Chapter 1 attention was drawn to the conflict between the SED and Wolfgang Harich in 1956, and between it and Robert Havemann in the 1960s. These outstanding cases stand for other, lesser ones. Among the list of emigrants one thinks of Alfred Kantorowicz, the internationally known expert on German liter-ature and life-long Marxist; Professor Ernst Bloch, another life-long Marxist, formerly of the faculty of Philosophy of Leipzig Univer-sity, who at 77 decided to stay in the West; Professor Hans Mayer, also of Leipzig and also a Communist; and Christa Reinig, the poetess who left East Germany in 1964. Frau Ingrid Ohlenschläger, who was well-known for her performances in the East Berlin poli-tical cabaret *Die Distel,* a National Prizewinner of the DDR, decided to stay in the West after a holiday in Yugoslavia in 1965. At that time she summed up the situation as follows : 'I no longer wanted to say things I did not believe. As a doctor or a technician one can live fairly well in the DDR, as a writer or an actor one must prostitute oneself daily'.[23] Hard words, but words spoken by someone who regards herself as a socialist. For these emigrants are not anti-socialist but self-declared Marxists, some of whom had suffered a great deal under the Nazis for their views, who felt they could not engage in honest creative activity due to the pressures of the Party on them. They gave up security, high living standards, and honours, in order to live in West Germany, where they were unsure of their reception.

At the end of the war an army of intellectuals settled in the Soviet Occupation Zone, returning from all parts of the world.

[23] *Der Spiegel* (1 September 1965).

Many of them were people who had made their way fairly success-fully in the countries which had sheltered them. Yet their output in the DDR has often lagged well behind their earlier achievement. The most prominent names in this group are Anna Seghers, the late Arnold Zweig, Stefan Heym, Ludwig Renn, the late Johannes R. Becher, Friedrich Wolf, and even the late Bertolt Brecht. Finally, the themes are very often about life under Nazism, or in the case of the former emigrants, life abroad, or historical works.[24] One of the most successful East German novels of recent years, and an equally successful film, was Christa Wolf's *Der geteilte Himmel* (*The Divided Sky*), which sold more than 100,000 copies in 1963.[25] It deals with the problems of two young lovers when the man decides to go West and the girl feels she cannot follow. It may be significant that Christa Wolf has also had her problems with the Party. No one will doubt the need to deal fully with the Nazi period. No one will doubt that the dark era gives tremendous scope for revealing in literary form the appalling human and political problems. Yet too much emphasis on the Third Reich could be self-defeating. And, apart from strictly political matters, there are many contemporary problems which interest the people of the DDR : the problems caused by bad housing; the problems of the pensioners; the problems of broken homes; the problems of the working mothers; of the women of the 'missing generation'; of the war disabled; of loneliness on the new housing estates—quite apart from the 'eternal' problems of human relations.

The DDR's military intervention in Czechoslovakia furnished another cause of friction between the East German leaders and their élite. An article in the *Democratic German Report* of 13 November 1968 indicated that a number of young East Germans, mostly the sons and daughters of prominent SED members, issued leaflets and daubed slogans protesting against East German action in Czechoslovakia. Some of them were jailed for their activities. Such treatment is only likely to make matters worse, for these young people know their views are shared by the French, Italian, and British Communist Parties—three parties having fairly close relations with the SED—as well as the Romanian, Yugoslav, Albanian, and Chinese movements. They will find bitter irony in the fact that they have been punished for expressing views identical with those of the usually orthodox British CP :

---

[24] For a discussion of this see Alfred Kantorowicz, *Der Geistige Wider-stand In Der DDR*, Kammwegverlag, Troisdorf, 1968.
[25] *Profile of East Germany*, Harrap, London, 1966, p. 95.

The Executive of the Communist Party of Great Britain deeply deplores the military intervention in Czechoslovakia . . . The military intervention which took place had no support from any leading body in the Czechoslovak Communist Party or state and is opposed by them. No grounds have been brought forward that can justify this violation of the national sovereignty of the Czechoslovak people and Government. Equally deplorable is the interference from outside the country to remove some of the leaders of the Czechoslovak Communist Party and to prevent them carrying out their duties, less than three weeks before the Party Congress was due to open on September 9. This is a gross violation of the democratic rights of the Czechoslovak Communists.[26]

Clearly, the problems of the SED's relations with its cultural élite remains. As the protests over Czechoslovakia show, its solution is likely to become more, rather than less, urgent as the new, educated, Marxist-orientated, and impatient, generation rises. Having been constantly exhorted to read Marx, Luxemburg, Thomas Mann, and Bertolt Brecht some of them have come to take the state's idols seriously and believe with Brecht's Galileo, 'I believe as scientists we have not to ask where the truth may lead us'.[27]

One final question needs to be considered in relation to the East German élite: do they represent a privileged bureaucracy in Trotsky's sense or a 'new class' in the sense of Milovan Djilas?

'According to the conditions of its daily life, Soviet society is', wrote Trotsky in 1936,

already divided into a secure and privileged minority, and a majority getting along in want. At its extremes, moreover, this inequality assumes the character of flagrant contrast. Products designed for broad circulation are as a rule, in spite of their high prices, of low quality . . . Characteristic of the present Soviet epoch are . . . military clubs chiefly for officers . . . One of the very clear, not to say defiant, manifestations of inequality is the opening in Moscow and other big cities of special stores with high-quality articles under the very expressive, although not very Russian, designation of 'Luxe' . . . Limousines for the 'activists', fine perfumes for 'our women', margarine for the workers, stores 'de luxe' for the gentry, a look at delicacies through the store

[26] Reports on the prosecution of the East German protesters appeared in *The Times* (23 October 1968) and in various West German papers. The statement of the British CP appeared in *Marxism Today* (October 1968), pp. 294–5.
[27] Brecht, *Versuche 19*, Suhrkamp Verlag, (West) Berlin, 1955, p. 40.

windows for the plebs—such socialism cannot but seem to the masses a new re-facing of capitalism.[28]

It would be strange if Trotsky's observations of Russia in the 1930s fitted completely East Germany in the 1960s and to be sure they do not. Russia and Germany have different traditions, and Russia then was still more agrarian than industrial while the DDR is part of an old-established industrial society. Having said this one can find many points of similarity between the inequalities noted by Trotsky and what one sees in the DDR. In contrast to the Soviet Union of the 1930s, although one does not notice great extremes of wealth in the DDR in the 1960s, one does notice differences. But as in the Soviet Union then and now the élite of the DDR have their special clubs such as the magnificent one visited by the writer at Dresden, quartered in an old royal palace set in spacious grounds. There are the expensive 'exquisite' shops and the 'Interhotels'. There are the 'Intershops' stocked up with Western goods and DDR goods of export quality for the lucky few with Western currency. The latter are the very few part-owners of firms engaged in the export trade, and the scientists and writers whose work appears, with official blessing, abroad. They are also allowed to spend money abroad. There are these and others who are sent off on delegations to the non-socialist world, a privilege in a travel-hungry state. It is also easier for some than for others to get places in the sanatoria and holiday homes run by the trade unions and other organizations, and there are different categories of resort and accommodation. Here it is important to remember that virtually all accommodation at the resorts is controlled by state or 'mass organizations'.

In general one can say that the top people of the DDR, as the top people of the Soviet Union, greatly benefit from knowing each other. They can smooth each other's paths. They can save each other time and frustration by cutting corners. The right contact can be very useful in jumping the queue for a car, getting treated by a top doctor, getting a larger flat, getting one's son on the right course in the right educational establishment. The differences between the best-off and the poorest in the DDR are not as great as those in most Western European countries or the USSR or the USA. A new class has not yet developed, it has not yet had time for stability. And, socialist measures apart, East Germany is so short of skilled people at all levels that there is room for a great deal of social mobility upwards.

28 L. Trotsky, *The Revolution Betrayed*, New Park Publications, London, 1967, pp. 116–20.

6 * *

Chapter 3

The Constitution: Democratic Centralism

The 1949 Constitution

EAST GERMANY has had two constitutions. The first was that of 1949 which came into operation with the setting up of the republic. The second was introduced in 1968. According to East German theory, whereas the constitution of 1949 was meant to reflect the 'anti-fascist democratic order' of the German Democratic Republic, the new constitution is supposed to mirror and aid the DDR's development to a full socialist society. The earlier constitution was modified on a number of occasions to express the changing structure of East German economy, society, and state from a merely anti-fascist order to a higher order based on the 'dictatorship of the proletariat' and the 'transition to socialism'. East German theorists do not give a precise date for the introduction of the dictatorship of the proletariat, that is, of people's democracy, in their part of Germany, but the change was certainly under way by 1952 when the SED decided to build the foundations of socialism in the DDR.

The DDR constitution of 1949 resulted mainly from discussions in three German People's Congresses (*Deutsche Volkskongresse*) carried on among representatives of the parties of the then Soviet Zone on the initiative of the SED between 1947 and 1949. Invitations were extended to parties and personalities in West Germany to attend these congresses but, apart from the Communist Party and a few neutralists and other dissenters, they were ignored. In May 1949 the people of the Soviet Zone were called upon to elect from a single list delegates to the 3rd People's Congress. According to the official result, just over two-thirds of the 90-odd per cent of the electorate who voted recorded their approval of the list. In the West the validity of this result has not gone unquestioned.[1] The

---

[1] Siegfried Mampel, 'Die Entwicklung der Verfassungsordnung in der sowjetisch besetzten Zone Deutschlands von 1945 bis 1963', *Sonderdruck aus Jahrbuch Des Offentlichen Rechts Band 13*, J. C. B. Mohr (Paul Siebeck), Tübingen, 1964, p. 509.

3rd German People's Congress now agreed a constitution worked
out by a 32-member committee of the 2nd Congress and headed by
Otto Grotewohl. It also elected from its midst a German People's
Council (*Deutscher Volksrat*) of 330 members. In this council the
SED had only 90 official representatives but there is little doubt it
had an absolute majority through its members among the representatives of the mass organizations : the trade unions, the youth
movement, the women's league, the league of culture, the association of Nazi victims, and so on. In October 1949 this council
declared itself a provisional People's Chamber (*Volkskammer*) or
parliament of the German Democratic Republic. This was a matter
of weeks after the setting up of the (West German) Federal
Republic. The East Germans claimed their actions in setting up the
Democratic Republic constituted an answer to the 'state of national
emergency' which 'had been created by the formation of the separ-
atist western state'.[2] By 1951 the character of the East German
state was described in an official publication in the following way :
'The abolition of the reactionary class of Junkers, the removal of
the big industrialists from their positions of power, made possible
the development of a peace economy free from crises. The democratic reform of the schools was a decisive factor for the erection in
Germany of a new social order. This is an antifascist democratic
order in which the united working class holds the decisive positions
of power'.[3]

A liberal would consider the formal text of the East German
constitution of 1949 as democratic as most. According to Article 50
the highest organ of the republic was the parliament, that is, *Volkskammer*. This chamber comprised (Article 51) deputies (*Abgeord-
nete*) elected at universal, equal, and secret elections which were to
take place every four years. The deputies were to be subordinated
only to their consciences. The *Volkskammer* elected its own *Präsidium*, in which all parties having 40 or more deputies were represented, to conduct its business and maintain discipline. It also
elected the government (*Regierung*). Article 63 gave the chamber
all the usual powers vested in an elected chamber : the right to lay
down the fundamentals of government policy; the right to ratify,
check, and dismiss the government; the right to make laws; the
right to decide the budget, economic plan, loans, and credits, and
the ratification of treaties; the right to proclaim amnesties; the

[2] *The Development Of The German Democratic Republic,* published by
the German National Preparatory Committee for the 3rd World Festival of
Youth and Students for Peace, Dresden, 1951 (?), p. 19.
[3] Ibid., p. 21.

election of the members of the high court and their dismissal; the election of the President of the Republic at a joint session with the *Länderkammer*. In order to carry on these activities the chamber elected 16 committees (*Auschüsse*), including three which carried on the work of parliament when it was not in session. In addition, according to Article 66, the *Volkskammer* elected a constitutional committee, in which all parties were represented according to their parliamentary strengths, to determine the constitutionality of laws and to see to it that elections were properly conducted. This committee also contained three members of the supreme court.

The constitution of 1949 dealt generously with deputies. Under Article 67 they were granted immunity, while Articles 69 and 70 gave them a tax-free allowance and the right to free travel on all public transport. Article 68 granted candidates to the chamber time off work on full pay to prepare their election campaign.

The original East German constitution like that of West Germany was based on the assumption that the German Republic was a collection of states or *Länder*. It too made provision for a chamber of states (*Länderkammer*) similar, but not as powerful, as Bonn's *Bundesrat*. Articles 71–80 set out the position of the *Länderkammer*. It consisted of representatives delegated for the legislative period of the People's Chamber by the state assemblies (*Landtage*). Each state had the right to send one representative per 500,000 inhabitants and in any case at least one delegate. The chamber of states had the right to introduce bills and had certain delaying powers (Article 84).

The Prime Minister of the German Democratic Republic was, according to Article 92, to be chosen by the parliamentary group having the largest number of members in the *Volkskammer*. Ministers had to be members of the chamber. Remarkably, Article 92 also gave the right to all groups having at least 40 members to be represented in the government. This was probably agreed to ensure the co-operation of the bourgeois parties in the single-list elections. It could also indicate that at this stage the SED was still prepared to face Western-style elections in which it would be in a minority. Thus should it have found itself in a weak position it would still have a right to be included in a government. The constitution put the government in a fairly strong position. Under Article 95 a Prime Minister could not be dismissed until a successor had been found. A similar clause in the West German constitution seeks to protect the Federal Republic from the situation which arose in the Weimar republic in which Prime Ministers were toppled before successors were appointed. No doubt East German constitutionalists had this problem in mind. Article 97 of the East German constitution named the Prime Minister as the chairman of the government and Article 98 gave him the right to determine the general lines of government policy. The government was to decide policy by majority vote with the Prime Minister having the casting vote in the case where equal votes were cast for opposing resolutions.

The President of the Republic was covered by Articles 101–5 of the 1949 constitution. His role was largely ceremonial.

The constitution of 1949 made the same claim as the 'Basic Law' made, and makes, for the Federal government of Bonn. It considered the Democratic Republic as the nucleus and legitimate centre of all Germany and proclaimed Berlin the capital. The preamble of the constitution asserted that it was 'the German people', without further qualification, who 'have given themselves this constitution'. Article 1 said that 'Germany is an indivisible democratic Republic; its constituent parts are the German states. The Republic decides on all matters essential for the continued existence and development of the German people as a whole'. The text did not indicate the area in which the constitution was valid. Article 1 also claimed, again like the Bonn constitution: 'There is only one German citizenship'.[4]

Centralization and Restrictions

Such was the formal structure of the East German state as set out in the 1949 constitution. Between 1949 and the introduction of the new constitution in 1968 it underwent a number of important modifications. The first of these was in 1952. In that year a law was passed by the *Volkskammer* abolishing the five state assemblies (*Landtage*) and replacing them by 14 district assemblies (*Bezirkstage*). This was presented as a measure of democratization aimed at bringing more citizens into the process of government. Western critics saw it as a means to destroy the potentially powerful *Landtage*, replacing them by smaller, weaker bodies. From 1952 the members of the *Länderkammer* were elected by the district assemblies until, in 1958, the chamber of states was abolished.

The structure of the 'government' of the DDR changed considerably during this period. From 1950 it was increasingly referred to as *Ministerrat* or Council of Ministers, rather than *Regierung* or

[4] The texts of the 1949 constitution used are *Die Verfassung Der Deutschen Demokratischen Republik*, VEB Deutscher Zentralverlag, Berlin, 1955; *Constitution of the German Democratic Republic*, VEB Deutscher Zentralverlag, 1962.

government. A law of 1954 laid down that the Council of Ministers sets up from among its members a *Präsidium* to carry on its work between its meetings and generally to organize its work. The importance of the *Präsidium*, which meets about once a week, was stressed in the law of 17 April 1963. Clause 9, paragraph 3, states that the decisions of the *Präsidium* are to be treated as decisions of the whole Council of Ministers. The size of the *Präsidium*, about 11 members, as against that of the full Council, some 49 in April 1966, obviously suits it for effective decision-making. Laws of 1954 and 1958 gave the Council of Ministers the right, widely used, to issue decrees (*Verordnungen*) having the force of law. Since 1963 the Council of Ministers has been mainly concerned with economic and educational spheres of policy, that is, with carrying into effect the reforms associated with the New Economic Policy. These changes brought the East German governmental structure closer to the Soviet model. Owing to the work of the *Politbüro* of the SED and, in recent years, of the *Staatsrat* or Council of State, the Council of Ministers is not quite a government in the Western sense. In many respects it appears as a body which gives practical shape to the decisions reached by the other two organs. But certainly in particular fields, above all in the economy, its importance should not be underestimated. It is much more of a SED-dominated body than the Council of State and is very much a body of economic experts at a time when economic problems are considered all important. Both these facts make it an organ of considerable weight.

The Council of State represents another modification of the 1949 constitution. It was set up in 1960 after the death of Wilhelm Pieck, the DDR's first and only President. Both according to the constitution and in practice, Herr Pieck played only a representative, symbolic role. The Council of State has both in theory and in fact more significance than President Pieck had. First of all, it has all the functions carried out by the late President. Its Chairman represents the DDR abroad. The Council appoints the DDR's ambassadors and receives foreign diplomats on behalf of the republic. It ratifies international treaties. It convenes the *Volkskammer* and has the right to carry through referenda. It can reprieve those sentenced to death and proclaim amnesties. It also confers honours. Secondly, the Council of State has a general responsibility for the affairs of the state when the chamber is not in session. To enable it to do this job it can issue orders which have the force of law and it can interpret existing laws. Thirdly, it is responsible for working out the general lines of policy in many 'non-political' areas—family affairs, crime prevention, consumer problems, education, etc.

Fourthly, it is supposed to identify more closely the non-Marxist, non-SED elements in political life with the state by giving them representation at its head. Fifthly, it provides an important organizational tie-up and system of direct communication between the highest ranks of the SED and the highest representatives of the remaining middle class and Christian sections of the population. Sixthly, it has important powers in national defence and national emergencies. Finally, the *Staatsrat* was probably set up as a result of the criticism of the 'cult of personality'. Had Ulbricht taken over the Presidency and retained his post as First Secretary of the Socialist Unity Party this move would have been interpreted as part and parcel of the 'cult', even though, traditionally in Communist states, the position of Head of State was purely ceremonial. As it is, Ulbricht can co-ordinate and discuss in the Council of State, at the same time emphasizing that the leadership of the state is a collective effort and not merely centred on one man. Some Western observers believe that the Council in fact strengthened Walter Ulbricht's position because in it there are very few of his colleagues from the SED, few comrades therefore to contradict him as most of his 'bourgeois' colleagues, in the Council, are unlikely to do so in any fundamental way.[5] One could of course argue the converse that the many powers of the Council and its wide membership emphasize that the DDR is on the way to a more democratic form of government than known there before.

Little space need be given to the East German parliament, the *Volkskammer,* for, up to 1968, it had played a purely formal, exclamatory, role. The many situations of discussion and disagreement which the formal provisions of the 1949 constitution were meant to deal with did not arise. The People's Chamber's 500 members have met once or twice a year unanimously to adopt measures put before them by their leaders.

What about the rights of the citizen as reflected in the 1949 constitution of the German Democratic Republic? Article 6 guaranteed equality before the law. Article 7 pronounced men and women equal. The secrecy of the post, personal freedom, and the inviolability of the home were proclaimed by Article 8. Freedom of opinion and expression, including freedom of the press, were the substance of Article 9. Articles 12 and 13 laid down the right of free association and the right to strike and to organize trade unions was explicitly covered by Article 14. Articles 16 to 19 guaranteed

[5] Ernst Richert, *Macht ohne Mandat, Der Staatsapparat in der Sowjet- ischen Besatzungszone Deutschlands,* Westdeutscher Verlag, Cologne, 1963 pp. 74–8.

the working people their rights at their places of employment as well as their right to receive insurance to cover old age, illness and unemployment, and, in the case of women, pregnancy. The rights of foreign-speaking minorities were set out in Article 11. (These are the Sorbs, the numerically weak Slav people who have survived for centuries in what is now East Germany.)

The family and the mother were given formal recognition under Articles 30 to 33 of the constitution. Article 33 protected children born out of wedlock, laying down that neither they nor their parents should suffer any disadvantage. Education was subject to a relatively large slice of the constitution and was covered in Articles 34 to 40 inclusive. Under Article 34 academic freedom was guaranteed. Article 37 set out the role of school and parents in education : 'The school educates youth in the spirit of the constitution to become responsible independently-minded human beings who are able and willing to integrate themselves into the life of the community. As the agency of culture the school has the task to educate youth in the spirit of friendship and peaceful companionship among the peoples, real democracy and true humanism. The parents co-operate, through the parents' councils [*Elternbeiräte*], in the education of their children'. Children whose social conditions were a disadvantage educationally were given special attention in Article 39. Finally, on education, Article 40 guaranteed the right of the religious denominations to conduct religious instruction and, in fact, more space was given to religion than to education in the 1949 text.

'Every citizen', stated Article 41, 'enjoys full freedom of conscience and belief. The undisturbed practice of religion stands under the protection of the Republic'. The principle of the separation of Church and state was laid down by Article 43. The same Article guaranteed the right to set up a religious organization and protected such bodies at law. It also gave the religious denominations the traditional right to collect the 'church tax' (*Kirchensteuer*) from their followers. Church property was protected by Article 45 and Article 46 gave the Churches the right to conduct religious services, as required, in public institutions such as hospitals and prisons. At the same time it pointed out that no one can be forced to attend such services. Article 44 took up religious instruction in schools again and accorded the denominations the right to use school premises for the purpose of giving such instruction. Such instruction was to be given by the nominees of the Churches themselves. No one could be prevented from or forced to take part in such instruction. Until a child was 14 years of age the parents had the right to decide whether or not it should have religious instruction.

A closer examination even of the formal provisions of the constitution of 1949 reveals that there were certain sections which, although agreed to by many East German politicians at the time for the best of motives, could, and did, seriously limit the rights of the citizens. Article 6 was probably the most noted example of this. As we have seen, it guaranteed all citizens equality before the law, but it went on to state: 'Incitement to boycott of democratic institutions and organisations, incitement to the murder of democratic politicians, the propagation of militarism, racialism, hatred of other peoples or creeds, and all other such actions which are aimed against equality [before the law] are crimes in the sense of the criminal code. The exercise of democratic rights in the spirit of the constitution is not incitement to boycott'. When this was included in the original constitution in 1949 many politically aware East Germans simply accepted this as being aimed at preventing the kind of political violence typical of the Weimar republic and preventing a recurrence of the horrors of the Nazi régime. No doubt it was used to counter such elements on the right but, in addition, there is evidence that it was also used, particularly during the Stalinist period proper, against Social Democrats who refused to accept the Unity Party as the sole representative of the working class, and against liberals and others who regarded the official 'bourgeois' parties as mere satellites of the SED.

The second part of Article 8 gave the state the right to restrict the rights of the individual, mentioned in the same section of the constitution. This, however, is something which has happened not only in East Germany or other Communist states. In both West Germany and Britain, for instance, the secrecy of the post has been interfered with. Such interference has made East Germans most reluctant to correspond with those in the 'Capitalist West' except when they do so to sponsor the régime's campaigns.

As far as freedom of religion is concerned, whereas Article 41, as mentioned above, guaranteed that freedom, it went on to state that religious institutions, organizations, and religious instruction must not be misused for party political or unconstitutional purposes. However, the religious denominations had the right to make known their point of view regarding the fundamental questions facing the people. It is difficult to object to such a stipulation as such. Even the Bad Godesberg Programme of the West German SPD warns about the misuse of religion for party political or anti-democratic

purposes.[6] And in West Germany the Catholic hierarchy have, time
and again, sought to intervene in party politics to the advantage
of one party.[7] The East German Socialist Unity Party equipped
itself to deal with this situation. However, much here depends on
interpretation and, to say the least, many Christians in both parts
of Germany are not convinced that the reference in Article 41 to
the misuse of religion was always used as originally intended.[8]
(More will be said about the Churches in East Germany in
Chapter 4.)

Another controversial Article of the East German constitution
was number 10 which guaranteed every citizen the right to emigrate
but went on to say that laws could be passed to limit this right.
Such laws were introduced in 1954, 1956, 1957, and 1963. Since
1957, anyone convicted of attempting to go to West Germany without official permission faces up to three years' imprisonment.[9] In
theory it is of course possible to get such permission but in practice
the authorities are not likely to grant many such requests. One
group of people who do get permission to leave are those over 65.
Since November 1964 very many elderly East Germans have visited
relatives in the West, few have decided to stay there. No doubt many
of these felt they could not get used to a new environment at their
time of life. Although of small comfort for East Germans who want
to emigrate, East German travel restrictions are, *in principle,* no
different than those imposed by other régimes in both Communist
and such Western-allied nations as Portugal, Spain, Greece, Turkey,
Iran, etc.—they all issue passports on a purely political basis and
only allow emigration at the state's convenience. It will be worth
returning to this theme when we consider East German elections.

Western estimates[10] of the number of political prisoners in East
Germany in 1965 were from 6,000 to 8,000 and some of these were
those who had broken the passport laws. Who were the others?
The Western organization 'Amnesty International' reported : 'A
large proportion of those arrested for crimes against the state are
charged under Paragraph 14 of the Supplementary Penal Code
with espionage. This may include anything from the passing on of

[6] 'Grundsatz Programm Der SPD', *Vorstand der Sozialdemokratischen Partei Deutschlands,* Bonn, 11/59, p. 21.
[7] See, for example, the comments of *The Times* (30 June 1958). Also *Political Studies* (October 1959), S. K. Panter-Brick's comments, p. 262.
[8] Karl Wilhelm Fricke, 'Selbstbehauptung und Widerstand in der Sowjet-ischen Besatzungszone Deutschlands', *Bonner Berichte Aus Mittel- Und Ostdeutschland,* Bonn and Berlin, 1966, p. 43.
[9] See the comments in *Prison Conditions In East Germany* compiled by Amnesty International, London, August 1966.
[10] Ibid., p. 14.

quite harmless information to individuals in the West or contact
of any sort with West German political parties, religious groups or
other organisations, to the kind of paid espionage activity which is
punishable in any country in the world'.[11] It also reported that now

> the general pattern is one of increasing moderation. So far as is
> known the death sentence has not been imposed on anyone (except
> Horst Fischer who was recently sentenced to death on account
> of his war crimes) since 1962 ... More recently the State Council
> appear to have been trying to implement their declared policy
> of enforcing 'socialist legality' by education and persuasion
> rather than by harsh retributive measures. One result has been a
> noticeable decrease in the numbers of political offenders served
> with prison sentences.

It is also only fair to mention here that in West Germany, too, many
people suffer in exactly the same way as in East Germany for 'passing on of harmless information' and 'contact' with political organizations in the other part of Germany, as well as for activities which
'endanger the state' and for advocating communism or supporting
the platform of the DDR. Between 1956 and 1968 the Communist
Party was banned in West Germany and those accused of activities
on its behalf risked imprisonment. Such activities would not be a
criminal offence in the democracies of Western Europe. This is not
just a theoretical possibility. The much respected Hamburg weekly
Die Zeit on 20 November 1964 quoted official figures indicating
that in 1963 10,222 actions were started against people alleged to
have committed treasonable offences of one kind or another. In
many cases these actions were against more than one person. In
1961 a total of 442 people were sentenced for various categories
of 'treason' in West Germany. Admittedly, the sentences were relatively mild.

One final limitation of the political rights of the individual contained in the old East German constitution was found in Article 13.
Its second paragraph stated, 'Nominations for the *Volkskammer*
can only be proposed by organisations which according to their
constitutions desire the democratic development of society and
whose organisation covers the entire territory of the Republic'. This
paragraph obviously bolstered existing organizations and parties
and made it very difficult to form any opposition to East Germany's
version of the 'Grand Coalition'. Even had there been no other
obstacles, it would, for instance, have been sufficient to prevent the
SPD, which was allowed to exist in the Eastern sector of Berlin

[11] Ibid, pp. 11–12.

until 1961, but not in the rest of East Germany, to put up candidates for the *Volkskammer*.

Elections: Much Ado About Nothing?

Article 3 of the 1949 constitution declared 'All power derives from the people'. In accordance with this the deputies of the People's Chamber are elected by all those citizens over the age of 18. In reality, the East German electoral system must be one of the régime's weakest, and most disagreeable, features. Apart from the elections to the *Volkskongress* in 1949 described above, elections to the *Volkskammer* have taken place in 1950, 1954, 1958, 1961, 1963, and 1967. All these elections had certain common characteristics. Firstly, the electors had to approve or reject a single list of candidates drawn up from the recognized parties and mass organizations. Secondly, there were overwhelming turnouts of electors and, thirdly, the electors gave overwhelming support to the official list. At the election of 1950, for instance, 98.5 per cent of the electorate voted; of these 99.7 per cent voted for the official list. In the new chamber the SED got 100 seats, 60 went to the CDU, 60 to the LDPD, 30 to the NDPD, and the other 150 to the mass organizations—trade unions, youth movement, co-operatives, etc., and the Farmers' Party (30), all of which were SED-dominated. At the elections which followed there were only very slight fluctuations in turnout and majorities for the official candidates. At the last election in 1967 98.82 per cent of the electorate voted. The National Front candidates received 99.93 per cent of the votes. The largest number of votes against the official candidates on this occasion were cast at Dresden, where 362 such votes were recorded. These represented 0.14 per cent of the valid votes.[12] A new feature of this election was that there were more candidates than seats in each constituency. In theory this could have given the electors at least some choice of candidates. In practice, however, the candidates who failed to get seats were recognized as replacements in case any of the others were, or became, unable to carry out their duties. After the 1967 election the SED continued to dominate the chamber through its control of the parliamentary groups of the mass organizations. The chairmen of all these parliamentary groups in 1967 were members of the SED. The Unity Party was awarded 129 seats (including its Berlin representatives who are still given only a non-voting status). Each of the other parties—CDU, LDPD, NDPD, and DBD—got 52 each. The four mass organizations were given 164 together. There is

---

[12] *Die Volkskammer Der Deutschen Demokratischen Republik 5. Wahlperiode*, Staatsverlag Der Deutschen Demokratischen Republik, Berlin, 1967

no indication on what basis these seats were allocated—other than the *a priori* assumption that the SED is the strongest. It is in membership, but this is no objective criterion as the parties are not in free competition for membership.

How are the DDR's fantastic election results achieved? To what extent are they a measure of popular will? Given the lack of choice on polling day, why bother to hold them?

The writer has been fortunate enough to talk to two persons— one anti-Communist and one non-Communist—who have acted as election officials in East Germany. Both assured him that on polling day there is in no sense any attempt to falsify the results of the poll or to intimidate electors in the polling stations. The results are achieved by a maximum of organization, flexibility, propaganda, social pressure, and, of course, by the impossibility of any open opposition. In all parts of the republic an army of agitators seeks to explain the issues to their fellow citizens and on the day to ensure that they vote. Most of the tenants in most blocks of flats, the majority of the electorate today, are organized in *Hausgemein-schaften*, that is in block communities. These are not just organized for electoral purposes. They have a permanent basis and exist ostensibly to bring the tenants closer together. They hold social gatherings and discussion groups. At election time they try to make all the necessary arrangements to ensure a complete turnout of voters in their respective blocks. For instance, the East German illustrated *NBI*, 16/1968, reported on the plebiscite to decide on the new socialist constitution. In this report it mentioned how the *Hausgemeinschaft* of Buchholzer Strasse 84 in Berlin-Niederschön-hausen organized itself for polling day. At 9 a.m. on the great day the tenants assembled with their children and went off to the polling station with flags flying, slogans displayed. At the polling station they were met by the local Free German Youth glee club. Having done their patriotic duty they returned to their chairman's flat for a drink. Should there be difficulties in looking after the babies or a need for transport the block community can make the necessary arrangements. Persons who have shown reluctance to take part in the serious discussions and the ballyhoo which have led up to the election or plebiscite can be sure that a local National Front or party official will 'knock them up' on the day. The issues will be put to them with deceptive and disarming simplicity: 'Are you in favour of Peace and peaceful construction?' or 'Are you against American aggression in Vietnam?' It never occurs to the zealots that, as was the young worker with whom the writer spoke in Magdeburg, one can be against both a constitution which does not grant the right to strike *and* American Vietnam policy. In 1954, to give just one other example of how the issues are presented, a plebiscite was held in which the electors were asked, 'Are you in favour of a peace treaty and the withdrawal of the occupation troops?' or 'Are you in favour of EDC, the Bonn Treaty and of the occupation troops remaining for 50 years?'[13]

Another aspect of good organization is provision for enough polling stations. In East Germany they not only have many polling stations, but they set them up in hospitals, nursing homes, and other institutions where the staff and inmates might otherwise experience difficulty in casting their votes. The East German electoral law also seeks to ensure a maximum vote by enabling citizens to vote, at *Volkskammer* elections, at any polling station in the republic. This is to give transport workers and those on shift work the chance to cast their votes. Normally polling stations are open from 7 a.m. to 8 p.m. but local electoral commissions can decide to open the stations earlier and can extend voting beyond 8 p.m. Voting also takes place on a holiday, thus giving people more time and even less excuse for not going to the polling station. Given the massive campaign, both organizational and political, it is not difficult to understand the high participation in the poll. After all, the participation in West German elections is higher than most. And in Austria, that other Germanic state, turnout at post-war elections has never dropped below 94 per cent and in three elections reached 97 per cent.[14] In Austria, apart from any Germanic 'sense of civic duty', there are also the same well-organized electoral machines, the same high percentage of voters who are enrolled members of a party, and, over much of the period, the same kind of coalition politics which one would expect would make the electorate apathetic. (Unlike in East Germany, there is, however, competition on polling day.)

Having got the electors to the polls how do the East German parties ensure that they vote the right way? Apart from the 1968 plebiscite on the new constitution, normal East German elections to the *Volkskammer* have been held under conditions which would discourage opposition. The fact that the voters have been presented with no opposition candidates would tend to make those who were opposed to the régime apathetic. Why run any risk, however small, if there is no chance to change anything? In any case to oppose means to draw attention to oneself by going into the cubicle to

---

[13] *Democratic German Report* (11 June 1954).
[14] Blecha/Gmoser/Kienzl, *Der durchleuchtete Wähler,* Europa Verlag, Vienna, 1964, p. 31.

amend the ballot paper. All that those who support the National Front candidates usually have to do is to collect their ballot papers from the clerk and put them into the box. Particularly if one goes to vote with one's colleagues at work or one's neighbours one would feel worried about possibly being the odd-man-out.

At the plebiscite to decide the socialist constitution the electorate had to mark their ballot papers for or against the proposed constitution. This also meant the privacy of the polling booth or cubicle. Once again there was the high state of organization and the full weight of the mass media brought to bear. In many areas the campaign for the socialist constitution was linked with the campaign against the murder of Dr Martin Luther King.[15] On this occasion of 98.10 per cent of the electorate who voted, 'only' 94.54 per cent of these voted for the constitution. The lowest vote in favour was recorded in East Berlin where only 90.96 per cent of the votes were for the constitution. In all, 11,536,265 East Germans cast their votes for the constitution, 409,329 against. The most enthusiastic supporters of the new constitution appear to have been the people of Rostock where 96.53 per cent voted for it.[16]

These elections and referenda lose much of their credibility when one recalls the large numbers of East Germans who left the republic before 1961. Between 1953 and 1961 over 2 million East Germans opted for the West. Now few of these were political refugees in the strict sense. Research carried on by the West German Ministry for All-German Affairs shows that of some 2,800 refugees who left the DDR in July 1961, 343 left to join their families already in West Germany; 205 said they hoped to improve their living standards; 63 sought to evade arrest for non-political reasons; 53 had marital difficulties; 19 had work to go to in West Germany; 14 wished to emigrate overseas; 68 had been refused permission to go West legally; 41 had failed to get into university; 137 were dissatisfied with changes in their salaries or status or had been made redundant; 140 had broken the pass laws, which could mean they had drawn attention to themselves for frequent unauthorized visits to the West. Among those who gave what could be called political reasons were 27 Jehovah's Witnesses; 59 who wished to avoid military service; 57 who claimed to have resisted the régime; 44 (presumably former) political prisoners; 195 whose firms or farms were being nationalized or taken over by co-operatives. There were another 528 who objected to pressure to take part in the mass organizations or to do other social work. The latter category could have included those

[15] *Neues Deutschland* (7 April 1968).
[16] Ibid.

who simply rejected the régime and those who were indifferent and wanted to live a quiet life. More disturbing were the 135 who claimed they had been called upon to work as informers for official bodies.[17] This investigation indicates that many who moved from East to West would probably have been on the move even if Germany had not been divided for reasons similar to those of the 1.2 million Britons who emigrated during 1953–61.[18] In other words, the refugees are proof that far more East Germans have been dissatisfied with conditions in the DDR than the elections there indicate. However, many of them may not have made a conscious political choice, and had their grievances been dealt with quickly, they might now have been living as reasonably contented citizens of the DDR. That this interpretation is plausible is shown by an earlier survey of the same West German Ministry. It showed that 35 per cent of the questioned refugees were 'Marxist' in their outlook. Only 35 per cent were completely free of the East German ideology. The same survey also led to the conclusion that the majority of refugees had left for non-political reasons.[19] Finally, about 25 per cent of the refugees were from the lost territories behind the Oder-Neisse frontier.[20]

Given the lack of choice on election day in East Germany why stage such an elaborate display? Firstly, of course, because the East German régime like most others wishes to show the world and its own people that it is a legitimate system of government because it has the backing of the people. Secondly, the elections are designed to raise the political consciousness of the masses. In the months which precede the election countless meetings will be held to discuss the programme of the National Front. Thirdly, the elections serve as an opportunity to renew the republic's parliamentary representatives. Here the East German authorities would stress the importance attached to the selection of the candidates *before* polling day. Just how this is done and how much influence local bodies have is difficult to say. There are indications, though, that in recent years greater attention has been paid to local susceptibilities. For instance, in 1958 the electors of Rostock rejected a number of candidates introduced to them at pre-election meetings.[21] These were candidates

[17] *Die Flucht Aus Der Sowjetzone Und Die Sperrmassnahmen Des Kommunistischen Regimes Vom 13. August 1961 In Berlin,* Bundesministerium für Gesamtdeutsche Fragen, Bonn and Berlin, 1965, pp. 21–2.
[18] Annual Abstract of Statistics, 1963, HMSO, p. 19, table 17.
[19] *Frankfurter Allgemeine Zeitung* (18 March 1957).
[20] *Die Flucht,* p. 18.
[21] Ernst-Wolfgang Böckenförde, *Die Rechtsauffassung im kommunistischen Staat,* Kösel-Verlag, Munich, 1967, p. 64.

for the district assemblies. And the correspondent of *The Times* on 17 September 1963 believed this was true in the 1963 elections.

> The régime is going out of its way to obtain as convincing an endorsement as possible. Election committees are to supervise the voting, and attempts are being made to appoint to them persons of independence and repute, not necessarily favourable to the régime... There are other indications that the communist leaders are attempting to avoid riding roughshod over voters' susceptibilities. In some factories, for instance, when too strong objections were voiced to the official candidates, others were substituted.

East German propagandists also argue that, in any case, the East German parliament, and therefore elections to it, have not got the same function as Western parliaments, and that there are other opportunities for participation by the masses in the decision-making process of the republic.

Roughly between 250,000 and 350,000 East Germans take part in the republic's regional and local organs of government. The German Democratic Republic is divided into 15 regions (*Bezirke*), including East Berlin, each of which has a regional parliament (*Bezirkstag*), as well as many other smaller units (*Kreise* and *Gemeinde*). As the law of 17 January 1957 dealing with these bodies pointed out (paragraph 1 of Article 5), they are subject to Democratic Centralism, that is, they are responsible to those who elected them, on the one hand, and to the higher organs of government on the other. Subject as they are to a hierarchical system of control, responsibility, and command, they form an integral part of the central administration. Local government in the British sense is unknown. The decisions which these East German bodies make must not in any way contradict those of the higher organs, according to Article 5, paragraph 3, of the above-mentioned law. The law of 1957 gave the *Volkskammer* the job of supervising the activities of the regional governments. This duty was transferred to the Council of State by a law of 20 September 1961.

Even if the regional and local organs of government in the DDR were not legally subject to Democratic Centralism they would still be so *de facto*, owing to the Socialist Unity Party's control of these bodies. For instance, out of 2,829 members of the regional parliaments in 1965 730 were elected as SED candidates. A further 643 were elected as candidates of the trade unions and the FDJ. The women's movement and the German Cultural League had 33

7 * *

places and the Farmers' Party 285. The bourgeois parties had together 840 members.[22]

In view of the emphasis being given in East Germany to decentralization and to the dialogue between rulers and ruled it seems likely that the local and regional organs of government are now playing a part not only in helping the central authorities execute certain responsibilities: maintenance of law and order, civil defence, revenue, town and country planning, traffic, education, public works, health and welfare, youth and sport, the contribution of local enterprises to the general economy, the control and satisfaction of local consumer wants; but also act as organs for the ventilation of local and individual grievances.

Apart from this hierarchical system of local and regional organs there are also the trade union committees at all levels and the committees of the other mass organizations. Once again, although the trade unions too are operated according to the principle of Democratic Centralism, there have been indications recently that the factory committees have served as useful organs for the expression of discontent. This is equally true of the works' courts in which employees judge their colleagues accused of minor offences.

The Constitution of 1968

Having considered the theory and practice of the East German constitution up to 1968 let us now examine the second, 'socialist', constitution of the DDR. But first, let us try to fathom why East Germany has been given a new constitution at this particular time. It was at the VII Congress of the Socialist Unity Party that Walter Ulbricht first hinted that a new constitution was on the way. He said:

> For some time now, it has been apparent that the present constitution of the DDR no longer accords with the relations of socialist society and the present level of historical development. The fact is that our present constitution dates from the period of the anti-fascist democratic period, from which we have gone a long way as is well known. In the intervening period there have been additions and implementation regulations through laws which have been unanimously adopted by the *Volkskammer*. The working out of a new and appropriate constitution, however, presupposes that the basic problems of the new period have matured to a great extent. I am of the opinion that this will be so in the near future. It will therefore be the task of the newly elected

[22] *SJB der DDR*, 1966, p. 582.

People's Chamber to decide when the preparation of a new constitution of the DDR will begin.[23]

One year later the new constitution was already in force. This was unusual haste even though, according to official estimates, during the year of discussion there were some 750,000 meetings attended by around 11 million people.[24] No doubt the official reason given, the development of the DDR into a socialist society, was part of the reason for the new constitution. The DDR was certainly in economic, social, and political terms a markedly different place in 1968 from what it had been in 1949. Another possible reason for the change was the fact that certain other socialist states had given themselves new constitutions in the sixties. More important, the new constitution would emphasize the sovereign nature of the DDR, distinguish it clearly from West Germany, and underline the existence of *two* German states. This has been an increasingly important theme of DDR policy since at least 1961. The policy-makers in East Germany also probably felt that a new constitution would both emphasize to their own people that there was no going back on their version of socialism and, at the same time, offer them hope of better things to come. The idea, first expressed by Ulbricht in 1965, was that the DDR was now putting aside dictatorial methods and was developing into a state of the whole people, into a *Volksstaat*. With a measure of stability brought about by properity and a number of fairly popular reforms, such as the family law, already in operation, it could be argued that the time was right for such an undertaking. The speed with which this was done was probably a sign of unease on the part of the leadership about developments in Czechoslovakia. The East German leaders felt obliged to play up their own adherence to developing socialist democracy, at the same time sticking to their own view of this.[25]

Already in Article 1 of the 1968 constitution it becomes clear that it is fundamentally different from the one it replaced. In the old constitution Germany was merely a 'democratic Republic' but the DDR is 'a socialist state of the German nation'. Power derives not just from 'the people' but from the 'working people' (Article 2) who are implementing socialism under the leadership of the 'Marxist-Leninist party' (Article 1). Thus the leading role of the SED becomes fundamental to the constitution. As one would expect, the section dealing with the economy (Articles 9–16) contrasts markedly

[23] *Neues Deutschland* (18 April 1967).
[24] Dietrich Müller-Römer, *Ulbrichts Grundgesetz Die sozialistische Verfassung der DDR*, Verlag Wissenschaft und Politik, Cologne, 1968, p. 25.
[25] Ibid., p. 29.

with Articles 19–29 of the old constitution. 'The national economy of the German Democratic Republic is based upon the socialist ownership of the means of production', says Article 9 of the present constitution. The old constitution said on the same subject, 'The system of economy must be based on the principles of social justice and ensure an adequate standard of living for all' (Article 19). The new constitution defines socialist property as nationally owned property, co-operative property, and property owned by the organizations of the people (Article 10). Surprisingly perhaps, the authors of the 1968 constitution, like their predecessors of 1949, find it necessary to list the type of property which is nationally owned, which includes virtually everything except the smaller enterprises and agricultural co-operatives. Article 23 of the first constitution dealt with nationalization of property and promised 'adequate compensation'. The 1968 constitution contains a similar clause. Article 16 states: 'Expropriations are permissible only for the public weal, on the basis of law, and against appropriate compensation. They may only be effected if the desired public purpose cannot be achieved in any other way'. This is obviously included to allay any possible fears East Germany's thousands of mini-capitalists might have. The socialist constitution says nothing about the right to inherit private enterprises though Article 11 guarantees the right of inheritance of 'personal property'. A whole series of rights contained in the old constitution is retained in the new: the right to education and leisure (Articles 25 and 34 respectively); the right to inviolability of the home (Article 37); the right 'to social care in case of old age and invalidity' (Article 36); the right to 'profess a religious creed, and to carry out religious activities' (Article 39); the right of the Sorbs 'to cultivate their mother tongue and culture' (Article 40). Certain other rights have been extended or given greater detail. The right of mother and child, for instance, under Article 38, to 'enjoy the special protection of the socialist state. Maternity leave, special medical care, material and financial support during childbirth and children's allowances are granted'. Certain restrictions contained in the earlier constitution on preaching racial hatred, militarist propaganda, and incitement to war, are renewed (Article 6). Certain important rights contained in the 1949 constitution have been reduced, countered by corresponding obligations, or simply dropped. The old constitution guaranteed, under Article 8, 'the right to choose one's place of residence'. Article 10 gave 'every citizen the right to emigrate'. Article 32 of the socialist constitution merely grants 'every citizen of the German Democratic Republic... the right to move freely within the state territory of the German Democratic Republic within the framework of the laws'. The right to work was guaranteed under the old constitution (Article 15). Now Article 24 states: 'Every citizen of the German Democratic Republic has the right to work. He has the right to employment and its free selection in accordance with social requirements and personal qualifications . . . The right to work and the duty to work form a unity'. Like many other aspects of the DDR constitution, this is similar to what the Soviet constitution of 1936 has to say on this subject (Articles 12 and 118). In the USSR this duty to work has been used against prostitutes, vagrants, and beatniks. Both the Soviet constitution and the present DDR constitution presume that the socialist economic system can maintain full employment. Thus the right to work is guaranteed by the intrinsic merits of the economic system rather than society merely saying that this should be so. This leads to a situation where the framers of these constitutions thought it unnecessary to guarantee state support in case of temporary or local unemployment. On this the 1949 constitution stated: 'By its guiding of the economy the state ensures work and the means of livelihood for every citizen. Where a suitable place of work cannot be made available the citizen will be provided with the necessary means of subsistence'. Up to 1968, however, a decree of 28 January 1947 and another of 12 July 1951 have provided insurance against unemployment.[26] This will presumably continue to be the case. The fact that the individual is not entirely free in his choice of work is implied by reference in the present constitution to right to employment and its free selection 'in accordance with social requirements'. Thus the appropriate authorities have the right to direct teachers to their first jobs after the completion of their training. Redundant workers—there have been some due to the changing nature of the economy—can be directed to new work, etc. A right which has completely disappeared from the constitution is the right to strike. 'The trade unions are guaranteed the right to strike', stated Article 14 of the old constitution. The theory now is that if the workers went on strike they would be striking against themselves because most of the means of production are owned by the state, their state, the state of the working people. Should grievances nevertheless occur in individual factories the workers can sort them out through their trade union representatives. Logical though this theory may be, it is doubtful whether it would convince many Western trade unionists, socialist or Communist. As far as the trade unions are concerned the consti-

[26] Dietrich Müller-Römer, *Sonderdruck Aus Die Grundrechte In Mitteldeutschland*, Verlag Wissenschaft und Politik, Cologne, p. 103.

tution (Article 44) sees their main tasks as playing 'a determining role in shaping socialist society, in planning and management of the national economy, in the implementation of the scientific-technical revolution, in the development of working and living conditions, health protection and labour safety, cultural working environment, and cultural and sports activities of the working people'. The trade unions also administer under Article 45 the social insurance system. In so far as the 1968 constitution names the existing trade unions as 'the all-embracing class organization of the working class' it precludes the setting up of other trade union organizations.

The normal rights included in the earlier constitution—free speech, freedom of the press, the right to assemble peacefully, the right of association—also have their place in the present constitution. They can only be exercised, however, 'in accordance with the spirit and aims of this Constitution' or 'within the framework of the principles and aims of the Constitution'.

The main change in the constitutional structure of power is that the People's Chamber and the Council of Ministers have lost some of their formal power to the Council of State. Of the People's Chamber the present constitution states:

> The People's Chamber is the supreme organ of state power in the German Democratic Republic. It decides in its plenary sessions the basic questions of state policy.
> The People's Chamber is the sole constitutional and legislative organ in the German Democratic Republic. No one can limit its rights.
> By its activities the People's Chamber implements the principle of the unity of decision and enforcement (Article 48).

The People's Chamber can hold plebiscites, it cannot be dissolved except at its own request (Article 64), it 'determines by means of laws and decisions the aims of the development of the German Democratic Republic in a final manner binding on all' (Article 49). According to Article 50 it also 'elects the Chairman and members of the Council of State, the Chairman and members of the Council of Ministers, the Chairman of the National Defence Council, the President and judges of the Supreme Court and the Attorney-General. They can be recalled at any time by the People's Chamber'. Finally, it approves state treaties and decides on the state (*Zustand*) of the defence of the DDR (Articles 51 and 52). The socialist constitution of the DDR spells out the wide powers of the Council of State and its Chairman. For instance, it has decisive influence on legislation: 'The Council of State deals with bills to be submitted to the People's Chamber and submits them for discussion by the committees of the People's Chamber' (Article 70). It calls elections, interprets the constitution and laws, 'takes fundamental decisions on matters relating to the defence and security of the country and organizes national defence with the help of the National Defence Council', whose members it appoints (Article 73). In all these matters the chamber has, in theory, the final say. 'In case of urgency', it is also empowered under Article 52, 'to decide on a state of defence'. Nowhere does one find any reference as to how the Council of State is to reach its decisions or what constitutes a quorum. One learns only that 'The Chairman directs the work of the Council of State' (Article 69). This is somewhat in contrast to the earlier constitution which set out how the 'government' (*Regierung*) was to operate. As for the Council of Ministers, which grew out of the old *Regierung*, as we saw above, it has lost much of its standing since 1949. The new constitution makes it a little more dependent on the Council of State. 'The Chairman of the Council of Ministers is proposed to the People's Chamber by the Chairman of the Council of State . . .' (Article 80). The Council of Ministers, on the other hand, is somewhat more independent of the chamber than under the old constitution. There is no provision for removal between elections. In fact, Article 80 states clearly, it is elected 'for a term of four years'. But it is 'responsible and accountable to the People's Chamber' (Article 80). The Council of Ministers' tasks are set out by Article 78 as follows : to organize, 'on behalf of the People's Chamber, the execution of the political, economic, cultural and social tasks of the socialist state and the defence tasks assigned to it'. It further 'works out scientifically based prognoses, organizes the economic system of socialism and directs the planned development of the national economy'. In other words, a body primarily concerned with economic affairs.

East German parliamentarians are not seen as representatives of local communities but of the 'whole people'. But they must 'maintain close contact with their electors. They are to heed their proposals, suggestions and criticisms and to ensure conscientious attention to them' (Article 56). They must also 'hold regular consultation hours and discussions and . . . report to their electors on their activities'. If they do not they can be 'recalled' (Article 57). They retain their immunity and other privileges granted under the 1949 constitution and now 'are entitled to refuse to testify concerning persons who have confided facts to them in the course of their duties as deputies, or to whom they have confided facts in the course of their duties as deputies, and about these facts themselves' (Article 60).

The legal system of the DDR is given greater attention in the socialist constitution than it was in that of 1949. The theory is that legality, the rule of law, and the fulfilment of the constitutional guarantees depend much more on the existence of a socialist society and on the participation of the citizens in the law, than on the integrity of a small corps of professional lawyers. This is implied or stated in Articles 86, 87, and 88. Article 92 sketches the system of courts : 'Jurisdiction in the German Democratic Republic is exercised by the Supreme Court, the District Courts, the Regional Court and the social courts within the framework of the tasks assigned them by law. In military matters jurisdiction is exercised by the Supreme Court, military tribunals and military courts'.

Article 101 tells us that 'Special courts are inadmissible'. The Supreme Court is the highest court and directs the jurisdiction of the other courts. It is responsible to the People's Chamber and between sessions to the Council of State (Article 93). Judges must be persons 'loyally devoted to the people and their socialist state, and endowed with a high measure of knowledge and experience, human maturity and character'. And, 'The democratic election of all judges, lay judges and members of social courts guarantees that justice will be administered by men and women from all classes and sections of the people'. The framers of the socialist constitution of the DDR have looked to the Soviet Union for an institution to safeguard 'the socialist state and social order and the rights of citizens'. This is the state attorney's office. The office, states Article 97, 'supervises the strict adherence to socialist legality on the basis of laws and other statutory regulations. It protects citizens from violations of the law. The state attorney's office directs the struggle against penal offences and ensures that persons who have committed crimes or other legal offences are called to account before the court'. The East Germans, however, retained the old German term *Staatsanwalt-schaft*, the term used in the 1949 constitution, instead of the Russian term 'procurator-general'. Articles 105 and 106 mark an improvement in the rights of individuals who feel they have cause to complain against decisions of public bodies or who have suffered from 'unlawful actions of employees of state organs'. Now 'liability lies with the state organ whose employee caused the damage. The conditions and procedure of state liability are regulated by law'. It remains to be seen how effective such guarantees will be, but a West German legal expert has commented : 'If one looks at the development of the legal protection against administrative measures in Middle Germany [i.e. the DDR] since 1945, one finds that since the low ebb of 1952 . . . an upward development towards modern, impartial solutions has begun . . . which has found expression in the new constitution'.[27]

Unlike the constitution of 1949 and unlike the constitution of West Germany, the present DDR constitution recognizes the division of Germany :

> The establishment and cultivation of normal relations and co-operation between the two German states on the basis of equality are national concerns of the German Democratic Republic. The German Democratic Republic and its citizens strive in addition to overcome the division of Germany imposed upon the German nation by imperialism, and support the step-by-step rapprochement of the two German states until the time of their unification on the basis of democracy and socialism (Article 8).

About the republic's defence Article 7 states : 'In the interests of the preservation of peace and the security of the socialist state, the National People's Army cultivates close comradeship-in-arms with the armies of the Soviet Union and other socialist states'.

The 1968 constitution of the German Democratic Republic is certainly more realistic about the real power relationships in the country than ever the 1949 constitution was. On the one hand, it recognizes the lack of effective power of parliament and, on the other, the very real power of the SED and, more particularly, through Democratic Centralism, of the leaders of the Unity Party. It emphasizes the wide powers of the Council of State and especially of its Chairman, Ulbricht. Readers will have their own views on just how democratic or socialist this constitution is. It is far from perfect. However, like most other constitutions it is flexible and will be more or less authoritarian, more or less democratic, depending on the direction East German society is going.

[27] *Ulbrichts Grundgesetz*, p. 57.

The Multi-Party System: The SED's 'Echoes'

I
N THE WEST many people wrongly assume that East Germany is
a one-party state. This is not the case. There are, in addition
to the SED, four other parties—CDU, LDPD, NDPD, and
DBD—as well as the mass organizations. In the Communist scheme
of things the continued existence of these parties has been very
useful. Firstly, they serve as a bridge between the DDR and similar
groups in West Germany and abroad. Secondly, they win for the
régime the active co-operation of people who would not care to
belong to a directly Marxist party anchored in the working class.
Thirdly, they act as a channel through which the grievances of the
'bourgeois' classes can be ventilated without conflict. Finally, they
are useful window-dressing, bolstering the régime's 'image' as a
truly democratic state.

Two of these parties, the Christian Democratic Union (CDU) and
the Liberal Democratic Party (LDPD), were founded after the war
and were very similar to such parties in West Germany at that
time. Like them they are largely middle class. They were soon
forced to shed their conservative and anti-Communist elements and
since about 1948 have existed largely as 'echoes' of the SED. The
National Democratic Party (NDPD), which has nothing to do with
the West German party bearing the same name, and the Democratic
Farmers' Party (DBD) were set up later, partly as counterweights
to the CDU and the LDPD, and partly to win new groups for the
régime.

Establishment Christians

As the West German Catholic journalist Walter Dirks, one of the
founders of the CDU, has emphasized, 'The CDU of the first period
was a "left-wing" movement—if only because the right-wing position was neither advocated nor capable of being advocated : the
fascist and reactionary rightists were overthrown, the capitalist
interests had no effect before the currency reform, the conservatives

were paralysed because in the ruins there was nothing to conserve'.[1] Some had been members of or influenced by the 'Confessing Church' which had opposed Hitler, some were strongly liberal democratic in the Weimar tradition, others had been connected with the July Plot against Hitler, still others were Christian Socialists. As Herr Dirks also emphasized, these Christian Democrats were sometimes joined by others—traditionalists, conservatives, anti-Communists rather than non-Communists, and industrial interests. In the West they gained the upper hand, in the East only those who were prepared to go along with the SED's interpretation of socialism were allowed to remain in the ranks of the East German CDU. From the sociological point of view, the CDU in Saxony-Anhalt, which contained 21 per cent of CDU members in the Soviet Zone, had the following social composition in 1947: 12.6 per cent workers; 18.4 per cent white-collar workers; 8.3 per cent civil servants; 13.6 per cent farmers; 9.6 per cent independent craftsmen; professional men 8.5 per cent; housewives 24.6 per cent; unknown 4.4 per cent.[2]

Among the founders of the CDU in Berlin and the Soviet Zone were Dr Andreas Hermes, a former Centre Party Minister in the Weimar republic; Ernst Lemmer, formerly of the moderate middle-class German Democratic Party; Dr Walther Schreiber, another Democratic Party politician; Dr Heinrich Krone, formerly of the Centre Party; and Jacob Kaiser and his wife, also former Centre Party members.[3] Lemmer, Kaiser, and Krone later became prominent in Bonn. Altogether the founders of the CDU in Berlin consisted of 21 former Centre Party members, about the same number of conservatives, and eight or nine former members of the German Democratic Party.[4]

On 22 July 1945 the founders held their first public meeting in what is now the theatre of the *Berliner Ensemble*. Already on 22 June in an appeal to the German people they said they wished to unite 'the Christian, democratic, and social forces to co-operate in building a new homeland'. They wanted religious instruction in schools to be an integral part of education, thus renewing an old policy demand of Christian politicians. In economic affairs they

[1] As given in Ossip K. Flechtheim, *Die Deutschen Parteien Seit 1945 Quellen Und Auszüge*, Carl Heymanns Verlag K G, Cologne, 1957, p. 125.
[2] Ibid., p. 57.
[3] Ernst Deuerlein, *CDU/CSU 1945–1957 Beiträge Zur Zeitgeschichte*, Verlag J. P. Bachem, Cologne, p. 44.
[4] Norbert Mattedi, 'Gründung und Entwicklung der Parteien in der Sowjetischen Besatzungszone Deutschlands, 1945–49', *Bonner Berichte Aus Mittel-Und Ostdeutschland*, Bonn and Berlin, 1966, p. 35.

moved in a socialistic direction to the extent that they demanded
state ownership of natural resources and wanted monopolies firmly
under state control. They advocated the quite revolutionary step of
a united trade union movement embracing all workers and white-
collar employees. They announced their intention of working together with other political parties, of which there were then only
two, the Social Democrats and the Communists.[5] No doubt this
programme represented a compromise between the more leftward
elements and the conservatives, the latter sensing they could not be
too far out of step with the general socialistic mood of the times.
In the British Zone the CDU adopted a more left-wing programme
which, however, was dropped once the CDU were in power in
Bonn. The first Berlin conference of the Christian Democrats in
June 1946 ratified the theses of 22 June.

The CDU leaders in the Eastern Zone were soon in conflict with
the Soviet military administration. The two leaders, Hermes and
Schreiber, had opposed the expropriation of large landholdings, a
measure which was probably one of the most popular the Soviets
carried through, and in December 1945 the Soviet authorities made
use of the right they had reserved themselves to remove them.[6]
They were replaced by Kaiser and Lemmer. The new leaders also
opposed the land reform. At the CDU's second conference in September 1947 they opposed the Oder-Neisse Line, called for the
Soviet Zone's participation in the Marshall Plan, and opposed
'dogmatic Marxism'.[7] Obviously, it was only a matter of time
before the leaders faced a show-down with the Soviets and the
SED. It came in December 1947. The Soviets refused to have anything more to do with them. This made the continued working of
the party difficult and, as in all such cases, encouraged factions and
in-fighting. A five-man committee took over the running of the
party. This included the general secretary, Dr Dertinger, and the
future leader of the party, Otto Nuschke. The party now started to
take a more positive attitude towards Soviet policies. Under the
influence of Nuschke it decided to take part in the 2nd People's
Congress. At the CDU's third conference in September 1948
Nuschke emerged as chairman. The East-Zone CDU took part in
the setting-up of the DDR in 1949 and accepted the Oder-Neisse
frontier in 1950 when it was finally agreed by the Polish and East
German governments. The CDU was awarded four posts in the

[5] Mattedi, op. cit., p. 37.
[6] *Die Sowjetische Besatzungszone Deutschlands in den Jahren 1945 bis
1954 Eine chronologische Übersicht*, Bundesministerium für Gesamtdeutsche Fragen, Bonn and Berlin, 1961, p. 27.
[7] Ibid., p. 59.

first DDR government of 1949. Nuschke became a deputy Prime Minister, Dr Dertinger became the Foreign Minister, Luitpold Steidle took over the Ministry of Health, and Friedrich Burmeister received the Ministry of Posts. Nuschke, a former journalist and German Democratic Party deputy in the Prussian parliament from 1921 until 1933, continued as a deputy Prime Minister until his death in 1957. Dertinger, a journalist for the nationalist *Stahlhelm* movement before 1933, was arrested in 1953 as an alleged spy. After serving several years in prison he was pardoned. Steidle, a *Wehrmacht* officer, had been captured by the Soviets at Stalingrad and was persuaded to carry on anti-Nazi propaganda. He remained Minister of Health until 1958 and is still one of the leading members of the CDU. Burmeister, a member of the German Democratic Party in the Weimar republic, remained a member of the East German parliament until 1958 when he retired owing to advanced age.

It was at a conference in Meissen in October 1951 that the East German CDU first came out in favour of socialism based on 'Christian Responsibility'. The conference declared:

> The Christian must see the correctness of the basic economic analysis of Marxism-Leninism . . . Through the effort of the democratic forces after the breakdown of the Hitler régime, the anti-fascist democratic order came into being which found its first state in the German Democratic Republic. These efforts of the democratic forces are, for Germany, the way of overcoming the past and treading a new road. The CDU therefore supports this régime and works solidly with it.[8]

At the CDU's sixth conference in 1952 Herr Nuschke justified his party's position in the following way:

> We are in favour of socialism, since it creates the indispensable economic conditions, which are needed for the unfolding of genuine humanity . . . Already St Thomas Aquinas described the securing of a certain existence minimum as an indispensable prerequisite for a religious life. Under socialism man will be freed from that continuous and agonizing struggle for his bare existence. He will have time and leisure to devote himself to his family, his community and also to develop his religious talents . . . Through its merely formal clergyman's Christianity the bourgeois world allowed millions of people to perish every hour in shocking

[8] 22 *Theses Of Christian Realism,* Christlich—Demokratische Union Deutschlands, Berlin, 1952.

social misery; families were torn apart, millions of people were killed in murderous wars, a ruthless competition and exploitation became the basic principle of a social system. Through socialism man, who was created by God, with his genuine and natural needs, will again stand in the centre of all social labour.[9]

These Christian socialists of East Germany emphasize the early Church, the 'social problem' brought on by industrial capitalism, the pacific side of Christianity in a world of wars and rumours of war. They also felt a sense of guilt for the deeds done in the name of the German people and for the ambiguous role of the Churches in two world wars. Among the older generation of CDU politicians there were those, like Nuschke, who had worked for an understanding with the Soviet Union in the 1920s, an understanding which harked back to traditional Russo-German ties and found expression in the Rapallo Treaty of 1922. Doubtless the East German CDU contained, and still does, those who sought personal advantage by co-operation with the Soviets and domestic Communists (though those who went West certainly did well), no doubt it attracted businessmen who sought to save what was to save, but it also attracted some genuine Christian socialists and some of the remnants of the 'Easterners' of the democratic bourgeoisie of the 1920s. The party was fortunate in winning the co-operation of such outstanding personalities as Professor Emil Fuchs of Leipzig and Bishop Moritz Mitzenheim, the Evangelical bishop of Thuringia, men whose integrity has never been questioned.

These pro-SED Christians, and they are very much in the minority, would claim that co-operation with the state has paid off. Has it? How much freedom do the Churches enjoy in East Germany? Amnesty International published a report in August 1966 on 'Prison Conditions In East Germany', already referred to in the last chapter. The section devoted to freedom of religion stated:

The majority of Christians in East Germany are members of the Protestant (Evangelische) Church. Although this Church has been harried in various ways and with particular intensity at certain periods by the State and by the atheistic programme of the Party and the mass organizations, the Church as a whole has maintained its independence. The authorities, it seems, find it more expedient to brand recalcitrant clergy as 'reactionaries' than to make martyrs of them by imprisonment. Individual Christians may be said to enjoy freedom of conscience and reli-

[9] *Mitgestalterin der neuen Zeit,* CDU (East), 1965, pp. 15–16.

gion provided that the exercise of this does not bring them, in any other way, into conflict with the State.[10]

After dealing with the problems of Christian pacifists, referred to in a later chapter, it continued,

> The religious sect of Jehovah's Witnesses has been subjected to systematic persecution in East Germany since it was banned in 1950 and accused of spying for the Americans under the cloak of religion. Announcing this ban Dr Steinhoff, then Minister of the Interior, said that the sect was guilty of 'spreading illegal written material', of 'systematically inciting against the existing order and its laws under the cover of religious functions' and of 'serving the espionage service of an imperialist power'. Since the East German army (*Volksarmee*) is described as a 'weapon for peace' Jehovah's Witnesses have also been accused of 'incitement to war' on account of their pacifism. Some Jehovah's Witnesses in East Germany have been in prison almost continuously since 1939, having been imprisoned first under Hitler and then by the Soviet occupation authorities and the East German government.

The writer himself had the opportunity of discussing the position of the Churches with Catholic priests without any official of the régime being present or knowing about it. They, by no means enthusiastic about the DDR, confirmed the view that the authorities do not wish to create martyrs. They also said that in general the state did not interfere in the life of the Catholic Church and believed Christians were better off in East Germany than in the other East European countries.

During a Catholic pilgrimage in Erfurt in 1966, attended by an estimated 12,000, the writer introduced himself to a priest and was immediately invited to see the seminary, a pleasant modern building erected by the Catholic Church itself and run as a private institution. This is the only one of its kind in the DDR. Before the war all priests were trained in the Catholic heartlands of western Germany. The Catholic Church also runs a preparatory seminary for boys, a training centre for those called later in life, two lay seminaries, a college for religious teachers, 39 hospitals with a total of 12,000 beds, 113 old people's homes, and monastic and other institutions. These services cover roughly 1.6 million Catholics out of a population of about 17 million. The Catholic Church also

[10] Report confirmed by *Berlin Sowjet Sektor*, Colloquium Verlag, Berlin (West), 1965.

publishes its own press. There is the *St Hedwigsblatt,* named after the cathedral, which is published in Berlin, and *Tag des Herrn,* which appears in Leipzig. Both are weeklies. In the offices of *St Hedwigsblatt* the writer was assured that there was no formal censorship, but that the church journalists knew just how far they dared go. Generally speaking, they were allowed to attack atheism, but not the socialist system. The Catholic, and for that matter the Protestant, press not only brings new items about the Church in the DDR but also about Catholic activities throughout the world. Its tone is in keeping with the efforts towards greater Christian unity. For example, the issue of *St Hedwigsblatt* of 14 August 1966 contained a report of the World Conference of Churches held in Geneva at which there were Catholic observers. The paper reported that the conference condemned nuclear war and demanded a controlled system of non-proliferation. The conference rejected every form of racial discrimination and called for a programme of economic co-operation with the developing countries. With reports of this kind the Catholic press in East Germany will certainly not come into conflict with the authorities. However, a sign of the coolness of this press towards the régime may be gauged from the fact that the term 'DDR' does not appear in the *St Hedwigsblatt.* Nor is there any news of those Catholics and other Christians who advance the causes of the state.

The Evangelical Church, which is divided into eight provinces in the DDR and which together with the provincial sister Churches in West Germany form the Evangelical Church of Germany (EKD), runs over 50 hospitals, well over 300 old people's homes, nearly 200 apprentices' homes, convalescent homes, children's homes, and other institutions.

A CDU publication[11] claimed that in the DDR there are 27 theological and church magazines and newspapers with a total circulation of 360,000 which appear regularly. The CDU itself puts out six daily newspapers which carry news of the Churches and religious affairs. The same publication claimed that in the years 1961–2 the man Evangelical publishing house, 'Die Evangelische Verlagsanstalt', was responsible for 641 books of which a total of 6.3 million copies were printed. In the same years the Catholic publishing house 'St Benno' in Leipzig carried 262 titles involving over 2.7 million copies. It is also only fair to mention that the East German radio broadcasts religious services. Apart from the information activities by and for the Churches, the CDU 'Union Verlag'

[11] *Christen Und Kirchen In Der Deutschen Demokratischen Republik,* CDU (East), 1964.

in Berlin is responsible for a large number of books and other publications. In 1968 it was offering paperback biographies of such noted Christians as Karl Barth, George Bell, Dietrich Bonhoeffer, Pope John XXIII, Martin Luther King, Albert Luthuli, Martin Niemöller, Pope Paul VI, Albert Schweitzer, and many others.

One of the main causes of friction between the Churches and the state in East Germany has been the emphasis on atheism in schools and the exclusion of religion. But the CDU point out that the clergy have the right to use school buildings at the end of the school day for religious instruction. Apparently, the actual realization of this depends on who the local personnel are. At DDR universities there were in 1965 642 students reading (Evangelical) theology full-time, a fairly high number. There are also Christian youth groups and student chaplains active in East German universities which is just about unique in the Soviet bloc. Most of these students get state grants. There are also other Evangelical educational establishments and, as mentioned above, a separate one for the Catholics.

Another cause of friction has been the belief of the Churches that not enough money is set aside for restoration of old churches and building of new ones. The protagonists of Church-state co-operation claim the opposite. They argue that in the years 1958 to 1962 the state spent 6 million marks on such restoration and many times this amount, they claim, was spent by the regional and local authorities for the same purpose. This is still only part of the funds needed, the rest is provided by the Churches themselves. Among the recipients of state funds were Magdeburg Cathedral, the Marienkirche of Berlin, the Catholic Hofkirche in Dresden, and Freiberg Cathedral. The clergy too receive state funds from the traditional church tax which is still levied by the East German authorities. Obviously, those East Germans who do not wish to pay do not do so. The pro-state Christians also cite to their credit the fact that there are no clergy in jail in East Germany,[12] and the arrangement by which the over sixty-fives may go to West Germany.

Perhaps the most important grievance of the Churches in East Germany in recent years has been the difficulties placed in the way of churchmen wanting to attend church functions in Federal Germany, and vice versa. The SED's reply has been to criticize the stand taken by certain churchmen and by the Churches in West Germany on certain issues. They resent church dignitaries supporting refugee organizations, supporting the West German CDU, and appearing to support the military policies of West Germany by providing chaplains for the Federal armed forces.

12 Welles Hangen, *The Muted Revolution*, Knopf, New York, 1966, p. 19.

8 * *

Both pro- and anti-SED Christians have assured the writer that the East German régime is working for a *modus vivendi* with the Churches. In the case of the Catholic Church the conciliatory attitudes of Popes John XXIII (1958–63) and Paul VI (1963–) greatly helped. In the case of the EKD an important factor was the 1965 memorandum of that Church appealing for recognition of the Oder-Neisse frontier which helped to improve the atmosphere. The fact that the East German economy gains advantage from the financial assistance, given in 'hard' West marks, that both Churches receive from their West German friends also carries weight with the SED.

The East German state has greatly benefited from the assistance of its Christian supporters. The East German CDU has made a considerable contribution to representing the republic abroad, especially in neutral and Western countries which do not have diplomatic relations with East Germany. Pro-SED Christians have taken an active part in the World Council of Churches, attending, for instance, the famous New Delhi congress in 1962. They have helped to give the pro-Moscow World Peace Council respectability in the West. Their members, as Ministers in the *Ministerrat*, have been on official delegations not only to Moscow, Prague, and Warsaw but also to Cairo, Bogotá, and Nicosia. CDU general secretary Gerald Götting, one of the post-war generation of Christians, made much publicized trips to Dr Albert Schweitzer and was able to connect the latter's name with the DDR. At the eleventh conference of the CDU in 1964 there were Christians from socialist and non-socialist countries alike including officials of the French Catholic MRP. The twelfth CDU conference in 1968 also attracted a very mixed assortment of foreign guests from a number of West European countries and the Soviet bloc. From the non-Communist world the most significant guests were the Rev. Gunnar Dahmen, head of the religious affairs department of the Swedish Radio, and an impressive delegation from the ruling Christian Democratic Party of Chile.

Who are the members of the East German CDU today? The writer has not seen any published figures on the social composition of the party or on its size. But the party organ, *Union Pressedienst* (Heft/14, 1968) gave some details of the delegates to the twelfth congress, and information is available on the delegates to the 1964 congress. On both occasions the intelligentsia was strongly represented. In 1968 27 per cent of the delegates were said to be in this class, mainly teachers, engineers, and doctors. Another 10 per cent of the delegates in 1968 were co-operative farmers and a further

10 per cent, at the same congress, were craftsmen, private traders, private manufacturers, or part-owners of mixed enterprises. The occupations of the other delegates were not given but it seems likely that some of them were workers and considerable numbers were either full-time party officials or housewives. In 1964 30 per cent of the delegates were said to be women.[13] In 1968 this had been increased to 33 per cent. According to the official figures for the delegates at these two conferences official Christianity in East Germany does not appear to be in danger of dying out. Roughly 20 per cent of the delegates at both congresses were aged between 18 and 35.

As for the East German CDU's religious affiliations, Gerald Götting, the party's general secretary since 1949, summed up the situation as follows:

The Christian Democratic Union is not the party of a church; it is in no way the 'political section' of the church. The tasks of the churches differ from those of a political party in which Christians come together to fulfil a social function. We are in no way umpires in theological disputes. The decisive factor for us, must be the social and political conclusions which are drawn. Our members belong to different churches, and are adherents of many different theological standpoints. But all of them, whether they may be Barthians, liberals, followers of Bultmann, Neo-Thomists or members of the Free Churches, are united in the will to accept their Christian responsibility and to co-operate in developing our state, supporting its peace policy and helping to build socialism.[14]

Having discussed the Christians in East Germany it would perhaps be appropriate to say something about the place of the Jews in the DDR, before continuing our survey of the parties.

In the Democratic Republic there are eight Jewish communities—in Berlin, Schwerin, Magdeburg, Halle, Erfurt, Leipzig, Dresden, and Karl-Marx-Stadt. They have eight synagogues and a prayer house almost entirely paid for from state funds. Jewish cemeteries have been restored and there is a Kosher slaughter-house in East Berlin. All this despite the fact that the Jews in the DDR number only a few thousand. Dr Martin Riesenburger, East Germany's Chief Rabbi until his death in 1965, was, like Bishop Mitzenheim,

[13] *Für Deutschlands Frieden und Deutschlands Zukunft*, CDU (East), no date
[14] Gerald Götting, *Christians And Politics In the GDR*, Union Verlag, East Berlin, 1966, p. 147.

awarded the DDR's Order of Merit in gold. There was a time, in the early fifties, when the Jews of East Germany in common with those of the rest of Eastern Europe suffered owing to the suspicions engendered by the 'cult of personality'. At that time a number of Jews were arrested together with certain other people. Fearing a similar fate many leading Jews went West. Today, Helmut Aris, whom the author has met, head of the Jewish communities of the DDR, plays a leading role in the East German Peace Council and has been appropriately honoured. Most Jews in the DDR, Herr Aris told the writer, receive special pensions as victims of fascism and, despite East German attacks on Israel as a 'base for American Imperialism', Jews had nothing to fear in the German Democratic Republic. That there is no official anti-Semitism can be seen when one considers that there are a number of ethnic Jews who are prominent in East German life—Albert Norden, the son of a rabbi, a member of the *Politbüro* of the SED; Frau Wittkowski, formerly a deputy Prime Minister, now head of the state bank; Alexander Abusch, a deputy Prime Minister and member of the Central Committee; the writer Stefan Heym, film director Konrad Wolf, Supreme Court judge Kurt Cohn, and painter Lea Grundig.

Marxian 'Liberals'

The Liberal Democratic Party (LDPD) of East Germany, formed in 1945 as the successor to earlier German liberal parties, tended to be strongly democratic, in the Weimar sense, in favour of private ownership, mainly non-working class, largely Protestant or free thinking, and rather 'national' in outlook.

The first manifesto of the Liberal Democrats in Berlin in 1945 was notable for its vagueness. It talked about overcoming militarism and Nazi arrogance and the 'cultural resurrection of the German people' without saying how it would achieve such aims. Unlike the CDU it came out clearly for 'private property and the free economy'.[15] The party's principles agreed in 1947 talked about being for 'Western Christian culture' and the free economy 'which is as far away from an exploiting and anti-competitive capitalism as it is from enslaving state monopolism'. The state should use its power against new monopolies and misuse of economic power for anti-democratic, anti-social, and anti-peace purposes. It opposed the welfare state in favour of voluntary self-help and was for religious

[15] Wolfgang Hoffmann, LDPD, *Humanistische Und Revolutionär-Demokratische Traditionen Des Bürgertums*, Buchverlag Der Morgen, Berlin, 1965, pp. 237–40.

instruction in schools.[16] In both parts of Germany the two Liberal parties, the LDPD and the FDP, were subject to bitter internal strife between several rival factions. In the case of the LDPD, as pointed out above, there was soon no place for any elements who were not prepared to accept the basic propositions of the existence of an East German state, socialism, and the leadership of the SED. In the first chairman of the party, Dr Wilhelm Külz, who was a Minister in the Weimar republic, member of the German Democratic Party, and Lord Mayor of Dresden until dismissed by the Nazis, the Soviets and the SED appear to have had a loyal collaborator. He supported participation in the bloc of anti-fascist parties and the People's Congresses. He was attacked at the party's second conference in Eisenach in 1947 for his attitude but was re-elected First Chairman. Külz died in 1948 and at the party's third conference in February 1948 Professor Kastner and Dr Karl Hamann were elected co-chairmen. The party agreed to continue co-operation with the SED and CDU, and now accepted that natural resources and the large undertakings of the basic industries should belong to the people.[17] Kastner was made a deputy premier of the DDR in 1949 but expelled from the party in 1950. He later fled to the West where he died. At the LDPD's fourth conference in July 1951 Hamann and Dr Hans Loch were elected joint-chairmen. The party agreed to economic planning in the shape of the DDR's Five-Year Plan. In 1952 the LDPD's fifth conference resolved to participate in the building of socialism in the German Democratic Republic. In December 1952 Hamann, who was Minister of Trade, was arrested and charged with sabotage, owing to the difficulties in the distribution of certain foodstuffs in East Germany. Loch was now sole chairman of the LDPD as well as being a deputy Prime Minister; a lawyer in the Weimar republic and an emigrant in Holland for part of the Nazi period, he retained these positions till his death in 1960. An East German publication credits him with being chiefly responsible for turning the party into an ally of the working class, the SED, and socialism.[18] In 1957 the LDPD accepted the leadership of the SED and recognized that socialism could only be built 'on the basis of the revolutionary and scientific theses of Marxism–Leninism'.

After Loch's death in 1960 the chairmanship of the party was taken over by Dr Max Suhrbier. Born in Rostock in 1902, Suhrbier got his doctorate of Law in 1925 and worked in different admini-

---

[16] Hoffmann, op. cit., pp. 237–40.
[17] Die Sowjetische Besatzungszone, p. 97.
[18] Hoffmann, op. cit., p. 257.

strative posts from then until 1945. The other two key figures in
the LDPD are Dr Manfred Gerlach, general secretary since 1954,
and Professor Johannes Dieckmann, one of the two vice-chairmen
since 1949 until his death in 1969. Gerlach was born in Leipzig
in 1928, the son of a skilled worker. When he left school in 1944 he
became a junior civil servant. Dieckmann, whose antecedents were
mentioned in Chapter 2, like Gerlach consistently pursued a pro-
Soviet, pro-SED policy. The LDPD's highest elected organ is the
political committee, *Politischer Ausschuss,* of the executive,
Vorstand, which elects it. It has 20 members. In 1965 five of these
had started their careers as lawyers, three as economists, two as
journalists. The rest gave their professions as, one of each, bookshop owner, teacher, salesman, white-collar worker, pharmacist,
civil servant, co-operative farm chairman, college-educated farmer
and manager, part-owner of a mixed enterprise.[19] The latter,
Edmund Pech, was the only member listed by Western researchers[20]
as having been a member of the Nazi Party, which he joined in
1941 aged 20. Of the political committee members, seven were
under 40 in 1965, eight were between 40 and 50, three were in
their sixties, and two in their seventies. Eighteen members are said
to have joined the party or presumably its youth movement, between 1945 and 1947. The 66 ordinary members of the executive
had very similar backgrounds to those of their colleagues on the
political committee, though they tended to be a little older, the
oldest being Otto Krauss, aged 80, a former bank director. Western
researchers claim that one of these 66 members, Werner Hacker, a
hairdresser, had been a nominal member of the Nazi Party.

It is difficult to know exactly who the ordinary members of the
LDPD are. A survey carried out in February 1949 showed that
14.1 per cent of the members were workers, 11.9 per cent farmers,
28.6 per cent white-collar workers, 2 per cent from the professions,
13.1 per cent housewives, 12.4 per cent small traders, 0.9 per cent
owners of industrial firms, and 10.1 per cent 'others'.[21] The LDPD
newspaper, *Der Morgen,* which is about the best all-round paper
in East Germany, reflects strongly the interests of the professional
man, the trader, and the middle-class housewife. In many respects
the Liberal Democratic Party is appealing to the same kind of

[19] *Zwanzig Jahre Liberal-Demokratische Partei Deutschlands,* LDPD,
Buchverlag Der Morgen, Berlin, 1965, pp. 272–88.
[20] All information regarding former membership of the Nazi Party in this
Chapter is taken from *Ehemalige Nationalsozialisten in Pankows Diensten,*
Fünfte, ergänzte Ausgabe, Untersuchungsausschuss Freiheitlicher Juristen, 1
Berlin (West) 37.
[21] Hoffmann, op. cit., p. 36.

people as the East German CDU. As the policies of these parties, and indeed all parties in East Germany, are identical it is difficult to see on what basis a person chooses one rather than the other. Among older people it is probably largely a matter of tradition. Among younger people it is likely to be a question of whether they feel strongly or not about Christianity, which party approaches them, whether their superiors feel they would be of more use to the state in one party or another.

Apart from its activities within the DDR, the Liberal Democratic Party has proved a very useful vehicle for presenting the East German view of the future of Germany to the West German middle class. In 1956 the party entertained three leading members of the West German FDP—Mende, Scheel, and Döring—in Weimar where they discussed the German problem. In 1963 officials of the LDPD exchanged views about the same problem with representatives of the FDP and the West German Liberal students.

The Liberal Democratic Party sees this dialogue with West Germans as one of its main functions. A party publication setting out its tasks stated that one of these was 'to win over the nationally orientated middle class in West Germany for the overcoming of militarism and for the democratic re-unification on the basis of the German Plan of the People and to convince them that the development of the German Democratic Republic serves the future happiness of the entire German People'. The Liberal Democrats of East Germany justify their support for socialism on the grounds that only through socialism can the democratic ideals of the progressive Liberals of 1848 and 1919 be fulfilled, and only through world socialism can peace be secured once and for all.

National Bolshevists

The National Democratic Party (NDPD) was founded in 1948 with the specific intention of trying to win support among the former 'other ranks' of the Nazi Party and former officers and professional soldiers of the *Wehrmacht*. On the face of it this would have seemed a hopeless, thankless, fruitless, and even politically dangerous, task for any Marxist–Moscow orientated organization. Traditionally the German Nationalist and Nazi right had detested Marxism and despised both the workers and the Slavs. Why should they now heed the call of a régime which supported German dismemberment and had branded the organizations they had served criminal, prevented many of them continuing in their professions and disowned their wartime sacrifices? More so as in the West a régime was rising which was more indulgent, demanded a return of former German territories, and recognized that in most cases they had 'only been doing their duty' and had 'only been serving their country' between 1939 and 1945. This West German régime either provided them with at least decent, and often generous, pensions or reinstated them in their old professions.

That the National Democratic Party of East Germany has enjoyed some moderate success is due to a number of factors. The first of these is connected with one of the lesser-known byways of German intellectual history, the phenomenon of National Bolshevism.[22] Certainly since the time of the Napoleonic wars, when both Russia and Prussia had to fight for their independence from France, there had been a pro-Russian wing among the German aristocracy and German conservatives. Apart from this common experience these German conservatives shared a common, authoritarian, view of the state with their Czarist colleagues. One would have expected any feeling for Russia to have died in these circles with the death of Czarism and the subsequent rise of Bolshevism—after all, did not Bolshevism threaten Germany? The great majority of German rightists thought it did and had a closed mind on the subject. However, the political situation was complicated by the Versailles Treaty which appeared to many Germans to herald the national enslavement of Germany. Both Russia and Germany appeared to be the victims of the Western powers. This could lead some influential Germans to the view that, although it was necessary to crush the German Communist Party at home, Germany and Russia could conceivably work together for their mutual benefit. This actually happened in the shape of secret military co-operation between the Red Army and the German armed forces, the *Reichswehr*, in the 1920s. In 1933 such co-operation was ended by Hitler. Some German rightists went further than merely advocating co-operation between the two states; they believed that something similar to the Bolshevik system was necessary in Germany to save the nation. This was National Bolshevism proper. The earliest advocate of this seems to have been a right-wing university professor, Paul Eltzbacher, who published a pamphlet in 1919 called *Der Bolschewismus und die deutsche Zukunft* or 'Bolshevism and the German Future'. Two other National Bolshevists were the dissident Communists Laufenberg and Wolffheim. Other rightists who adopted this view included Captain Josef Römer, who joined the KPD in 1923 and died resisting Hitler; *Reichswehr* officer and former Nazi Richard Scheringer, who went on working for communism in West

---

[22] See Arthur Spencer, 'National-Bolshevism', *Survey* (October 1962). In the same issue F. L. Carsten deals with 'The Reichswehr and the Red Army'.

Germany after the war; Ernst Niekisch who, having been imprisoned by Hitler, became a professor in West Berlin after 1945; and many who later became part of the resistance group known as *die Rote Kapelle.*

The East German National Democratic Party could then call on a fairly lengthy, and authentic, tradition and ideology. The other weapons in its ideological armoury are the activities of certain German officers and soldiers who were prisoners of the Soviets, and the 20 July plotters against Hitler. Right from the start of the German invasion of the Soviet Union German Communists in Moscow carried on propaganda activities either over the radio or in the front line. Although there were cases of German soldiers, and even officers, going over to the Soviets out of disgust for the war, it was only after Stalingrad that the German emigrants in Moscow started to make any impression. The National Committee for a Free Germany, *Nationalkomitee Freies Deutschland*, was set up by emigrants and prisoners-of-war in July 1943. Its aim was the withdrawal of the *Wehrmacht* to behind Germany's frontiers and the overthrow of Hitler. A little later the League of German Officers, *Bund deutscher Offiziere*, was established as part of the same movement. General von Seydlitz, a member of an old German officer family, became its president; General Elder von Daniels and Colonels Steidle and van Hooven became vice-presidents. Another aristocratic officer who helped form both organizations was Major Egbert von Frankenberg und Proschlitz, who joined the Nazi Party in 1931 and the SS in 1932. During the war he was a *Luftwaffe* pilot. Among the others who later joined were Major-General Arno von Lenski, also a Nazi Party member and also from an old military family, who joined the *Bund* early in 1944; Colonel Adam, another professional soldier, NSDAP and SA member; Lieutenant-General Vincenz Müller, a professional soldier who surrendered against Hitler's orders; several military chaplains; and, last but not least, after the execution of some of the July plotters, Field Marshal Paulus, who commanded the Sixth Army at Stalingrad. Naturally the League regarded the July plotters led by Colonel Count Schenk von Stauffenberg as their own.[23]

Many of these officers later took part in the founding of the National Democratic Party, especially von Lenski, Adam, von Frankenberg, Professor Rühle, also an officer at Stalingrad, Dr Heinrich Homann, formerly a major, Friedrich Pfaffenbach, a former captain, and others. Not all of these officers who later played

[23] Wilhelm Adam, *Der Schwere Entschluss*, Verlag der Nation, Berlin, 1965, pp. 412–13, 395, 420, 423.

a political role in East Germany opted for the NDPD. A few like Colonel Steidle, mayor of Weimar, joined the CDU. Others like Job von Witzleben, who became a colonel of the East German Army, joined the SED.

At the foundation of the National Democratic Party in April 1948 the three members who emerged as its leaders were Dr Lothar Bolz, a lawyer who had been expelled from the legal profession by the Nazis and spent several years in Moscow; Professor Heilmann, a former Nazi Party member; and Dr Koltzenburg, before 1933 a member of the small German State Party. Bolz became the First, that is Senior, Chairman of the party and has retained this position ever since. Between 1953 and 1965 he was the Foreign Minister of the German Democratic Republic.

Not all the leading members of the NDPD then are former officers or former Nazis, in fact most of them are not. Out of its 50 members of the East German parliament in 1963 only 14 had been members of the NSDAP. Thirty-three had served in the war and seven of these were members of the Free Germany Committee. (Five of them had been in the Nazi Party.) The parliamentary group of the NDPD contained two members who had spent most of the Hitler years in concentration camps and one who was an emigrant. The NDPD elects at its four-yearly *Parteitag* a *Hauptausschuss* (head committee) to run its affairs; this committee, which meets once a quarter, in turn elects a *Vorstand* or executive. Of the members of the *Hauptausschuss* who were also in parliament—18 of them—five had belonged to the NSDAP, but these same five all joined the Free Germany Committee, as did two others who were not Nazis. Both former concentration camp inmates and the former emigrants were members of this committee in 1963. Of the other nine members, two had been too young to be politically active before 1945, and the remaining seven do not seem to have been in any way active. Of the members of the *Vorstand* in parliament—seven of them—only one, Homann, had been in the NSDAP. The emigrant Lothar Bolz was party chairman, and both former concentration camp prisoners were members. One of the other three had been too young to be politically active in the Third Reich and one, not a Nazi Party member, had worked with the Free Germany Committee.

Although the NDPD was set up to try to integrate the former nominal Nazis, professional soldiers, and the like into the structure of East German society, and has had some success in doing this, the leadership of the party, in the *Vorstand*, is firmly in the hands of people the SED can trust because of their social and political backgrounds. Even at the *Hauptausschuss* level, the 18 parliamentary members of this committee contain fewer former NSDAP members among them than does the West German cabinet formed in 1966.

Little more need be said about the NDPD. Its policy is exactly the same as that of the Socialist Unity Party, but in its tone it is a little less 'class' orientated, a little more 'national'.

> Our German Democratic Republic is the legacy, in the form of a state, of the best sons and daughters of our people, however much their struggles and sacrifices often seemed in vain. In the DDR lives the spirit of the revolutionary peasant armies of Thomas Müntzer, lives Ulrich von Hutten's 'I have dared!' In it lives world-wide Humanism of Luther, Melanchthon Erasmus, Leibniz, Herder, Lessing, Schiller, Goethe, and Humboldt. In it lives the revolutionary world of the music of Handel, Bach, and Mozart, lives Beethoven's *'Seid umschlungen, Millionen!'*, in the DDR lives the spirit of the fighters for our national liberation, the spirit of Stein, Arndt, Fichte, Clausewitz, Scharnhorst, Gneisenau, Blücher and Schill, York, Jahn, and Friesen. In it lives the spirit of the *Vormärz*, lives the spirit of Heine, Herwegh, Freiligrath, Weerth and Büchner, lives the spirit of the fighters of the revolution of 1848/49. Above all, is our German Democratic Republic the legacy of the best sons and daughters of the class, which is its leading strength, the German working class. It is the legacy of the two greatest sons of the German people, Karl Marx and Friedrich Engels, the intellectual creators of Marxism, according to whose principles already today 1,000 million people are building socialism and hundreds of millions of working people in the capitalist world are struggling for socialism....[24]

Like the East German CDU and LDPD the National Democratic Party also sees as an essential part of its task the winning over of particular groups in West Germany, in this case, 'the former and present supporters of German militarism and imperialism as well as the members of the commercial middle class and the intelligentsia...'[25]

West German sources estimated that by 1953 the NDPD had

[24] *Die National-Demokratische Partei Deutschlands in unserer Zeit,* Dokument des Achten Parteitages, Erfurt, 25 bis 27 Mai 1963, NDPD, pp. 5–6.
[25] See *Satzungen Der National-Demokratischen Partei Deutschlands Beschluss des Achten Parteitages,* Nationales Druckhaus VOB National, Berlin C 2, pp. 6–7.

about 100,000 members, rising to about 120,000 three years later.[26] Considering the party's rather narrow appeal it seems unlikely that these totals have been exceeded. Like the other parties in East Germany, the National Democratic Party has its own press, its main organ being the *National-Zeitung*.

Socialist Farmers

One might suppose that the Democratic Farmers' Party (DBD) had an advantage over the three 'bourgeois' parties of the DDR in that its appeal is to a fairly compact social group with not much competition. Yet in practice the DBD is not all that strong. It was set up in 1948 in an attempt to gain the farmers and farm workers for the SED's brand of socialism. Most East German farmers, like most European farmers, tended to be conservative and a considerable number of them had been pro-Nazi. Many regarded the SED as a party of atheistic town-dwellers and proletarians, whom they distrusted. To leave the farmers to the CDU and the LDPD, even though these parties were in close alliance with the Unity Party, seemed in those days potentially dangerous. On the other hand, the building up of a farmers' party under SED hegemony would represent a weakening of the two bourgeois parties in the bloc, in any future parliament and government. So the DBD was set up with a blood transfusion from the SED. All this does not mean that politically active farmers and farm workers are only found in this party. For a variety of personal, practical, and political reasons there are farmers in all East German parties. And the Democratic Farmers of the DBD are not all farmers—at least not all those who represent the party in the *Volkskammer* are. Roughly half the DBD deputies started life in urban homes or had fathers with non-agricultural occupations. Many of the others grew up to have agricultural occupations themselves. About half of the 51 parliamentary members elected in 1967 were journalists, party functionaries, experts, academics, or state officials. Of the rest the majority were chairmen of co-operative farms.[27] The chairman of the Democratic Farmers is Herr Ernst Goldenbaum. He was born, the son of a worker, in 1898. After serving in the First World War he became first a worker and later a farmer. He spent most of the period of the Third Reich in prisons or camps. Like the other parties of the National Front, the DBD holds one of the deputy chairmanships of the Council of State.

[26] *SBZ von A–Z*, Deutscher Bundes-Verlag, Bonn, 1966, p. 334.
[27] The professions of these members are contained in the official handbook of the *Volkskammer*.

No published figures are available but it seems unlikely that up to now the DBD has achieved widespread membership among the farmers of East Germany. It must have been difficult to get initial support in 1948 because of the existence of the other three parties. Since then the Farmers' Party has supported all the SED's plans for the transformation of agriculture on co-operative lines without so much as a murmur of opposition, even though this policy faced the scepticism of many farmers. Thirdly, since 1945 there has existed the VdgB, the Association of Farmers' Mutual Aid, an organization devoted to farmers' problems through which they help each other. However, the fact that the DBD has such a relatively large representation in the *Volkskammer* and among its deputies there are so many well-qualified people, is a sign that the leaders of the DDR have found it a convenient vehicle through which to advocate and organize the transformation of agriculture. They are no doubt looking to the future and this is reflected by the considerable number of young, qualified, DBD members in the People's Chamber. The DBD has as its main newspaper the *Bauern-Echo*.

Despite their diverse origins, the differences in their 'images', the slight formal differences in their constitutions, the four parties of the DDR which are the allies of the SED in the National Front have consciously accepted a secondary and subservient role in the affairs of state. There can be no question of their striking out in an independent way. Although there is some overlapping in the type of members they attract, their spheres of operations are fairly narrow and have been worked out by the SED in the National Front. Only the SED, for instance, is allowed to organize in the economy, the police, and the armed forces. The same is equally true of the 'mass organizations' in East Germany which also have representatives in parliament : the trade unions (FDGB), the German League of Culture (DKB), the Free German Youth (FDJ), and the Democratic Women's League (DFD). It is true, too, for such organizations as the *Friedensrat der DDR*, the Peace Council of the DDR, a body with considerable funds which employs many talented people who put the DDR's point of view through contacts with peace organizations around the world. Essentially these organizations play the same role as the four political parties—they have their allotted segments to influence in the direction of *sozialistischer Aufbau*, socialist construction, and the *Kampf um den Frieden*, the struggle for peace.

Chapter 5

The New Economic System: A New Catechism?

I T WAS difficult to know what to call this chapter to convey
accurately the way in which the New Economic Policy is presented to the East German people. It might have been called
the new ideology, though it is not new in the sense of contradicting
Marxism, for it is not intrinsically at variance with the thought
of Marx. More accurately perhaps, it might have been called the
new panacea, for this is the impression given in official pronounce-
ments about it. The new catechism? Yes, catechism in the sense
that so many people whose job it is to explain it, and so many who
have to learn about it, talk about it in parrot-like fashion. Perhaps
this is due to the fear of falling into 'revisionist' or 'dogmatist' ways
of thinking by thinking for oneself. Perhaps it is in some people a
sign of indifference—sometimes learning a lesson off word for word
is the easiest way of doing one's duty and one can be sure of being
right. Much of the flood of official literature on the subject does
not help very much, being written in sloganistic 'party Chinese'.
The SED is now plugging the New Economic Policy in the same,
total, somewhat suffocating way it plugged its earlier campaigns.
And although experts in East and West believe, on the evidence so
far, rightly, that it is a great improvement on past economic management policies, some East Germans remain unconvinced. 'We
have heard it all before' is the typical remark of the sceptical. Because all earlier panaceas have been presented with the same
totality, the same confidence, with the same artificial zeal, there is a
certain 'sales resistance' on the part of many East Germans. What
then is this new policy? How did it originate? What did it replace?

End of Dogmatism

That old party hand of the post-war generation, Professor Otto
Reinhold, together with his colleague Wolfgang Berger, in a brave
attempt, have tried to show that the New Economic System of
Planning and Managing the Economy—*das neue ökonomische*

System der Planung und Leitung der Volkswirtschaft or *NöS*—is very largely an organic—the authors' word—development of past policies, rather than a break with the past. The authors admit that 'although today there can hardly be differences of opinion about the fact that in its time Socialist political economy bore certain dogmatic and schematic features. . . .' at the twenty-first meeting of the Central Committee, at the end of 1954, 'the main point found expression in the demand of Walter Ulbricht to increase the profitability of the nationalized undertakings and to carry through the [principle of] economic accountability in the factories'. They quote Ulbricht as saying that the workers should be made more 'materially interested', which means in Western parlance paid according to results, in the fulfilment of the *Gewinnplan*, the plan of net income of the enterprise. Berger and Reinhold then claim that 'already with this quotation it is clear how misleading the claim of West German critics of the New Economic System is that to emphasize the role of profit means a break and a denial of previous SED economic policy'.[1] Now it is true to say that for most of its existence the Soviet system, and its imitators in Eastern Europe, always tried to make the workers 'materially interested'. In fact Western trade unionists were often shocked by what they regarded as 'state capitalism' in these countries. But, as we shall see, rewards, including bonus payments, were awarded both to individuals and to plants, on the basis of overfulfilment of certain strictly laid down production targets, targets which put the main emphasis on quantity rather than quality. Within this narrow framework there was also competition between plants. The system did not take into account real economic costs and took little account of quality. Most East Germans interested in such matters would probably admit in private that Otto Reinhold and Wolfgang Berger put too much emphasis on the continuity of SED economic policy, and too little on the dogmatism and rigidity of the past. A good many Western economists would agree with them when they go on to argue, in justification of past policies, that the strictly centralized economy of the past, with its emphasis on growth at almost any cost, is necessary or at least feasible in a backward economy. Dr Margaret Miller admirably sums up the state of the argument in her book on the Soviet Union's New Economic System. She says:

[1] Wolfgang Berger and Otto Reinhold, *Zu den wissenschaftlichen Grundlagen des neuen ökonomischen Systems,* Dietz Verlag, (East) Berlin, 1966, p. 10.

There is general agreement among students of Soviet economics that the hectic pace of development imposed heavy sacrifices on the Russian people. There is much disagreement, inevitable in view of the difficulty of assessing the evidence on Soviet economic activities, about the degree of efficiency with which planning has done the job, and whether other methods would have been more efficacious. Some hold that a slower rate of development, with more attention paid to consumer needs, would have yielded better results from the strictly economic point of view. Such differences of opinion are now of interest only as a background to the changes introduced in 1962. On the broad effectiveness of the industrialisation drive in achieving the politically-inspired aims of the government there can be no doubt.[2]

And again, 'the very success of industrialisation established an economy so large and complex that it could no longer be administered in the old way without a degree of loss, inefficiency and inconvenience intolerable to people and government alike'.[3] These remarks apply equally to East Germany even though there the economy was not backward in the sense of the Russian economy before 1917, but weak in basic industry and ravaged by the war and its aftermath.

The East German economic reforms followed those introduced in the Soviet Union in 1962 as a result of the thoughts of Professors Liberman and Nemchinov. In the DDR the two chief architects seem to have been Erich Apel and Günter Mittag together with a whole group of experts—ten alone received the 'Order of Labour' for their work.[4] As in the Soviet Union pilot schemes were tried before any changes were introduced throughout the economy, and such experimentation has become, so official publications claim, a normal part of the East German administration of the economy.

With the introduction of the New Economic Policy most of the old economic institutions have been retained but some of their functions have been changed. At the head of the system is the Council of Ministers (*Ministerrat*). Since February 1963 'the management of the national economy is the main function of the *Ministerrat and its Präsidium*'.[5] It now has the overall responsibility

[2] Margaret Miller, *Rise of the Russian Consumer*, Institute of Economic Affairs, London, 1965, p. 18.

[3] Ibid., p. 43.

[4] Berger & Reinhold, op. cit., p. 28.

[5] 'Richtlinie für das neue ökonomische System der Planung und Leitung der Volkswirtschaft', *Beschluss des Präsidiums des Ministerrates der Deutschen Demokratischen Republik vom II,* July 1963, Dietz Verlag, (East) Berlin, 1963, p. 21.

for : the full exploitation of the economic laws of socialism; the rapid carrying through of technological and scientific progress and the raising of productivity; the further development of the material-technical basis; the development of the leading branches of the economy; the accumulation of capital, the raising of its economic effectiveness, and its intensive use. Until December 1965 the *Volkswirtschaftsrat*, or Economic Council, had the responsibility for working out the details of the plan but it was abolished and its functions taken over by eight new Ministries for : basic industries; electrical and electro-technical; light; food; chemical; heavy machines and installations; iron ore mining and metallurgy; machine building and vehicles. There are, in addition, other Ministers concerned with the economy : the chairman of the State Planning Commission; his deputy; the Minister for the Guidance of Regional and Local Councils; the Minister for Science and Technology; the Minister for the Construction Industry; the Minister of Finance; the Minister in charge of the Office for Prices; the chairman of the Agricultural Council; the Minister of Foreign Trade; and certain deputy Prime Ministers.

As far as economic planning is concerned, there is the State Planning Commission (*die Staatliche Plankommission*). Its job is to work out the long-range plan (*der Perspektivplan*), which is supposed to be different from the earlier type of rigid, five-year plans. As an official publication tells us :

> Obviously long-range plans once established do not represent an unchangeable magnitude. That is why the competent authorities, working together with research institutions, the managements of industrial branches and factories take into consideration new factors, both in regard to the establishment of long-range and annual plans. A purposeful operating system of information contributes to the solution of this problem according to schedule. New methods are currently being worked out to increase the scientific character of planning. Thus input and output balances are being developed with a view to bringing out the complicated national economic interrelations. The process of reproduction and its most important details are represented in models, and important economic processes are mathematically formulated.[6]

And we are assured : 'The problem thus does not consist in the rigid planning of every product or every minor economic process for many years in advance, but rather in envisaging coordinated

[6] *The GDR—A Modern Industrial State,* Verlag Zeit im Bild, Dresden, August 1966, p. 44.

9 * *

measures ensuring a high degree of national economic efficiency
and which on the other hand offer a wide scope of development to
individual or collective initiative'.[7]

The Ministries are responsible for the more detailed planning,
each in its own sphere. Under the eight industrial Ministries are 80
associations of nationalized enterprises—*Vereinigungen Volkseigener
Betriebe* (VVBs). These associations are not new, but they have a
changed role under the New Economic System. Up to 1963 the
associations were regarded as *administrative* organizations financed
from state funds. Now they are being regarded much more as
business organizations, 'socialist trusts', with their own financial
means concerned with putting those means to the best use and
showing a profit. 'Profit is the decisive criterion for judging the
economic achievement of the VVB.'[8] The VVBs are now responsible for their own marketing and, in co-operation with the appropriate authorities, for market research, advertising, the profitability
of their exports, aftersales service, efficiency. All these responsibilities now fall, in the first place, on the shoulders of the 80 general
directors, *Generaldirektoren*, of the VVBs who thus each become
a kind of socialist tycoon. They are aided by a technical director,
a production director, an economic director, a director for procure-
ment of supplies and marketing, a chief bookkeeper (or accountant),
and the head of the Technical Control Organization (TKO) of the
VVB. The latter keeps a check on the quality of the production. In
each individual factory there is a works-manager (*Werkleiter*) who
is responsible to the general director. This type of industrial management is not unlike the type of set-up in the big West German
trusts today and in the concerns of pre-war Germany with its
emphasis on the sole responsibility, or better, individual responsibility of the general director and the technical competence of the
whole management team. It contrasts sharply with the idea still
prevalent in much of British industry of the amateur, self-made
man, or man of general education. (Though it is only fair to say
that many of these directors will have got to know their industry
at the bottom, combining practical work with the academic study.)
It is worth mentioning here that since August 1968 East German
publications have once again stressed the importance of central
control over the 'socialist enterprises'. They have denounced Czech
views of 'decentralization' and 'self-administration of socialist enterprises'. The present East German formulation says that 'socialist
enterprises as well as towns and communities are self-responsible

[7] *The GDR—A Modern Industrial State*, p. 45.
[8] 'Richtlinie', p. 28.

socialist communities of citizens within the framework of central state planning and management, but are not autonomous islands which are left to their fate'.[9]

Key Role for Banks

In the new scheme of things the central bank will play a key role. It will be a little less like a small-town savings bank and a little more like a great commercial bank. No longer will the VVBs be directly linked with the state purse. Under the new order they are directly tied to the industrial branches of the central bank which now have the job of granting credit and carrying through an annual audit of the VVBs. The banks now have the power, and indeed the duty, to discriminate when granting credits by using the rate of interest to punish, prod, and reward the VVBs for their varying performances. The banks are also, as agents of the Council of Ministers, responsible for collecting VVB profits for the State.

If then the profits go to the state, how are profits a useful tool to spur on the VVBs? Under the New Economic System wages and salaries are effected much more by the fate of profits than under the old system. Starting at the top, the general director's salary consists of a basic amount with the possibility of a large bonus varying with the profit. His managerial colleagues are in the same position. As for the work-people, quality gets a much higher rating in judging their performance than in the past. It is not true to say that in the past quality did not matter, but it got a much smaller rating in the rush to produce more—production became a fetish. Now there is a much more positive attempt to reward quality. A worker is given a certain number of a particular good to produce in a specified amount of time, and in a given quality. Nowadays the checkers will be looking to see whether the worker has improved on the quality of the article as much as on the quantity asked for. East Germany is now concerned—one could almost say obsessed—with trying to reach the highest world standards in every branch of production. Important responsibilities in this respect are given to the German Office for Measurement and the Testing of Goods, *Das Deutsche Amt für Messwesen und Warenprüfung*. Its job is to set standards and to grade the articles produced by the various VVBs accordingly. In each VVB and in each factory the *TKO-Leiter*, Head of Technical Control, has obligations to the *Amt* and is, in a sense, its local agent. This interest in standards started in 1958 and not just with the *NöS*.

[9] 'The Role of the Socialist State', speech by Walter Ulbricht, 12 October 1968, Verlag Zeit im Bild, p. 20.

The New Economic System will not mean any price competition among the plants of the 80 VVBs. Prices will continue to be fixed from the centre by the *Amt für Preise*. However, prices are being systematically investigated to make them conform much more than in the past to the actual costs of production.

The industrial price reform, introduced in several steps, is also associated with this process; it is envisaged to eliminate the glaring disproportions resulting for certain reasons from the differing relations between production costs, sales prices and state subsidies. It is noteworthy that these regulations, which are in conformity with national economic interests and are of benefit to *all*, should be compensated for by an economic use of material in production and are not reflected by continuous price increases in retail trade. The price structure of the DDR is stable but not rigid.[10]

Put another way,

An industrial price reform had become necessary because in the past many industrial prices did not reflect real values. Many products of basic industry such as coal, power, gas and potash were sold to industry at old pegged prices below production costs. The lignite mines needed large state subsidies because industry paid for a ton of lignite only 3.51 marks (regardless of quality and rising production costs). Since the coal was so cheap many factories made no serious attempt to economise in the use of fuel. Today a ton of lignite costs between six and nine marks, and the factories are forced to be economical.[11]

The beginning of a reform in the house-building industry means that the rents in the flats built in the last few years are higher than those built before 1963. It is claimed that the industrial price reform will not make much difference to the retail price of consumer goods although there have been certain slight increases. The retail price index has developed in the following way in the sixties : 1960—100, 1965—100.3.[12]

Under the new scheme of things all the employees are supposed to help in drawing up the plans and in the management : ('Alle planen und leiten mit'). This is regulated by a law passed by the *Volkskammer* in November 1966 which lays down the election of production committees (*Produktionskomitees*) by the employees of big enterprises. These committees have an advisory and a checking

[10] *GDR—A Modern Industrial State,* p. 45.
[11] *Democratic German Report* (14 July 1967).
[12] *Wörterbuch Der Okonomie Sozialismus,* Dietz Verlag, (East) Berlin, 1967, p. 362.

or control function. They are supposed to : participate in the work-ing-out and, later, carrying-out of the enterprise's yearly and pers-pective plan; help in improving quality of production; check that contracts are being carried out; help in the training and develop-ment of the cadre; check to ensure that the working and living conditions of the employees are improving as planned.[13] Another organ of employee participation is the 'social council' or *Gesell-schaftlicher Rat* in the VVB. Officially these councils are to see to it that the activities of the VVBs do not conflict with those of society. But according to the official list of their responsibilities their work seems to overlap with those of the production committees. Apart from representatives of the VVBs these councils are com-posed of representatives of the trade unions, the FDJ, the local branches of the trading organizations, and so on.[14] There are also other, somewhat more specialized, committees in the VVBs and the individual factories as well on which the employees are repre-sented. There is no question here of anything resembling 'workers' control' on the Yugoslav model or even the more limited 'co-determination' which exists in West Germany.

Foreign trade in the German Democratic Republic is of course a state monopoly. But here too changes are taking place within the framework of the New Economic System. There is now a special bank, *Deutsche Aussenhandelsbank AG,* to deal not only with the formal side of arranging payment between the DDR and its trad-ing partners but also to encourage foreign trade through a more imaginative credit policy. Under the new economic régime the VVBs or certain large, specialized, industrial bodies may soon have the chance to deal directly with foreign markets. Up to now they have had to deal with certain centralized foreign trade bodies. Obviously, this tends to slow down the import-export trade. At the VII Congress of the SED Ulbricht promised that this matter was under review. Already an experiment had been carried out, success-fully, with Carl Zeiss of Jena, the optical equipment firm, under which Zeiss had been allowed such direct contact and initiative. The SED leader said that the experiment 'makes new considerations necessary so as to take similar steps especially where in large export enterprises or complexes favourable prerequisites exist or can be created for taking over the functions of export directly'.[15] However,

[13] *Wörterbuch,* p. 374.
[14] Ibid., pp. 166-7.
[15] 'Social Development In The German Democratic Republic Up To The Completion Of Socialism, Speech by Comrade Walter Ulbricht at the Seventh Congress of the Socialist Unity Party of Germany', Verlag Zeit im Bild, Dresden, 1967, p. 192. Also in *Die Wirtschaft* (20 April 1967).

since the showdown with Czechoslovakia in August 1968 the state monopoly in foreign trade has been strongly emphasized again. Dr Grete Wittkowski, president of the state bank, underlined this in an interview published in *Der Morgen* (4 December 1968). She stressed also that there could be no convertibility for the East German mark.

Private Enterprise: 'The Red Dior'

Although 87.9 per cent of the DDR's industrial production in 1966 was credited, by the *Statistisches Jahrbuch der DDR, 1967,* to state or co-operative enterprises, and though 83.8 per cent of all employees worked in such enterprises, the majority of firms were still either completely private or mixed state-private undertakings. In 1966 the semi-private firms employed 344,602 factory and office staff against over 2,700,000 in the non-private sector. A further 98,000 were employed by private firms. The private and semi-private firms tend to operate in the consumer goods sector, in certain fields which are traditional in East Germany—toy making, furniture, textiles, glass and leather, camping equipment, light engineering. They include such firms as the clothing firm 'Lucie Kaiser', which exports to North America, Holland, Belgium, Sweden, Norway, and West Germany, as well as to the other socialist states; Adolf R. Both KG of Thalheim, which exports its travel goods to over 20 countries; Gebr Weissbach KG of Karl-Marx-Stadt, which produces boiler equipment; and Max Grumbach KG of Freiberg, producers of agricultural machinery. Probably the best-known of these industrial firms is that of Heinz Bormann. The author had the opportunity of meeting Herr Bormann who told how, as a former wartime lieutenant, he turned to his father's business to start patching Red Army uniforms. By the sixties West German firms were dubbing him the 'Red Dior' because of his spectacular export successes around the world, particularly in West Germany. Since 1956 his firm has been a mixed enterprise. He told the East German magazine *Freie Welt* (4. Maiheft, 1967) that before the state bought a share in his firm he had 160 employees, a turnover of 1.8 million marks, and no exports. In 1967 his clothes were known in 30 countries, he had 400 employees, and produced 10 million marks-worth of goods. The same magazine stated that he was exporting 130,000 dresses to the USSR alone. Bormann is a member of the executive of the National Democratic Party of (East) Germany. The largest of the mixed enterprises is the Otto Schüngel KG in Burkhardtsdorf in the south of the DDR. It makes plastic packaging, foam rubber, and allied products. The manager and part-owner—and in all cases the private part-owner appears to do the managing—is Herr Otto

Schüngel, a member of the CDU and its executive. He talked, in an interview reported in the *Democratic German Report* (20 October 1967), of his firm's progress:

> I went into partnership with the state in 1958, at which time the value of our annual output amounted to 3.6 million marks. This compares with 56 million marks' worth a year, and production will go on increasing. We employ today twice the number of people ... 520 members of the staff ... The state has bought 63 per cent of the firm, and we stick to this relation when it comes to investing new capital ... I draw a fixed salary as works manager, plus a corresponding percentage of the profits. I cannot complain. I could, if I wanted to, put all my money into a savings bank, and in due course it would grow to a tidy sum. Of course, there is a limit to everything, which in my case is the sliding scale of tax. So my money is mainly ploughed back into the business.

More remarkable is the case of Karl Barth of Leipzig. He abandoned his plastics moulding works in 1960 and went to West Germany. He encountered many difficulties there and returned to the DDR. According to an East German pamphlet, *From Germany To Germany*, published in Dresden in 1965, he was welcomed back and got his factory back as a mixed enterprise.

Why should the SED have decided to tolerate these remnants of private ownership of the means of production? The system had been used by the Communists in China and probably for the same reasons. Many of these enterprises were so small that it would have been difficult to fit them into a nationally owned structure; yet the state felt it was so short of the things they produced that it dare not close them down. Secondly, the Communists recognized the advantage of retaining a manager who knows his firm intimately and is interested in it. Will these enterprises survive? It certainly seems likely that they will do so for the present because of the increasingly undoctrinaire approach of the SED to economic matters and because of the priority given to raising living standards quickly. The relevant clause in the 1968 DDR constitution seems tacitly to admit this. And Herr Bormann, for one, told the writer that he expected his son to succeed him. This is one of the reasons why people like Bormann have been prepared to go along with the state. Another reason is that the job they are doing is the one they know, and presumably like, best. And, relative to DDR standards, the rewards are high. Another convincing reason, given by Herr Barth, important when one remembers that these are relatively small undertakings, is that in the DDR they do not have to fear competition or bankruptcy. Whether, in the long run, they will be taken over by state enterprises, and in many cases such state enterprises are already part-owners, or whether they will be built up into separate state enterprises in keeping with the rationalization of production demanded by the New Economic System is impossible to say.

The New Economic System is relatively new and is still developing. It is therefore difficult, and perhaps unwise, to attempt to evaluate how it operates in practice, apart that is from the cautious statement that it appears to be an improvement on the old régime. There are still a number of questions about the New Economic System for which the author did not find answers. For instance, if profitability is to determine, through the bonus system, the final level of incomes, will this not be unjust, and perhaps even bad, economically, to those in industries where, because of the nature of the industry, profits are bound to be low? Why should automobile workers, for instance, earn substantially more than so many others? Under the New Economic System the banks seem to have a great deal of power. This would be controversial in any society. Are the banks equipped to carry on such responsibilities? They are perhaps less equipped in the DDR than in Western countries. As Ulbricht has himself admitted, 'All this means that the comrades in banking will have to adjust very quickly to this new function of the banks in the economic system and consequently will need to alter thoroughly the mode of work they have so far been accustomed to.'[16] Will they be able to do this in the short run? There is also the problem of overlapping functions in the new system. There would appear to be need of still further streamlining of the actual machinery of the NöS. The SED and other East German leaders do, however, seem to be aware of this problem. Nor should it be forgotten, when pointing out the new initiative released, the new flexibility, of the NöS, that there are still severe limits on the initiative of the VVBs and their managers. The new industrial price reform will force them to consider ways and means of economizing on fuel, but could they, for example, forsake home-produced lignite for foreign-produced oil? Such a change could be in the interest of the VVB but not in the interest of the economy as a whole. Yet one of the slogans of the NöS is that it will bring the

[16] 'Social Development', p. 138; also in *Die Wirtschaft* (20 April 1967); see also *Aus erster Hand Neues Okonomisches System, Eine Information über die DDR*, Staatssekretariat für gesamtdeutsche Fragen, (East) Berlin, 1966; Erich Apel and Günter Mittag, *Neues Okonomisches System und Investitionspolitik*, Dietz Verlag, (East) Berlin, 1965.

interests of the VVB and the individual in line with those of society. Another important limitation on the VVBs is that they cannot readily purchase foreign patents even if through their exports they earned the necessary foreign currency. It must be admitted, however, that the DDR does buy a considerable number of foreign patents. Another problem in the domain of foreign trade is the lack of freedom of the VVBs to sell where they like. The trade treaty of 1965 and subsequent ones with the Soviet Union must substantially reduce their scope for enterprise in the hard currency areas. The arrangements with the Soviet Union, let it be admitted, do enable particular industries and the economy as a whole to plan with safety for some time into the future. Finally, in connection with the New Economic System, one can ask, 'Is it socialism? Or is it a partial return to capitalism?' Again this is a very complex problem but this author sees no contradiction between the new arrangements and the doctrine of Marx. The means of production remain in the hands of the state on behalf of society, and the profits, apart from incentive bonuses and the like, are handed over to the state—though this in itself is not necessarily socialist in the sense of Marx and Engels.

Chapter 6

The Other German Economic Miracle?

Early Difficulties

MOST PEOPLE outside the Communist world, and a good many in it, if asked to name a country which had undergone a tremendous economic upsurge in the post-war period, would undoubtedly and unhesitatingly say Germany. If questioned further they would mention they meant *West* Germany. And if questioned further still they would probably reveal that for them the German economy meant Gründig, Volkswagen, and, above all, Krupp. They would not know that, although East Germany cannot compete in sheer size with the Federal German Republic's economic capacities, and that although its rate of growth has not been as spectacular as that of West Germany, its economic achievements are nevertheless, in certain respects, remarkable. In fact it is said to be among the top ten industrial nations of the world, producing, *per capita,* in 1965, more steel than Italy, more electricity than West Germany, and more cement, TVs, refrigerators, and washing machines than Britain. On the same *per capita* basis it was ahead of the Soviet Union but behind the United States. In the Communist world, according to a Soviet survey given prominence in the London *Economist* of 28 May 1966,

In industrial development east Germany emerges as the indisputable leader of the socialist countries, with a level of production per head half as high again as Russia's in 1963. The finding seems plausible: it underlines the importance of keeping east German economic potential within the Soviet orbit, quite apart from any political-ideological considerations. By now east Germany has far out-distanced its sluggish competitor for leadership in this field—Czechoslovakia. These two are followed by Poland and Hungary only with a considerable lag ... The Rumanian level is only half that of the Russians and barely one third of the east German. Even Bulgaria's industrial rank is as much as one quarter higher. It is also startling to be reminded that industrial output per head in Jugoslavia is lower than in Bulgaria : this is a striking example of the disparity that can exist between economic and international political status.

Both, then, in the Communist world and in the world as a whole the DDR is a force to be reckoned with in industrial terms. Why should this be regarded as remarkable?

The DDR's rulers took over a territory suffering from war damage and the cost of enormous reparations to the Soviet Union and Poland. The area also lacked raw materials, experienced a chronic shortage of labour, and had some of its valuable industrial and agricultural products drained off through its Berlin frontier.

Official East German publications estimate that in 1946 the then Soviet Zone was producing, in industrial terms, only 42 per cent of what it produced in 1936.[1] The West German Ministry for All-German Affairs puts East German losses in industrial capacity due to war damage and reparations at double those of West German industry.[2] Production of cement, for example, was in 1946 a mere 570,000 tons as against nearly 1.7 million in 1936. Production of steel was 152,700 tons and 1,198,600 tons in those years respectively. Production of electricity fell from 14,000 GWh in 1936 to 11,536 GWh in 1946. Car production dropped from 60,849 to 1,439 vehicles in the same years, and the number of pairs of shoes produced, to take another random example, slumped from 15,341 to 5,540.[3]

An American expert, Professor Hans Apel, writing in *Challenge*, the economic affairs magazine of New York University, in November 1963, after describing recent East German economic progress, characterized the different starting points of the two parts of Germany as follows :

> In contrast to the US, the Soviet Union was itself greatly impoverished by the war and had neither the resources nor the inclination to assist in the rebuilding of East Germany. Naturally enough, the Soviets were primarily interested in reconstructing their own economy and their policies were directed towards achievement of this foremost objective. This Soviet attitude had far-reaching effects upon the East German economy . . . Immediately at the war's end, East Germany was subjected to a general

[1] Handbuch der Deutschen Demokratischen Republik, 1963, p. 335.
[2] *Sowjetische Besatzungszone von A–Z*, Herausgegeben vom Bundesministerium für Gesamtdeutsche Fragen, Bonn, 1966 (henceforth *SBZ von A–Z*), p. 206.
[3] Statistisches Jahrbuch der Deutschen Demokratischen Republik, 1966, pp. 25–7 (*SJB*).

requisitioning and pillaging of practically everything that seemed
useful to the Soviet occupation authorities. . . . The dismantling of
large industrial plants . . . was systematically and ruthlessly carried out. . . .

The US gave West Germany over 4 billion dollars in aid
between 1945 and the terminal date of our assistance programs
to Germany in 1955. . . .

As far as dismantling of industrial installations for reparations
is concerned, another American authority claims that there were
six waves of dismantling by the Soviets, the last of which was in
1948. He writes: 'In the light of the appalling wreckage inflicted
upon the Soviet Union by the German invaders, it is of little
wonder that East German industry became the object of feverish
activity of dismantling crews almost immediately. One can clearly
distinguish six waves of dismantling, first growing and then weakening in intensity.'[4] In the first wave alone, he continues, 460 larger
industrial plants were taken from Berlin. 'Within the Soviet zone
of occupation, the following were chief targets: coal mine installations, railway repair shops, power plants, and highly developed
technical plants, such as Zeiss (optics) at Jena, Ohrenstein und
Koppel (locomotives) at Potsdam, and the great electro-technical
works of AEG and Siemens-Halske.' Later dismantling affected
everything from breweries to railway track of which 32 per cent of
the total was taken.[5] Apart from reparations in the form of dismantled equipment, the Soviets also took reparations from current
production. Owing to the confused conditions after Germany's
surrender, secrecy, and different methods of calculation, no one
knows precisely just how much was taken from East Germany by
the Soviets. Estimates vary. Ulbricht is reported to have said that
in 1948 reparations plus occupation costs in 1948 took 25 per cent
of net production.[6] The official East German figure for total reparations payments is $4,300 million.[7] Our American authority puts it
at $10,429.12 billion at 1938 prices.[8] Whatever the figure was it
was certainly enormous. The *Manchester Guardian* on 7 October
1959 graphically summed up the importance of these reparations
and the miracle of overcoming their burden on the tenth anniversary of the setting-up of the East German state: '. . . in their own

[4] Heinz Köhler, *Economic Integration in the Soviet Bloc with an East
German Case Study*, Praeger, New York, 1965, p. 14.
[5] Ibid., p. 15.
[6] Ibid., p. 35.
[7] '20 Jahre Danach, Sonderheft 1 1965', *Deutsche Aussenpolitik*, p. 111.
[8] Köhler, op. cit., p. 29.

way the East Germans, too, have brought off a minor economic miracle. The Russians, by way of reparations, had taken one half of the fowl for cooking, leaving the other half for laying eggs—and it started to lay again. The East Germans restored their dismantled factories. They built industries where there were none before. They have made their rump State economically viable . . .'

The *Manchester Guardian* here touched on the third aspect of East Germany's economic difficulties, the fact that before the war the area which is now the DDR was heavily dependent on raw materials imported from West Germany and Silesia which is now in Poland. East Germany was not, as is so often believed, an area without industry. In 1944, 25 per cent of the population living within Germany's 1936 borders lived in East Germany, yet 28.9 per cent of the same area's total industrial output originated there. East Germany then produced 24.5 per cent of German basic industry output, 25.5 per cent of food, drink, and tobacco industries, 30.1 per cent of metal-working industries' output, and 35.3 per cent of that of light industries.[9] Nevertheless, for all this industry, East Germany produced only about 2 per cent of Germany's hard coal and only about 8 per cent of its pig-iron production. And although one-third of German motor-vehicle production was the responsibility of factories now in East Germany, only one-seventh of the supplying enterprises, for such things as tyres, sparking plugs, and other engine parts, were there.[10]

Before the war in 1938 16.6 million people lived in what is now the German Democratic Republic. Owing to the movement of German population westwards from the areas taken over by Poland, the USSR, and Czechoslovakia, and from the other countries of Eastern Europe, as well as the natural increase in population, this area had over 19 million inhabitants in 1948.[11] By 1955 the population of the DDR had fallen to 17,832,232 and at the end of 1964 it had dropped still further to 17,011,931. In 1967 it numbered 17,082,300.[12] The decline of the East German population by about 2 million was the result of a further shift of population from East to West Germany plus low reproduction rates. This second movement of population was brought about by a number of factors. Many left in the belief that they would enjoy higher living standards in the West, others left for political or religious reasons. Both

---

[9] Köhler, op. cit., pp. 12–13.
[10] *Wirtschaftsterritorium Deutsche Demokratische Republik Autorenkollektiv*, Verlag Die Wirtschaft, (East) Berlin, 1962, p. 142 (henceforth *Wt–DDR*).
[11] *Wt–DDR*, p. 59.
[12] *SJB*, 1957, p. 10; *Statistisches Taschenbuch der DDR*, 1968 (*STB*).

these groups have been dealt with at length in earlier chapters. Here we need only remind ourselves of factors which influenced many people in the early years after the war. One of these was fear of what life under the Russians would be. Many Nazis and former officials of the Hitler régime thought they would fare better under the Western Allies than under the Soviets. Certain social groups lost their property and positions as a result of socialistic measures carried out in the Soviet Zone. Later certain groups suffered as a consequence of the SED's Stalinist interpretation of the 'Dictatorship of the Proletariat'. Many Germans from the lost territories and Eastern Europe went West because the Federal Republic made better provision for them than did the East German Republic. Finally, in the early years it was easy to cross the demarcation line between East and West and even possible to get property across, and, due to wartime evacuations, the Germans had become, psychologically speaking, mobile.[13]

The East German authorities have tried to persuade some of these refugees to return to the DDR. Occasionally they have been successful with small businessmen who were offered their property back. They also had some success with those former DDR citizens who found it difficult to fit into the life of West Germany. In addition, some West Germans emigrated to East Germany either because of job difficulties, as in the case of miners for instance, or for political reasons. The official East German population figures given above would suggest that their numbers were limited.

In view of the close ties at official level between the DDR and the régimes of Eastern Europe one might have expected that the East German authorities would have imported labour from their relatively overpopulated and underdeveloped neighbours. For whatever reasons, such a solution to the labour shortage which has arisen from the lack of population was rejected up to the 1960s. Particularly since the introduction of the New Economic System in 1963 there appears to have been some rethinking on this matter and one hears of limited exchanges of labour usually for specific projects of limited duration. *Die Wirtschaft* on 17 October 1968 reported the arrival of young workers from Hungary to spend several years working in the industrial undertakings of the DDR. It emphasized that they would be given industrial training, would be treated as equal members of the community, and would eventually return to their homeland.

[13] *Frankfurter Allgemeine Zeitung* (18 March 1957); see also Ernest Richert, *Das zweite Deutschland Ein Staat der nicht sein darf*, Fischer, Frankfurt Main, 1966; for a discussion of this see pp. 93–4 above.

In summer 1966 the writer ventured into one of East Berlin's high-price luxury shops on the Unter den Linden. This shop stocked everything from furs to Meissen china. In it were three sergeants of the British military garrison buying expensive gifts. The chances are that they were paying in black-market East marks obtained in West Berlin at a fraction of their real worth. Immediately after the currency reform in the West in 1948, East Germany could not compete with West Germany in the variety of goods it provided for its people. Particularly short were textiles, cocoa and chocolate products, tropical fruits, good quality cigarettes and cigars, and durable consumer goods. The result was that many East Germans were quite willing to change their East marks for West marks at four to five for one in West Berlin. If grandfather wanted some cigars for his birthday or the girl-friend something to make her glamorous, or if baby would not eat potatoes but would eat bananas, or a sick relative needed a drug only obtainable in the West, why not change East marks occasionally? Other East marks arrived in the West with refugees and from *Grenzgänger,* those who worked in the West but lived in the East or vice versa. Although it might have been argued some years ago that one East mark was not worth one West mark, few would have argued that it was only worth one quarter of one West mark. As most East Berliners concerned only changed relatively few marks at a time, they did not feel the full impact of this unfair rate of exchange. Of what importance was the loss of all this currency to East Germany? Exact measurement is impossible but anyone seeing the effects in East Berlin in the fifties could not help feeling that this was something the East German authorities could not tolerate indefinitely. In the early fifties it meant that any West Berliner could make his income go farther by buying certain things in the East. This must have been useful to the large numbers of unemployed in West Berlin at that time, as well as to pensioners, students, and others on low incomes. It meant that, indirectly, the people of East Germany were giving a subsidy to the poor of West Berlin. It helped to demoralize the already hard-pressed East Berliners when, for instance, they went into restaurants and, after finding a table with difficulty, noticed the West Berliners around them ordering the most expensive items on the menu which *they* could not afford. Later regulations were introduced under which service was to be given only to those producing East German identity cards or valid visas. In practice it was easy to evade this rule. The Berlin Wall was in part the result of this evasion. The events of August 1961 greatly reduced this outflow but they could not completely stop it. Apart from a few authorized tourists, functionaries, artists, and businessmen, many East German pensioners visit relatives in the West; so do increasing numbers of seamen and rail employees. There are still West Berliners who work in the East who are partly paid in East marks. There are still buyers for black-market East marks: West German and foreign tourists; Allied servicemen, foreign workers employed in West Berlin. For political reasons the East Germans acquiesce in face of this situation.

East Germany suffers not only from having too few people, it also has the wrong kind. Out of every hundred Germans in 1939 67.5 per cent were of working age. By 1965 this percentage had dropped to 58.2. And although the percentage of children under 15 years-old has increased since 1939—23.2 as against 21.4—so has the percentage of old people—18.6 as against 11.1. Moreover, due to the war, the balance of the sexes has been upset. In 1939 there were 8,190,781 males and 8,554,604 females in the part of Germany which is now the DDR. In 1965 the figures were 7,783,347 and 9,264,586 respectively.[14] The working population of East Germany has to support a greater number of dependents than did the working force in that part of Germany in 1939. The labour force also contained a greater number of those working beyond the normal retirement age, more physically disabled and, above all, more female workers. In 1934 only 29.7 per cent of the labour force in what is now the DDR were females: in 1965 the figure was 47 per cent.[15] In industry, in 1952, 36.8 per cent of the labour force were women. By 1965 the percentages had risen to 40.3.[16] The percentage of women in the labour force of the Federal German Republic is only about 36.[17] These factors must to some extent reduce the effectiveness of the present labour force. They must, for example, help to explain the high rate of absenteeism in the DDR mentioned a few years ago.[18] Expanding the working population by use of female labour has meant calling on reserves of unskilled persons not used to the industrial process. Of necessity this involves high expenditure on training, nurseries, and other welfare measures for women.

[14] *SJB*, 1966, p. 518.
[15] *SJB*, 1966, p. 65.   [16] *SJB*, 1966, p. 65.
[17] *SBZ von A–Z*, p. 33; in 1963 the figure for West Germany was 35.7 per cent.
[18] *Worth Knowing about the Development and the New Economic System of the Planning and Management of the National Economy of the German Democratic Republic,* Leipzig, 1965, p. 58.

1.   1 May 1968, Marx-Engels-Platz, East Berlin: the armed forces
are an important symbol of DDR nationhood.
2.   5 July 1962. The People's Police reinforce the Berlin Wall at
Bernauerstrasse.

3. East Germany's education is supposed to link theory with practice, the classroom with society.

4.   Western educationalists are often impressed by the audio-visual aids in schools in the DDR. Here a foreign-language class is in progress.

5.   The Pentacon camera factory in Dresden. Optical goods are an important export; women are an important part of the labour force.

6. Double-decker carriages drawn by diesel engines are a characteristic feature of East German railways.

7. Harvesting potatoes in Schwerin: agriculture as East German publicists see it. Despite recent progress it will be some time before this picture is truly representative.

8.   Part of the chemical works Leuna II near Halle. The oil is pumped from the USSR. East Germany is a leading producer of chemicals.

9.   The DDR's main port, Rostock, largely developed since the war.

10. The new Foreign Ministry building in East Berlin with the river Spree in foreground.

11. Part of the restored Unter den Linden in East Berlin.

12. The Unter den Linden with the Brandenburg Gate from the Eastern side. The Berlin Wall is just out of sight.

13. Karl-Marx-Stadt (Chemnitz), the centre of the DDR's textile industry.

14. Members and candidates of the *Politbüro*, July 1968. Front row (l. to r.): Matern, Honecker, Ulbricht, Stoph, Ebert; 2nd row: Mittag, Hager, Verner, Mückenberger, Warnke, Neumann, Norden, Fröhlich, Grüneberg, Sindermann; back row (candidates): Axen, Ewald, Halbritter, Jarowinsky, Kleiber, Müller.

15a. Dresden, 1945. 14 square kilometres were completely destroyed.

15b. Dresden, 1965. The Old Market Place (Altmarkt) of restored Dresden.

16. A residential area of Dresden. 1966.

17. Halle, an important centre of the chemical industry. In the centre, statue of Handel, Halle's most famous son; on the right, the 'Red Tower', over 450 years old.

18. Otto Grotewohl. Wilhelm Pieck, Walter Ulbricht.

19.   Ulbricht's search for recognition: with President Nasser and Frau Lotte Ulbricht in Cairo, 1965.

20. Ulbricht as he is generally seen: SED VII *Parteitag*, April 1967. Front row, left to right: Hermann Matern, Yuri Andropov (USSR), Erich Honecker, Leonid Brezhnev, Ulbricht, Willi Stoph, Wladyslaw Gomulka (Poland), Friedrich Ebert, Jiri Hendrych (Czechoslovakia).

21. Ulbricht as he likes to be seen: the sportsman and family man.

22.   The late Bertolt Brecht and his wife, Helene Weigel, in 1954.
They remain East Germany's greatest cultural ambassadors.

23. The 'Red Dior': Heinz Bormann and his family, symbol of private enterprise in East Germany.

Political Investments

Taking 1950 as the base year, that is as 100, the official index of industrial production stood at 391 in 1965. The index for the basic industry stood at 361 while the metal industry index had risen to 561. The energy index for 1965 had reached 279. Light industry had not made quite as much progress and its index 'only' stood at 284, but the food industry had an index of 356.[19] Though one can argue about how these indices are arrived at they do at least show the general upward direction and the emphasis in the economy on some sectors rather than others. They do not tell us anything about the quality of the products produced. This should be remembered when considering the claim of an 'economic miracle'. One need only mention two points on this. Firstly, as noted in Chapter 1, in 1958 Ulbricht complained about East German products being behind world standards. Secondly, as in other Communist countries, certain modern industries such as petro-chemicals and electronics were neglected. These costly mistakes, which since 1963 the authorities have sought to correct, were perhaps inevitable given East German dependence on the USSR.

One of the main industries to benefit from East Germany's rapid post-war development was the iron and steel industry. In 1936 this area produced 898,000 tons of rolled steel. Yet despite wartime expansion the amount in 1946 was only 104,000. Heavy investments, particularly from about 1948 to 1958, increased production to 3,078,300 tons in 1967.[20] Before the war such iron and steel industry as there was, at such places as Brandenburg and Riesa, depended on imported fuel. The decision to rebuild, extend, and modernize the industry after the DDR was set up was an important political decision. It meant diverting a great deal of capital away from more popular projects such as consumer goods. It meant making certain calculations about the future of Germany. If the DDR was to become a viable economic entity, clearly its steel industry had got to be rehabilitated and extended. There has been a good deal of controversy about the extent of this development. It was embarked upon during the Stalinist era when according to Communist economic dogma every state should strive to build up the full range of industries whatever the cost and irrespective of what one's socialist neighbours were doing. The fact that this industry was developed under the influence of Stalinist autarkic principles has led many both inside and outside the DDR to question the economic

[19] *SJB,* 1966, p. 24.
[20] *STB der DDR,* 1968, p. 55.

10 * *

sense of such a course. That the East German government shifted
the emphasis in its investment policy away from the iron and steel
industry in recent years would seem to indicate that they are bow-
ing to that criticism. But given the division of Germany any East
German government, Communist or not, might have done the
same thing though not to the same extent.

East Germany now has three main centres of the iron and steel
industry. At Calbe an der Saale a completely new steel foundry
was built between 1950 and 1953, being the first foundry in the
world to be fuelled by brown coal. The second main centre, and
again completely new, is at Eisenhüttenstadt on the East German-
Polish frontier. This plant uses Soviet ores and Polish coke. The
third main centre is at Unterwellenborn at the south-western end
of the DDR. East Germany inherited this plant from the Third
Reich but it has been modernized and developed. Other pre-war
plants at Brandenburg, Hennigsdorf near Berlin, and Riesa have
likewise been modernized. In spite of all the investments and the
progress made, the DDR remains the world's largest importer of
steel and is likely to remain so for a long time.[21]

The development of the iron and steel industry meant also the
development of the fuel economy. This could not be done on the
basis of hard coal. There is such coal in Saxony but this coalfield
had no great importance before the war. The coal there has a high
ash-content and there is little which is really suitable for coking
except around Zwickau.[22] On the other hand East Germany is
well-endowed with deposits of brown coal. These have the advantage of being relatively easy to exploit though, traditionally, they
were never used for the iron and steel industry. A great deal of—
from the economic point of view questionable—investment resulted
in the development of the production of brown-coal briquettes
from 23,529,000 tons in 1936 to 60,380,000 tons in 1965.[23] Brown-
coal open-cast mining is carried on over a wide area of the
southern DDR but one name stands out in this context—the
'Schwarze Pumpe' complex at Cottbus. This is the world's largest
lignite processing plant and it was, for a time, East Germany's
biggest single investment. This plant came into operation in 1959.
About 60 per cent of East Germany's reserves are in the Cottbus
district. Brown coal now accounts for well over 80 per cent of
the DDR's energy requirements. As a source of fuel it remains

[21] Wt–DDR, pp. 97–103; Neues Deutschland (17 March 1965).
[22] Germany, Vol. III, Naval Intelligence Division, London, November
1944, p. 255 (NID).
[23] SJB, 1966, p. 25.

less economical than hard coal or oil and since East Germany and the other states of Eastern Europe started to rationalize their economies in 1958, there has been some slackening of the earlier enthusiasm for lignite. Oil is still of very limited significance, though the building of a refinery at Schwedt on the East German-Polish frontier makes it possible to use oil on an increasing scale. This refinery, which started work in early 1964, is one of the termini of the Friendship pipeline which starts at Kuibyschev, east of the Volga, and is said to be the longest in the world. The oil processed is used for fuel and for the development of the petro-chemical industry. The changing position of brown coal and oil is shown by the fact that in 1965 'Schwarze Pumpe' increased production by 2 per cent: at Schwedt processing of oil increased by 28 per cent. There is now also a pipeline from the Baltic port of Rostock to Schwedt. It was conceived as a crude-oil line for piping overseas crude to the inland refineries at Schwedt and Leuna. At the moment the future of this pipeline is in doubt. As far as is known no agreements have been signed with oil-producing states.

As mentioned above, on a *per capita* basis, East Germany produces more electricity than West Germany. To achieve this position it raised production of electricity from a mere 14,000 GWh in 1936 in that part of Germany which is now the DDR, to nearly 60,000 in 1967. In 1946 production had been reduced to 11,536 GWh. However, the increase in electricity has not kept pace with the increase of industrial production and its supply remains a problem. The electrical generating industry is closely connected with the brown-coal industry. Three of East Germany's biggest power stations, for example, are part of the 'Schwarze Pumpe' complex. The DDR's electrical supply industry is now connected to those of its East European neighbours and it imports electricity as well as exporting it to West Berlin. Since 1964 imports have exceeded exports.[24] The DDR also imports more gas than it exports and by 1972 will be receiving natural gas by pipeline from the USSR.

Another form of energy which the East Germans are developing is nuclear power. The DDR is known to be well-endowed with uranium deposits,[25] exploitation of which is in the hands of a mixed Soviet-East German company, the *Wismut*. Of East Germany's nuclear-power programme the London *Economist* (21 January 1967) wrote:

East Germany, after a six-year delay, put its pathetically small 70-megawatt pressurised light-water reactor at Rheinsberg (be-

[24] *SJB*, 1966, pp. 401, 407.   [25] *Wt–DDR*, p. 115.

tween Berlin and Rostock) into operation in May, 1966, and it is now supplying industrial and domestic power. The original agreement for the reactor was signed with the Soviet Union in 1957 with the hope that it would be operational by 1960, but somewhere along the line the delivery date became fussed over. The East Germans are now negotiating with the Russians to obtain a bigger reactor which ought to give them something in the commercial range of 350 to 700 megawatts.

Before 1945 the chemical industry was based on local raw materials—lignite, potash, and limestone. The most important, and famous, plant of the chemical industry at that time was the *Leunawerke* near Merseburg. This was actually set up during the First World War as part of Germany's drive for self-sufficiency. Oil was produced from coal and lignite by hydrogenation and in 1938 a production of 1,250,000 tons was achieved. This was used for synthetic gasoline, including aviation spirit, diesel oil, and benzol.[26] Leuna is once again important with a more varied production than before and a new complex, Leuna II, being developed. Leuna II's job is to process petroleum into polyethylene and other materials for plastics, and caprolactum for synthetic fibres (which were also produced in this part of Germany before the war). In both plastics and man-made fibres the DDR has made rapid progress. In plastics some East German processes have developed successfully enough to become attractive to chemical industries in advanced Western countries.[27] Roughly 13 per cent of the DDR's industrial production in 1967 were products of the chemical industry which was thus East Germany's most important industry.[28] In 1966 the chemical industry was the largest employer of labour with 282,038 employees. The development of this industry obviously makes good sense both because it is largely based on plentiful local raw materials and because relatively little labour is required proportionate to the value of its product—an important consideration in a country desperately short of labour.

The manufacture of electrical equipment is another industry which flourished before 1945 and which today is enjoying boom conditions. It was the third largest employer of labour in 1966, accounting for nearly 237,000 personnel. As before the war, Berlin

[26] *NID*, p. 267.
[27] A. Zauberman, *Industrial Progress In Poland, Czechoslovakia and Eastern Germany 1937–1962*, Royal Institute of International Affairs, 1964, p. 265.
[28] *STB*, p. 46; Economic Survey of Europe 1967, UN, New York, 1968, Chapter II, p. 15.

remains the main centre of the industry, accounting for something like a third of all production. In the capital, particularly at Treptow, Oberspree, and Köpenick, all parts of the electrical equipment industry are represented from electric lamps to cables, from transformers and high-frequency equipment to radio and television sets. The electrical equipment industry is also carried on in the outer suburbs of Berlin, such as Hennigsdorf. In addition, heavy generators are built in Dresden, electrical motors at Wernigerode, Osterwieck, and Oschersleben in the west of the DDR, lamps in Plauen, Zwickau, Dresden, and Eisenach, radio and television sets at Rochlitz, near Karl-Marx-Stadt, Stassfurt, and Dresden, and valves in Erfurt.[29] At the end of 1967 production started of the domestically designed medium-size computer Robotron 300. Up to 1970 200 units are to be completed mainly for the home market. Data-processing equipment is being produced especially for the export trade.

With over 206,000 employees in 1966 the general machinery industry was the fourth largest employer in that year. Not far behind was heavy machinery with another 185,500. It took seventh place after food and drink (200,000) and mining of all kinds (190,000). The East German machine-building industry is somewhat different from its parent industry. Before 1945 the machinery industry was mainly concerned with textile machinery, machine tools, and certain other light machinery. Textile machinery is still important but the industry has become more diversified. This industry like much of the East German economy has been affected by the division of the country and by reparations to the Soviet Union. The Soviet Union, and the rest of Eastern Europe for that matter, was, in the years just after the war, more interested in heavy machinery than in textile machinery or other machines for producing consumer goods. The result was that East Germany started to invest heavily in all kinds of heavy engineering for which it was not really suited. The East German authorities have already realized this. As a high-powered DDR survey in 1961 pointed out, the engineering industry turned out practically as many types of machines as the Soviet Union or the United States.[30] Clearly this could not be to the advantage of East Germany. The survey rightly explained that the republic should concentrate on high-quality machines requiring relatively little raw material. At that time East Germany was the seventh largest producer of machine tools and the third largest exporter, after West Germany and the USA. East

[29] *Wt–DDR,* pp. 146–8.
[30] *Wt–DDR,* p. 137.

Germany's main centres of production are, for machine tools:
Karl-Marx-Stadt, Magdeburg, Berlin, Leipzig, Plauen, Gera,
Meuselwitz, Aschersleben, Erfurt, Freital, Dresden; for mining
equipment, cranes, and heavy engineering: Magdeburg and Leipzig; for textile machinery: Karl-Marx-Stadt and the surrounding
towns; for pumping equipment: Halle, Salzwedel, Oschersleben,
Karl-Marx-Stadt, Zwickau, Gera, and Erfurt; for agricultural
machinery: Leipzig, Weimar, and Neustadt, between Dresden and
Bautzen.[31]

Apart from Krupp, Volkswagen, and Gründig, one German
industrial firm which is well-known abroad is Carl Zeiss of Jena.
Many of those who know of this firm probably do not realize that
Jena is in the DDR and that, despite the existence of a rival in
West Germany, the East German Zeiss is more truly the successor
of the pre-war firm. Its products are exported to 80 countries and,
apart from cameras, it produces a wide variety of optical equipment. A British scientific journalist has characterized this wide
variety in the following way:

> Each year the company has extended its scope and introduced
> new optical-based instruments for use by science and industry.
> Amongst them are electron microscopes of extremely high magni-
> fication, spectrographs and analytical instruments, and the light
> coagulator which provides a tool of high precision for the eye
> surgeons. The very latest developments from Zeiss are showing
> how electronics and optics can be combined to provide high
> speed analytical instruments suitable for the needs of automation.
> Techniques used include those of the Laser, which will be used
> to provide a monochromatic source of light of high accuracy
> for use in analysis of samples.[32]

Other enterprises in this industry are found at Dresden and at
Görlitz. In the East German economic system optical equipment is
grouped together with light engineering, the best known products
of which are office machines, clocks and watches—another traditional industry—and medical equipment, noted factories for the
manufacture of which exist in Berlin, Potsdam, and in Thuringia.
These sectors together employed 102,097 people in 1965. They
were thus about the tenth largest industrial employer.

Two industries which have fared quite differently, because of the
division of Germany, are shipbuilding and the automobile industry.
Before the war there was not much in the way of shipbuilding

---

[31] *Wt–DDR*, pp. 135–42.
[32] *Profile of East Germany*, chapter by J. H. Bonnett, pp. 53–4.

between the Elbe and the Oder, or rather, between what is now the
East German side of the Elbe and the Oder. At Rostock, on the
Baltic coast, there was the Neptun AG which built seven vessels of
19,700 tons gross in 1938. This compared with the Deutsche Werft
AG of Hamburg's 17 vessels of 149,720 tons gross in the same year.
The biggest ship built at Rostock before the war was the merchant
vessel *Vestvard* of 4,319 tons gross. It was completed in 1925.
The Neptun's production consisted of steam and motor-cargo
vessels and trawlers, dredgers, and tugs. There was also a smaller yard
at Rostock and other small ones at Stralsund and Warnemünde.[33]
The Neptun yard employed 5,000 workers at the end of the war.
In 1965 East German shipyards employed 38,180 personnel. East
Germany's biggest yard is the *Warnowwerft* at Warnemünde. This
yard builds 11,200-ton freighters, 10,400-ton freighters, and 9,500-
ton coal- and ore-freighters. The *Neptunwerft* now builds 3,000-ton
freighters and at Wolgast 500- and 750-ton coasters are built. At
Wismar river boats capable of carrying 335 passengers and at
Stralsund trawlers and other fishing vessels are constructed. These
yards were responsible for 198,000 tdw of new ocean-going and
coastal shipping in 1965—in all, 47 ships. In the same year 51
fishing vessels were completed; the total tonnage of these was not
disclosed.[34] Even though the East Germans are very proud of the
shipbuilding industry they have developed it is still much smaller
than those of the leading shipbuilding states—Japan, Sweden, West
Germany, France, and the USA. At the present time the DDR's
yards have no difficulty in finding customers. They mainly produce
for the Soviet Union, though they have found markets in the
Scandinavian countries and the Third World.

Before the Second World War about 30 per cent of German
automobile production—over 60,000 cars—came from what is now
the DDR. This industry was hit heavily by the division of the
country, for only 14 per cent of tyres were produced there, only 7 per
cent of sparking plugs, and only 13 per cent of lights.[35] In addition
to the shortage of these parts, the East German automobile industry
faced a crisis caused by lack of appropriate metals. With the
greatest of effort this, and many other problems, were mastered.
From a very low level in the immediate post-war years production
was built up to 111,500 cars and 29,900 trucks in 1967. The industry's structure was also rationalized. Despite this writers in *Die*

[33] *NID*, p. 306.
[34] *SJB*, 1966, p. 171; *The Motor Ship*, London (September 1963), spoke
highly of E. German yards.
[35] *SBZ von A–Z*, p. 147.

Wirtschaft (25 May 1967) were still worried about the types of vehicle being manufactured. To West Germans or Britons the East German industry must seem puny but it has been important in the East European setting. In 1964 the USSR produced only 185,200 cars, the DDR 93,000. The DDR's total was greater than those of Poland, Czechoslovakia, and Yugoslavia put together and the other East European countries manufactured almost no cars. On a *per capita* basis the DDR's total was many times that of the Soviet Union. Yet East Germany remains one of the most under-motorized of the advanced industrial nations. And its automobile industry has problems. Doubts are being voiced about the further extension of its main plant at Eisenach, near Erfurt. The physical structure of the plant and the local geography make this extremely difficult, say the doubters. Another problem is the provision for spare parts. Only 57 per cent of all lorries in use in 1965 were manufactured after 1955, over 20 per cent were of pre-1945 stock. Ten per cent of the passenger cars on the roads were likewise pre-1945. *Die Wirtschaft* (22 December 1966), from which these figures are taken, believes that the East German automobile industry could be ruined by having to provide spares for so many different types of vehicles. The obvious solution would be simply to force old vehicles off the roads. But East Germany is desperately short of automobiles and does not produce enough to cover its needs. For instance, according to *Die Wirtschaft* (17 November 1966), only one-third of the DDR's requirement of small trucks and vans is met from domestic production. Lack of hard currency, and perhaps political considerations, prevent imports from the West. Clearly the DDR ought to consider stopping exports—nearly 38,000 cars and almost 8,500 trucks in 1966—which many suspect have been sold at prices which do not reflect costs.[36] Commenting on both price and quality of these cars the British automobile magazine *Autocar* (13 July 1967), after carrying out road tests on the 1967 *Wartburg Knight*, said : 'This Wartburg is a fairly basic car in terms of what it can do and the way it is made. A lot of equipment is included for an extraordinary new recommended price and the car has a capacity of five people in reasonable comfort plus their luggage. It looks smart and there is a mechanical ruggedness that should make it very reliable transport.'

Failure and Success in the Air

Some employees of the automobile industry might fear a similar

[36] P.J.D. Wiles, *Communist International Economics*, Blackwell, Oxford, 1968, claims the DDR subsidizes both exports *and* imports (p. 134).

fate to their colleagues in the aviation industry, which died officially as a result of the new division of labour in the East European economic community after 1958. There was a whole series of aircraft factories in East Germany before 1945. The Soviet occupation authorities either dismantled them or turned them over to other uses. A start was made to build up a new industry in 1956. At Dresden production was begun on Soviet IL-14 airliners for the East German airline. By 1960 about 80 such machines had been constructed and a number of these were sold abroad. The East Germans even claimed to be producing an improved version of the IL-14. With the return of German technicians and designers from the USSR the DDR raised its sights. Plans were put into operation for an East German designed jet airliner, the B 152. A model of the plane, together with a full-sized cutaway of one of its motors, was displayed at the Leipzig Trade Fair early in March 1958. *The Times* (3 March 1958) wrote : 'It has been left to East Germany to surprise and impress, and this it has done with a model of a 72-seater turbo-jet airliner... The designer is Prof. Baade, who before the war worked for Junkers... Should it prove successful, the effect it will have in the Federal Republic where only light air-craft are being made, is likely to be not much less than that of the first sputnik.' The East German aviation industry suffered from raw material difficulties and from loss of personnel to the West. Develop-ment costs proved heavier than expected and it was decided that the project was too much of a gamble to be continued. The decline of this industry is illustrated by certain figures concerning aero-nautical students. In 1960 there were 467 of them at DDR univer-sities. In the same year there were 97 graduates. After the decision to wind up the industry the numbers dropped to three students and 76 graduates in 1961. There are no students of aeronautics in the DDR at the present time. At its apex the industry employed over 20,000 workers and technicians.

Notwithstanding the decline of the East German aviation industry the DDR's airline has continued to expand on a modest scale. When the East German airline started operations in 1956 it carried a mere 12,553 passengers. By 1958 this had grown to 194,669. Two years later 292,377 guests were recorded and two years after that 310,279. In 1964 the total climbed to 385,839. Thus in that year it beat the all-German record of the old *Lufthansa* which carried 323,100 passengers in 1937. How does the DDR firm's achievement match those (admittedly larger) airlines serving other (admittedly larger) states? The West German *Lufthansa* was responsible for nearly 3 million passengers in 1965. In the same year BEA transported 6,842,763 people, while *Interflug*, the East German company, booked 440,336. In 1967 *Interflug* claimed over 649,300 guests.[37]

It was in February 1956 that a DDR airline commenced regular international flights between Berlin and Warsaw. This was followed in May by services to Prague, Budapest, Sofia, and Bucharest. Regular flights to Moscow were inaugurated on the seventh anniversary of the setting-up of the German Democratic Republic on 7 October 1956. *Interflug's* further international development was hampered by West German representations to its allies and to other nations friendly to it. It succeeded, for instance, in making it very difficult for the East German airline to use the old name 'Lufthansa', which it claimed exclusively for its own airline. Strong West German pressure which was so successful in preventing *Interflug* from making regular appearances in West European capitals was less successful in keeping it out of the Afro-Asian states. In 1964 the East Germans began regular flights to Nicosia. After Walter Ulbricht, as East German Head of State, paid a highly successful visit to President Nasser in Cairo in 1964, there followed the inauguration of non-stop flights between Berlin and Cairo. In January 1966 flights were started to Damascus and in 1969 regular flights were due to start to Baghdad. East Germany, with Moscow's help, was also able to topple Bonn's monopoly of Germany's relations with Yugoslavia. Tito recognized the DDR and in April 1960 *Interflug* opened a line between Berlin, Belgrade, and Tirana. *Interflug* also carries on certain other regular flights to Africa as well as seven internal flights linking Berlin with the chief centres of industry and population. In addition, it has an industrial service, mainly helping with construction work, an agricultural and a medical service, as well as charter flights especially for the Leipzig Fair. In its early days the East German airline's difficulties were considerable. Air crews and ground personnel were not readily available. Pilots with war experience did not have experience of the latest planes. In any case, there was competition for trained people from the West German *Lufthansa*. Shortage of air crews led to first flights being made by Soviet personnel. But by the summer of 1957 German crews had completely replaced their Soviet colleagues. Another problem was airports. The new East German state found itself much worse off than West Germany in its inheritance. Germany's biggest pre-war airport, Tempelhof, is in West Berlin. And the next two largest are in the Federal Republic. The best the East Germans got was the Halle/Leipzig

[37] *STB*, 1968, p. 107.

airport which before the war was Germany's fourth largest. They
also got relatively unimportant airports at Karl-Marx-Stadt, Dresden, Erfurt, Magdeburg, and Rügen (the latter being taken over
by the Soviet forces). In Berlin they got Schönefeld, which before
the war was merely a works' testing field.

Foreign Trade: Moscow Holds the Strings

From what has already been said about the East German automobile industry the reader will have rightly concluded that motor
transport is still economically less important than the railway in
East Germany. Since the war there has been a great change in the
relative importance of the various routes. Before 1945, for instance,
the line between Berlin and the Ruhr was of the greatest importance particularly via Stendal—Hanover—Bielefeld. The Hamburg—
Berlin route was also very important. These lines have been
greatly reduced in importance owing to the division of the country.
So has the line from Leipzig and Halle to the West. On the other
hand, routes to the north-east, east, and south have greatly increased
their importance and the line from Berlin to Frankfurt/Oder is
now the most important one, being the main line via Poland to the
Soviet Union. The lines from Berlin to the north have also increased
in importance because of the development of the Baltic coast ports.
The East German railways suffer from a labour problem. An article
in *Die Wirtschaft* (1 December 1966), which was largely concerned
with inefficient use of rolling-stock, claimed that rail employees
lacked the necessary knowledge to do their jobs properly. As other
railways, the *Deutsche Reichsbahn* has embarked upon a programme of modernization. There are already container trains
operating on certain key routes. By the end of 1975 the last of the
steam engines is to be replaced. In that year 81.6 per cent of the
capacity of the railways will be based on diesel locomotives and
the rest on electric. Many of the new engines will be Soviet-built;
thus the DDR does not intend to expand its research and development establishments in this field.[38] The East Germans believe
further research would be costly relative to revenue, as they do
not expect many export orders. Little known is the fact that East
Germany has exported a great deal of rolling-stock. One authoritative Western report characterized the development in the following way: 'Although the industry was fragmented and largely
devastated by the war and its aftermath, a broad foundation of
railway works and design and production experience remained on
which to build. It has been developed into a rolling stock manu-

[38] *Neue Zeit* (9 June 1968).

facturing industry the equal of any in design, materials and work-
manship, and in advance of many in terms of productivity.' By
1966, according to the same source, the industry had a labour force
of 26,000 and was producing many types of vehicle

> including diesel and electric locomotives and a very high percen-
> tage of the more sophisticated types of rolling stock, such as
> restaurant and sleeping cars and refrigerated goods wagons.
> More than half the total production has been exported. Produc-
> tion has followed a continuously rising trend and was doubled in
> the years 1956–66 to a total of roughly 5,000 vehicles a year.
> The current five-year programme is planned to expand produc-
> tion by a further 80 per cent. The annual production of powered
> stock was increased dramatically between March 1966 and
> March 1967, from a total of 250,000 h.p. to 1 m. h.p. . . . the
> country's rolling stock industry is certainly among the most
> highly mechanised in the world. . . . Although the basis of present
> success was a succession of big orders from the USSR and other
> communist countries, the efficient designs and production meth-
> ods evolved to meet these commitments have given the East
> German industry a considerable competitive edge in bidding for
> orders in the traditional markets of Western manufacturers.

And East German rail vehicles 'are at work in 22 countries,
including Greece . . . Syria, India, Indonesia, West Germany,
Belgium, Norway, Brazil, Egypt and Iceland (on industrial lines in
this instance).'[39]

In 1952 the East German merchant fleet consisted of one ship
of 917 BRT. By 1965 its merchant fleet had expanded to 127 ships
of 485,325 BRT. This included a tanker fleet of 12 vessels with a
total tonnage of 95,711 BRT. Where does this put it in the
international league tables? In 1964, when the total East German
tonnage was 422,000 BRT, West German tonnage was 5,159,000
and that of the UK 21,490,000. In the same year Poland and
Yugoslavia, both of which had benefited from German reparations,
had total tonnages of 853,000 and 968,000 respectively. East Germany was, however, ahead of South Africa, another industrialized
yet relatively small state, and was catching up to Australia. Continued expansion is foreseen in the coming years. The port of
Rostock, East Germany's main sea outlet, has developed with the
growth of the merchant fleet. It undoubtedly became a prestige
symbol of the régime and by the end of the 1950s very ambitious
plans had been worked out for its development. Later the diffi-

[39] *Modern Railways, London* (July 1967), see also August issue.

culty of competing with the established ports of Hamburg and Szczecin (Stettin) was recognized and the plans were scaled down.[40]

The growth of East German maritime strength reflects the growth of East German trade with overseas nations. As one might expect in view of recent history, the biggest trading partner of the DDR is not overseas but in Eastern Europe, that is the USSR. Soviet-East German trade has long been a controversial matter. In the West it is often said that the Soviets exploit East Germany economically by forcing them to sell their sought-after industrial products at prices below those prevailing in international markets. The suicide of top East German economic planner Erich Apel at the end of 1965, just after he had been to Moscow to sign a new trade treaty covering the years 1966–70, renewed speculation in the West about this. Whole books have been written by Western specialists on East Germany's trade, books prepared on the basis of guesswork and analysis of inadequate official East German information. This writer, not a specialist in these matters, would not dare to embark on such an exciting yet unrewarding task. Before briefly outlining the DDR's trade relations he will, however, mention two salient results of Western research. One West German expert, Joachim Nawrocki, who enjoys the confidence of the Bonn Ministry for All-German Affairs, has decided that the evidence advanced to show that the USSR is still exploiting the DDR through their trade relations is inadequate and often misleading.[41] Secondly, another, equally respected, West German researcher estimates that even in the years 1955–9 East Germany suffered less disadvantage in its trade with the USSR than did the other states of the Council for Mutual Economic Aid (that is, all the European Communist states except Yugoslavia). And by 1959 the DDR had virtually eliminated any price disadvantage it had earlier suffered in this trade.[42]

East Germany like Britain and certain other countries is heavily dependent on imported raw materials. This means it must export on a large scale to pay for these. Moreover, the DDR is largely dependent on one country for such raw materials, the Soviet Union. This dependence is made worse by the need for the Soviet Union to act as political sponsor and protector. The Soviet Union

[40] Dr. Konstantin Pritzel, *Die wirtschaftliche Integration der Sowjetischen Besatzungszone Deutschlands in den Ostblock,* Bundesministerium für Gesamtdeutsche Fragen, Bonn, 1966, p. 224.
[41] Joachim Nawrocki, *Das geplante Wunder,* Christian Wegner Verlag, Hamburg, 1967, pp. 176–84. Sonderausgabe für das Bundesministerium für Gesamtdeutsche Fragen.
[42] Pritzel, op. cit., p. 261.

receives from the DDR roughly one quarter of her imports and the Democratic Republic is thus USSR's biggest trading partner. Certainly before 1956 the Soviet Union was able to get from Eastern Europe imports below world market prices. After that time, owing to Polish pressure in the first instance, trade exchanges among Soviet bloc countries were based to a much greater extent on world market prices.[43] The DDR's heavy Soviet orientation in its external trade has, says Herr Nawrocki, one positive side : the long-term contracts make planning of investments, production, and employment much easier.[44] Even so, many East Germans are still doubtful about the wisdom of doing such a large volume of trade with allied states—75.2 per cent of exports and 73 per cent of imports in 1967.

The DDR's trading relations have been looking up in the 1960s. After a slight deficit in its trade with the socialist countries in 1962 the DDR recorded surpluses in the years 1963–7. In its trade with the developing countries—just over 4 per cent of the total in these years—East Germany had surpluses from 1962 to 1967. With the capitalist states the DDR had surpluses between 1962 and 1965, but was in the red in 1966 and 1967.[45] One interesting aspect of East German trade is that although it is affected by politics, it is not based solely on political considerations. For instance, after considerable ups and downs, trade with Albania has tended to expand in the 1960s despite bitter political differences. This is also true of the higher volume of trade with Greece and Romania. Trade with Communist China has slumped owing to political differences and is now worth less than trade with such unorthodox Communist states as Cuba, Romania, and Yugoslavia, or, for that matter, with Holland or West Berlin. West Germany remains the DDR's biggest Western and NATO trading partner. In fact, East Germany does as much trade with the Federal Republic as it does with all the other NATO countries put together. This trade, which has been rising in the 1960s, is only a fraction of the trade between these two areas of Germany before the war. Still, it remains more important than trade with Poland.[46]

Scientific Farming

Finally, let us look at East German agriculture, another complex problem facing the East German government. In 1967 just

[43] *Der Spiegel* (22 August 1966). See also Economic Bulletin For Europe, UN, New York, November 1966, p. 13.
[44] Nawrocki, op. cit., p. 181.
[45] *STB*, 1968, pp. 115–17.
[46] Ibid., pp. 118–21.

over 94 per cent of East German agricultural land was collectively operated. Just under 7 per cent of this area was held by state farms and the rest by co-operatives. There are three kinds of co-operative. In type one members pool only their arable land, re-taining for themselves their livestock, machines, and orchards. In type two co-operative members pool their livestock, and imple-ments as well. In type three co-operatives all crops, livestock, and buildings are put into the common pool. In all three types mem-bers retain some animals and a small amount of land for their own use. In 1967 there were over 7,000 co-operatives of types one and two with over 292,000 members and nearly 1,500,000 hectares of land. The type three farms—nearly 6,000—had 678,000 mem-bers and almost 4 million hectares.[47]

In 1963 agriculture (including forestry and fishing) employed over 1,250,000, roughly 17 per cent of all employed persons. Yet this group contributed only 9.2 per cent of the total product.[48] This compares unfavourably with the performance of the agricul-tural sector in the advanced countries of Western Europe. As one British agricultural journalist recorded in 1966, 'With the same number of people three times as much land is farmed in the United Kingdom' than in the DDR.[49] Why should this be so and what is being done to change the situation? Much of the agricul-tural land of the DDR was part of large estates before 1945. This was especially true in the north, in Brandenburg and Mecklenburg. The other main features of this pre-1945 agriculture were the dependence on immigrant labour from Poland, state subsidies, and the emphasis on arable farming somewhat to the neglect of live-stock. In 1945 a great many Germans, as well as the Soviet occu-piers, thought it necessary to destroy the influence of the great estate-owners, so often used against the interests of the nation, by dividing up their properties. This, however, brought problems. Al-though some of the new small farmers were those who had farmed their own land before 1945 in what were now the lost territories, many were former landless labourers or ex-servicemen without agricultural experience. The new units were small, uneconomical, and under-capitalized. Agricultural machinery was lacking. Inevit-ably production suffered. Both for ideological and economic reasons the SED forced through the collectivization of the land at great speed in 1960–1. By no means all the farmers were in

[47] STB, 1968, p. 79.
[48] Handbuch der DDR, 1963, p. 392.
[49] Profile of East Germany, chapter by A. Kenworthy, p. 44.

favour of this and some left the land and killed their livestock.[50]
The amount of land under cultivation fell.[51] The new co-operatives
had, and still have, a labour problem. Many of the older farmers
are former labourers who find it difficult to change their ways
and who were not expected to use their initiative before the war.
Many are women who were also kept to the inferior and unskilled jobs on the farm before the war. The farm population is also
an ageing one. Many of the more enterprising young men and
women leave the land to seek the better life of the towns. Between
1952 and 1964 the numbers employed in agriculture, forestry, and
fishing fell from 1,700,000 to 1,314,000.[52] By 1967 they had fallen
to 1,203,000.[53] It has been difficult to find the farm managers with
the necessary human and technical skills to run the increasingly
complex co-operatives. Another problem was equipping the new
farms with sufficient machinery, fertilizers, protective chemicals,
and modern buildings to enable them to deliver the goods. Before
the war the territory of the present DDR imported some of its
meat from West Germany. The East German authorities have tried
to deal with this situation, made worse by the seizure of herds by
the Soviets in 1945, by increasing the number of livestock. This
they have succeeded in doing but only at the expense of
arable farming. According to West German sources, the number of
cattle increased from an average of 3,597,000 in the years 1935–8
to 4,682,000 in 1964. The number of pigs increased from 5,812,000
to 8,759,000, of sheep from 1,628,000 to 1,972,000, and the number
of fowl, 21,690,000 in 1938, to 38,210,000.[54] In 1967 there were
over 5 million head of cattle, over 9¼ million pigs, 1,818,000 sheep,
and 37,976,000 fowl.[55]

Great attempts have been made to get more qualified people on
the land. The number of graduates on co-operative farms increased
from about 1,500 in 1961 to over 4,400 in 1967. The numbers of
those who had completed courses at *Fachschulen* increased from
about 8,000 to over 19,800 in the same period. The number of
skilled workers advanced from 18,500 to 216,600. In 1967 roughly
about two-thirds of farm chairmen belonged to one of these
categories, 1,829 graduates among them. The fact that only 16

[50] Stefan Doernberg, *Kurze Geschichte der DDR,* Dietz Verlag, (East)
Berlin, 1964, p. 220.
[51] *STB,* 1964, p. 83.
[52] *SBZ von A–Z,* p. 274.
[53] *STB,* 1968, p. 81.
[54] *SBZ von A–Z,* p. 278.
[55] *STB,* 1968, p. 90.

of these were women, as against 20 in 1966 and 22 in 1965, shows the difficulties still to be overcome.[56]

Herr Nawrocki believes that, on the whole, the four years 1964–7 were good ones for East German agriculture in which much progress was made. He says that, owing to more machinery—120,000 tractors in 1967 against only 43,000 in 1960—more chemicals being used, improved prices for agricultural products, and, not least, a greater acceptance by farmers of the new system, pre-war levels have been overtaken and the gap between standards in East and West Germany reduced.[57] United Nations economists came to the same conclusions:

> Weather conditions on the whole appear to have been favourable. All-time record yields were obtained for the most important crops at levels which compare well with western European standards. The steady progress can be explained to a significant extent by improving soil fertility, resulting from considerable investment efforts in melioration works in the recent past, as well as by the consistent efforts to improve the general agro-technical level. The net of agricultural extension services is adequately organized and inter-farm co-operation for optimal utilization of available technical equipment seems to enable cultivation and harvesting to be carried out without undue recourse to temporary labour from other sectors.[58]

[56] *STB*, 1968, p. 81.
[57] Nawrocki, op. cit., pp. 143–4.
[58] Economic Survey of Europe 1967, UN, New York, 1968, Chapter II, p. 27.

11 * *

Chapter 7

Living Standards: Affluence Just Around the Corner?

D URING THE last few years East Berlin has been getting a face-lift. This work has been intensified since 1965 in preparation for the 20th Anniversary of the founding of the DDR in 1969. The most spectacular piece of this renewal is the television tower, which next to Moscow's is said to be the highest structure in Europe. The tower accommodates a café with 200 seats and a viewers' gallery. East Berlin's new face also includes hotels in contemporary style such as the *Unter den Linden* and *Berolina,* and most recently *Stadt Berlin,* and newish restaurants such as the *Moskau* and *Lindencorso,* which have modern lines and tasteful furnishings. In shops like *Havana* and *Delicat* on the restored Unter den Linden one can buy Cuban cigars, Western cigarettes, canned foods from East and West, delicacies from France, wines from West Germany, even Scotch whisky. Admittedly, most Western consumer goods are either not available or only available for the privileged few with 'hard', Western, currency. And even in these shops on the Linden, where Western currency is not required, prices are high. But they give the East Germans hope, hope that the less austere 1960s will turn into the increasingly affluent 1970s. The modern hotels, good restaurants, and luxury shops are, however, gloss—and even the gloss of East Berlin is not quite so glossy as that on the other side of the wall; more important is the living standard of the ordinary people. What has the DDR's tremendous economic expansion meant to the people of East Germany in terms of the homes they live in, the food they eat, the clothes they wear, their leisure and cultural activities? How does their standard of life compare with those in other countries?

It is extremely difficult to measure living standards. There is the difficulty of comparing like with like, of comparing the quality of one product manufactured in one country with that of a similar product made elsewhere. Statistics are another problem, being presented differently even in countries having the same economic, social, and political systems. Often they are arrived at by different methods of calculation. Then there is the argument about what to include, some items being more important to one nation than to the other. Nevertheless, despite these and other problems it is possible to make certain useful comparisons of living standards in the DDR with those of certain other countries.

Difficulties in Housing

First, let us look at housing. A visitor to East Berlin, Dresden, Leipzig, Erfurt, Magdeburg, and other East German towns might well either be shocked still to see marks of war or, if he still retains the 'normal' Western image of the DDR, he would be impressed by the apparently large numbers of modern looking flats of pleasing colours and satisfactory design. If on a visit to East Germany organized by an official body he would undoubtedly be taken to see Lütten Klein, near Rostock, and Halle Neustadt. Lütten Klein will eventually be a town of 150,000, while Halle Neustadt, which in 1968 had a population of about 20,000, will provide homes for 100,000 by about 1980.[1] In their different ways both these projects are things the DDR can be proud of, but they tend to give an over-optimistic impression of housing conditions in East Germany. Housing must be one of the most pressing problems in the DDR today. An official survey carried out in 1961 spotlighted the shocking state of affairs which existed at that time. It revealed that of East German dwellings or *Wohnungen* only about 22 per cent had their own baths, only about 33 per cent had their own indoor lavatories, and that about 33 per cent had no piped water.[2] By way of comparison, in West Germany in the same year 52.4 per cent had baths, 76.5 per cent had lavatories, and all but 3 per cent had running water. In England and Wales at that time 78.7 per cent of dwellings possessed baths (not counting showers), 90 per cent had lavatories (here the figures do not distinguish between indoor and outdoor), only 2 per cent were without piped water. No doubt had Scotland and Northern Ireland been included the British figures would have been somewhat worse. In 1960 85.2 per cent of homes in the USA had baths or showers, 86.8 per cent had lavatories (again no distinction between indoor and outdoor is made), and 94 per cent were supplied with piped water. The

[1] For Lütten Klein see *Der Morgen* (9 August 1968); for Halle Neustadt see *Union Pressedienst,* Heft 10, 1968.
[2] Statistisches Jahrbuch der *DDR*, 1963, p. 208 (henceforth SJB).

average number of persons per room in 1960–1 was 1.2, 0.9, 0.7, and again 0.7 in those countries respectively.[3]

Why is the housing position so much worse in the DDR than in the other countries mentioned? East Germany suffered a great deal from war devastation which Britain and the USA did not. It may also be the case that it was the houses in agricultural districts, generally of a poorer quality, which more frequently survived the war. Schwerin, for example, and Neubrandenburg, both agricultural areas, had the worst housing conditions in 1961. Berlin and Erfurt were the best placed. Even so, of 442,292 homes in the capital, only 205,407 had their own bath, only 315,997 had their own indoor WC, and about 14,000 were without piped water. Another factor which probably worsened the East German figures was the division of larger houses to create more homes without providing extra services.

These factors would not explain the difference between housing standards in East and West Germany. Apart from a poor inheritance made worse by the war the situation has been aggravated by the large number of buildings, pre-war and post-war, occupied by the Soviet forces, and, above all, by East Germany's poor housing record. The DDR has lagged behind the nations of both Western and Communist Europe in house-building for most of the time since the war. Between 1945 and 1961 573,841 dwellings were constructed. From 1962 to 1965 a further 307,400 homes were completed.[4] This is well below the levels of construction, proportionate to population, of most European countries in those years. Moreover, the number of homes built in recent years has fluctuated downwards as well as upwards. It reached a peak in 1961, when 92,000 dwellings were constructed, fell to 87,200 in 1962, fell again to 76,000 in 1963, rose slightly to 76,600 in 1964, reached only 68,200 in 1965, slumped to 65,300 in 1966, and rose to 76,300 in 1967.[5] In 1961 West Germany built 565,000 dwellings or 100 per 10,000 of population. The DDR's total represented only 54 per 10,000 inhabitants. By 1964 the gap between the two parts of Germany had widened still further. In that year West Germany erected 623,000 dwellings or 107 per 10,000 citizens, the DDR only

[3] British Annual Official Handbook, 1966, HMSO, p. 19; Statistisches Jahrbuch für die Bundesrepublik Deutschland, 1966, p. 76; USA: Statistical Abstract of the United States, 1967, US Department of Commerce, Washington, 1967, p. 729; average number of persons per room, Statistical Abstract of the United States, 1967, pp. 890–1 (these figures are taken from the UN).
[4] 1945–61: *SJB*, 1963, p. 208. 1962–5: *SJB*, 1966, p. 241.
[5] *Statistisches Taschenbuch der DDR*, 1968, p. 71 (*STB*).

76,000 or about 45 per 10,000.[6] Homes have also got somewhat smaller in recent years. In 1963 the DDR completed only 76,000 homes but created 4.2 million square metres of living space. In 1967 76,300 homes were built, but these amounted to only 3.8 million square metres.[7]

If the situation is to get better in the DDR much more home-building will be required, for the bulk of the present housing stock is old. The 1961 survey of East German dwellings showed that 21.7 per cent of them were pre-Franco-Prussian war origin, another 23.3 per cent were built between 1870 and 1899, 19.7 per cent dated from between 1900 and 1918, while 13.6 per cent had been erected during the Weimar republic. Hitler's Reich was responsible for 11.2 per cent and 10.5 per cent were post-war buildings. Many East German homes, the survey indicated, were small. Of a total of 5,447,122, there were 731,644 with only one room, 2,105,506 with two, 1,691,063 consisted of three rooms, 633,026 managed four, and 285,883 had five or more rooms. On 31 August 1967 *Die Wirtschaft* reported that 60 per cent of East German homes were built before 1918, 24 per cent between 1914 and 1945, and 16 per cent after 1945. It further reported that only 27 per cent had baths, only 37 per cent had WCs, and that 32 per cent had no running water. The paper indicated that in provision of baths and WCs East Germans were worse off than Austrians, Czechs, Frenchmen, Swedes, and West Germans (among others).

Poor housing is part of the price the East Germans have had to pay for their post-war industrial revolution, involving so many slow maturing, and in some cases ill-advised, projects. More could have been done with the resources used until about 1956, for manpower and materials were wasted on monumental blocks of flats which few people really liked and which are costly to maintain. This must not be exaggerated, however, for most of East Germany's building has been done since then. Shortage of skilled labour, partly caused by loss of labour to the West, also slowed down many building projects.

The DDR is trying to rationalize its building methods by increasing use of pre-fabricated parts. In 1967 over 54 per cent of all homes completed were constructed in this way. According to *Die Wirtschaft* (1 August 1968), many housing projects were still behind schedule and the issue of 7 November accused some East

---

[6] *Sowjetische Besatzungszone von A–Z*, Bundesministerium für Gesamt-deutsche Fragen, Bonn, 1966, p. 546 (henceforth *SBZ von A–Z*).
[7] *STB*, 1968, p. 71.

German builders of taking longer than their West German colleagues.

As compared with the citizens of Western countries, the East German people enjoy the doubtful privilege of paying only modest rents for their homes. Most of them are rented accommodation, though the rents for new flats have been increased since the reforms started in 1963. As a proportion of their incomes they also spend less on light, gas, and heating.

More Refrigerators and Fruit

At the V Congress of the SED in 1958 Ulbricht declared that the DDR's aim was to overtake the Federal Republic in provision of consumer goods by the early 1960s. This aim proved completely unrealistic. Even so, the DDR has made substantial progress in providing its people with the household gadgets of the affluent society. Of every 100 households in 1958 only 5.1 had television sets, whereas in 1965 the number was 48 per cent, In 1958 only 2.1 per cent had refrigerators, but in 1965 the figure was 26 per cent. Washing machines were found in 1.6 per cent of households in 1958. By 1965 the figure had risen to 28 per cent.[8] In Britain in 1965 88 per cent of households had television, 39 per cent had refrigerators, and 56 per cent washing machines.[9] By the end of 1968 44 per cent of East German homes had refrigerators, 43 per cent were equipped with washing machines, and 65 per cent possessed television.[10] By that year the DDR had just about caught up with the Federal Republic in providing its citizens with television and radio, but was still behind on other consumer durables.[11] By the 1960s virtually all homes in the USA had provided themselves with these goods.

The number of private cars available to East Germans has also been rising in the 1960s. In 1958 there were only 1.6 per cent of households which possessed a car. By 1966 the number had risen to 9.4 and in 1967 it was 11 per cent. This was still very small by West European or American standards. For instance, in 1965 there were 106 cars for every thousand inhabitants in the Federal Republic as against 34 in the DDR. The number in Britain in that year was approximately the same as in West Germany.[12] In the USA 79 per cent of families had their own car in 1966.[13] The

8 *SJB*, 1966, p. 442.   9 *Observer* (2 January 1966).
10 *Der Morgen* (8 February 1969).
11 Bruno Gleitze, *Das Wirtschaftswachstum in beiden Teilen Deutschlands,* Bonn, 1968, p. 23.
12 *SJB für die BRD*, 1966, p. 106.
13 Statistical Abstract, US, 1967, p. 565.

cars available to the private motorist are either the Trabant 601, slightly larger than the BMC Mini, or the larger Wartburgs manufactured at Eisenach. Much more expensive, owing to tax, are imported Czech cars, some of which also reach the private motorist. Few people are likely to buy imported Soviet cars as they are beyond the price even better-off East Germans can afford. Even when they have the money, East Germans expect to wait up to two years for delivery of the cars they want to buy. A few West German cars are seen with East German number-plates. Their owners have managed to persuade the authorities that they are gifts from West German relatives or friends.

Impressions and statistics confirm that East Germans are eating much better than they did ten years ago and better than they did even five years ago. The patterns of change which have accompanied the arrival of relative affluence in other countries are also noticeable in East German eating habits. Average consumption of meat, poultry, fish, eggs, and rice are up and have shown steady increases in the 1960s. Consumption of real coffee is many times higher than the modest levels of the mid-1950s. Again, as in other 'affluent' countries consumption of beer, wines, and spirits is increasing from year to year. East Germans are also eating, or drinking, about double the amount of cocoa products they did ten years ago. On the other hand, and once again in line with people in other advanced nations, East Germans buy less bread and potatoes than they used to. On the negative side, the citizens of the DDR seem to have certain difficulties in obtaining a regular and increasing supply of fresh fruit. In 1966 and 1967 the consumption of fresh fruit was only about half what it had been in 1960. Consumption of tropical fruit has fluctuated but improved steadily in 1965, 1966, and 1967. Whether East Germans get tropical fruit or not depends what happens to the DDR's relations with the Third World. These relations have been developing over the last ten years and this is reflected by the variety of foodstuffs from overseas in the shops. The difficulties of providing a reasonable amount of fresh fruit probably reflect the problems still to be solved on East Germany's farms. The amount of milk drunk tends to fluctuate, but it has tended to rise in the 1960s and is above what it was in 1955.[14] Already on 25 August 1965 the West German weekly *Der Spiegel* reported that the East German population was catching up with its relatives in the West in food consumption. According to the magazine the East Germans were at that time eating

[14] *SJB,* 1966, p. 442, and *STB,* 1968, p. 137.

more butter and nearly as much sugar and meat, and drinking almost as much milk as the West Germans.

One thing which is obvious to any visitor on even the most superficial of visits to the German Democratic Republic is that people are not as well dressed as in Western countries and that, apart from those in a few expensive shops, the ready-made clothes on display in shop windows are not up to the usual Western standards. Here again, things are very much better than they were. They could be even better. It is little known that the Democratic Republic has a really thriving clothing industry with an international reputation. As *Der Spiegel* (20 October 1965) has pointed out, millions of West German women do not know that the dresses they are wearing were made in the DDR—they are often not marketed under their own labels. Official East German trade returns show considerable exports of fabrics, ready-made clothing, and footwear to Holland, Belgium and Luxembourg, Austria, Sweden, and West Germany, as well as to the Soviet Union and Eastern Europe. This is not so surprising when one considers that the textile industry in East Germany has been responsible for a number of technical innovations in the last twenty years. The best known of these is the introduction of 'Malimo' machines, named after the inventor Heinrich Mauersberger of Limbach, which do a combination of sewing and knitting. They turn out a material which is 'popular because of its interesting structure and softness. It is easy to wash and iron and hardwearing. Malimo materials are made from wool, cotton, acetate and other chemical fibres.' These machines have been exported to twenty-odd countries, including Switzerland, Spain, and Britain. At least one American firm, Frompton & Knowles-Malimo Inc. of Worcester, has bought the licence.[15] The DDR has also started to manufacture cheap, throwaway, dresses made of artificial fibres. In 1966 the DDR produced 85.3 million pairs of women's stockings and exported over 44 million pairs of them, nearly 32 million pairs to the Federal Republic. In 1964, when the DDR total was nearly 37 million pairs exported, West Germany exported $43\frac{1}{2}$ million pairs—a record. In 1966 East Germany also exported over one million pairs of leather shoes.[16] The DDR's efforts in this field were only possible on the basis of austerity at home. Stockings, for instance, cost several times what they do in West Germany and this is a cause of discontent among women in the DDR. In a report pub-

[15] *Democratic German Report* (15 May 1968).
[16] *The German View* (26 May 1965) for the West German figure; *SJB*, 1967, pp. 397, 403.

lished in *Die Wirtschaft* (1 August 1968) the East German Central Statistical Office admitted that the demand of the people for high-quality clothing, shoes, and furniture was not always met.

East Germany is said to be the world's largest exporter of furniture and most East Germans say this is one record they could do without. Production in the mid-1960s was considerably above what it was a decade earlier. Despite the large volume of exports the supply to the home market appears to have improved, though there is still a good deal of grumbling about price. East Germany is rightly proud of its imitation Persian carpets and some of these too have found their way on to the British market as well as to West Germany, Austria, and Sweden. The quality of carpets available for the home market appears to have improved but, in view of the official figures, it is difficult to see how the quantity in the shops has increased since 1955. In that year 5,069,000 square metres were produced of which 1,518,000 square metres were exported. In 1965 the figures were 11,296,000 and 4,865,000 respectively.[17] Certainly some imports were made though it is not clear how many.

Another way of looking at the movement of living standards is to compare the movement of wages with that of prices. If we do this in the case of the DDR we find that the wages of production workers, men and women, rose by 132 MDN in the five years from 1955 to 1960, and by 73 MDN between 1960 and 1965. In terms of the wage index the progress was as follows: 1955, 100; 1960, 130.4; 1965, 147.1.[18] The cost of living index stood at 110.1 in 1955, dropping to 100 in 1960, and rising slightly to 100.4 in 1965.[19] According to these official figures, therefore, more progress was made in the first five years under review than during the second. These indices would seem to contradict our earlier figures concerning consumer goods. This is because they fail to take into consideration the effective purchasing power of the East German mark (MDN). Then so many things which are now on display in East Germany's stores and shops could not be seen. Those who could went to shop in the West. East Germany's trade balance was passive, yet the government was forced to increase wages owing to losses of manpower through the open frontier. It may also be the case that the high home-building peak reached in 1960 was the result of pressure from below because, as we have seen, home building has declined since the Wall. To a much lesser extent we see this in terms of the amount of money spent on social welfare

[17] *SJB*, 1966, pp. 173, 405.
[18] Ibid., pp. 200–1.
[19] Ibid., pp. 439, 32.

and health. Though expenditure on these items has risen continuously over the decade, the amount of the increase has slackened
off since 1960.[20] The luxury shops, over 300 of them, that are
mentioned at the opening of this chapter, are also the result of
pressure, pressure from the relatively well-paid intelligentsia who
before the Wall shopped in West Berlin. The effective cost of
living in 1955, particularly for all those buying in the West, was
probably a good deal higher than what is shown in the official
index. Hence East Germans are likely to be better-off now, compared with a decade ago, than the official indices of prices and
wages show.

A Comparison with the West

An interesting West German comparison of living standards in
the Federal German Republic, Britain, and East Germany covering the year 1963 is worth looking at. This survey showed that
wages of industrial workers were higher in Britain than either West
Germany or the DDR. In that year Germans in East and West
worked roughly the same number of hours, but British workers put
in just over an hour extra a week. West Germans enjoyed the
longest holidays, followed by the East Germans who in the course
of a year got several days more than their British colleagues. East
Germans, according to this survey, got higher sick pay than
Britons though slightly less than West Germans. Retirement pensioners also did best in Federal Germany and worst in East Germany.[21] By 1968 both West Germans and East Germans had
increased their lead in shorter hours over the British. The East
Germans got a statutory five-day week in September 1967, covering all industrial employees at a time when many British workers
still did not enjoy this. They had also narrowed the gap between
themselves and the West Germans on holidays. However, the
situation in East Germany is not quite as good in respect of free
time as these figures would suggest. Many East Germans are
under strong pressure to give up some of their own time for various
social and political purposes.

In the field of medical care, which must also be counted as part
of living standards, East Germans, like West Germans, benefit from
Germany's traditionally high facilities. Until the Berlin Wall, the
DDR was suffering from a 'brain drain' among doctors, but since
then, an official West German publication reports, 'there is a

[20] *SJB*, 1966, p. 32.
[21] *Scala International*, Frankfurt/M, English edition, July 1965.

rapidly growing number of doctors and dentists.'[22] The number of doctors available to the East German population is still lower than in West Germany. In 1964 there were 947 inhabitants to a doctor in East Germany, only 696 to a doctor in the Federal Republic, and about 662 in the USA. In Britain in 1963, according to the UN, there were 840, in Sweden 960, and in USSR only 510.[23] In the same year there were 1,030 inhabitants to a doctor in the DDR. By 1965 this had dropped to 869.5 and in 1967 to about 750.[24] East Germany also provided more hospital beds for its citizens than most other countries in the 1960s, though here the position has deteriorated slightly. In 1961 there were only 106 hospital beds for every 10,000 Britons, as against 121 for every 10,000 East Germans. In 1964 the number for East Germans was the same as in 1961 and the West German figure was 106 per 10,000.[25] By 1966 there were only 119 beds for every 10,000 inhabitants in the DDR.[26]

The East German education system, also part of living standards, is discussed separately.

East Germans have many more opportunities for entertainment than most people in the West would imagine. At the 'high-brow' level there are 93 professional theatres, for instance, including several for children, and puppet theatres, as against about 200 in the UK.[27] In other words East Germany has more proportionate to population. The same is true of professional orchestras. Of course there are strong theatrical and musical traditions in Germany, but it is part and parcel of the East German state's policy to foster these. Nor must it be thought that East Germans are subjected to Communist ideology in the theatre. True, there is nothing which openly contradicts that ideology. But East Germans have access to a wide variety of plays, and films and books for that matter, from the non-Communist world. In 1964 the following foreign ensembles gave guest performances in the DDR: The Belgium National Theatre; Ballet ensemble of the Helsinki National Opera; Ballet ensemble of the Royal Opera of Sweden; Theatre Workshop of London; Opera Nazionale Italiana; Athens Piraikon Theatre; Chitrasena Ballet of India; Dancers of Ceylon; Singing and dancing ensemble of Burma; Royal Ballet of Cam-

---

[22] *SBZ von A–Z*, p. 173.
[23] *SJB für die BRD*, 1966, p. 39* for East and West Germany; UN Yearbook, 1965, p. 666, for UK, USSR, US, and Sweden.
[24] *SJB*, 1966, p. 34 for 1965; *STB*, 1968, p. 153 for 1967.
[25] *SJB für die BRD*, 1966, p. 44.
[26] *STB*, 1968, p. 153.
[27] *SJB*, 1966, p. 478.

bodia; National Ballet of Senegal; Stanislavsky Musical Theatre of Moscow; and Theatre on the Balustrade of Prague.[28] On another level, Louis Armstrong, Acker Bilk, Marlene Dietrich, and Juliette Greco have performed in East Germany. Most of Britain's 'new wave' films have been shown as well as many films from France, Italy, West Germany, and the USA too. Here financial considerations are easily as important as political ones. Among Western authors published in recent years are Dürrenmatt, O'Casey, Graham Greene, John Steinbeck, and Alan Sillitoe. Statistics about other forms of entertainment, such as dancing, are harder to come by. Using his knowledge of both countries, the writer believes East Germany has no cause for embarrassment.

Sport is another traditionally well-developed form of entertainment in Germany and Ulbricht and his colleagues have paid due tribute to this tradition. Today, with 10 per cent of the population actively taking part, there are some 1,800,000 members in 7,000 clubs.[29] Fees are negligible, facilities, by most standards, lavish. Most of the money to provide these facilities comes from the government, from industry, and from the state-run football pools. East Germany could boast of having, by the end of 1964, 202 stadia, 927 sports grounds, 8,772 practice grounds, 4,247 gymnasia, 62 indoor swimming pools, 663 outdoor pools, and 23 cycling tracks.[30] These are not just meaningless figures, they have produced results. In Melbourne in 1956, East Germans won one gold, four silver, and two bronze medals. In Rome four years later they took three gold, nine silver, and seven bronze. Even more medals followed in Tokyo and these successes were followed up in Mexico. In the 1968 Games they won nine gold, nine silver, and seven bronze, finishing in fifth place. This compared with West Germany's five gold, ten silver, and ten bronze. The West Germans were placed eighth in the medals table.

Poor Outlook for Holidays Abroad

As far as living standards are concerned, one of the biggest single causes of discontent is the difficulty East Germans experience in going on holiday, in particular in going abroad. As prosperity develops in the DDR increasing numbers of East Germans reach the income level which in West European countries enables people to holiday abroad. What is the position in East Germany?

[28] *Introducing The GDR*, Verlag Zeit im Bild, 1965, p. 75.
[29] *STB*, 1968, p. 150.
[30] *Profile of East Germany*, Harrap, London, 1966, p. 99.

The great majority of those who get away, apart from pensioners who are able to go either to West Germany or abroad, go to holiday resorts in the DDR under the auspices of the trade union movement. According to the East German economic paper, *Die Wirtschaft* (19 May 1966), over 3,800,000 East Germans took a holiday away from home in 1965, that is about 20 per cent of the total population. Of these over one million or 27.5 per cent enjoyed cheap holidays organized by the trade unions, over half a million or 15.2 per cent went on holidays through the official tourist agency, while another 650,000 (16.9 per cent) went to holiday homes run by their employers. Children and young persons made up another 22 per cent or 880,000 and they went through various official schemes or youth hostelling. Finally, 11.2 per cent—430,000—went camping, a popular recreation in Germany. These figures seem to ignore people visiting relatives in West Germany or abroad.

Although trade union holiday schemes, even more than holiday camps in Britain, have given many people the chance of a cheap holiday, many people would like to get away by themselves. This is not so easy to do. Hotel accommodation in the DDR is very limited. True, in the last few years some impressive hotels have been built and others renovated in East Germany's main towns, but these are meant mainly for German and foreign businessmen, and for foreign tourists. The tariffs they charge are high, though competitive by most Western standards. Even those who can afford the prices cannot always be sure of finding a room. East Germany can offer her tourists historical towns in plenty, a good stretch of Baltic coast where the sun does not always shine, and the scenic beauty of 'Saxony-Switzerland', but an increasing number of East Germans yearn for more, they want to get abroad. They hear from relatives in the West who have been to Spain, Italy, or France, and perhaps Yugoslavia, Bulgaria, and Romania too, and want to know why their opportunities are so limited.

The limitation of these opportunities is shown by the fact that in 1964 only 465,746 East Germans managed to get abroad as tourists. Their average stay was 4.2 days. Luckier were 95,635 of these whose visits lasted on average 13.6 days. In that year an estimated 4½ million Britons went abroad on holiday, in other words, proportionate to population, three times as many British people went abroad. The East German government, if not the people, may have been tolerably pleased with this situation, for in 1960 only 53,285 East Germans went abroad as tourists and in 1962 the number was only 47,948. Moreover, in 1965 the number of East German tourists jumped to 600,110, though the average length of their trips dropped to 3.8 days. But 122,764 stayed abroad for an average of 13.1 days. In 1967 over 604,000 East Germans went abroad with the official tourist agency.[31] In that year visas were abolished for East Germans visiting a number of socialist countries and many are said to have gone abroad privately, particularly to Czechoslovakia and Poland. The position then is improving and is likely to go on doing so, for as the East German economy gets stronger it can both find exports to pay for these holidays and build the facilities to attract more foreign tourists. Economics apart though, political factors are extremely important in explaining why East Germans have not made their appearance as tourists in Western countries. Here the question of recognition is a factor but not the important one East German spokesmen make out. Non-recognition does not prevent trade, though it probably makes it more cumbersome. Non-recognition probably puts off Western tourists from going to the DDR which in turn makes more difficult, for currency reasons, the flow in the other direction. However, the fact that few East Germans have visited Yugoslavia as tourists—a country with which the DDR has been enjoying 'socialist, fraternal, relations'—is an indication of the importance of political factors other than recognition.

At the present time East Germans can only travel in the 'socialist camp', the largest numbers going, up to 1968, to Czechoslovakia, Bulgaria, and Poland. Others visit the USSR, Hungary, and Romania. A handful have managed more exotic places such as Cuba and Mongolia. In addition, thousands of East Germans went abroad on cultural, party, parliamentary, and technical exchanges, quite apart from those on diplomatic or trade missions or studying abroad. Such travellers are mainly members of the intelligentsia going not only to Eastern Europe but to the West and especially to the countries of the Third World.

From being relatively good compared with those in the Western zones in the immediate post-war period, living standards in East Germany fell behind those of the West after about 1948–9. After 1953, especially after 1956, great progress was made in raising standards. But the crisis connected with the events of 1960–2 slowed things up. Since that time substantial improvements have been registered, though the housing situation remains critical.

[31] *STB*, 1968, p. 152.

Chapter 8

Education: Mixing Mental and Manual Labour

Education before 1945

O NE OF THE better features of the Soviet bloc states is the great educational revolution they have fostered. East Germany has also taken part in this revolution.

East Germany's education system today reflects its highly complex and developed economy with its great need for skilled labour of all kinds. Indeed, as we shall see, the state deliberately seeks to make the education system conform to the needs of the economy. The education system of the DDR also reflects East Germany's determination to overcome the legacy of Nazism and German imperialism, and the social revolution which has been under way in the DDR, and before 1949 in the Soviet Zone, during the past twenty years. Part and parcel of this revolution has been the harnessing of the school, college, university, and youth movement in the service of the SED's version of Communist ideology—the least desirable aspect of this great educational development. Finally, and not least, the East German educational system reflects the changing ideas on education within the framework of Communist ideology, including the interest in technical and industrial training which finds expression in traditional Marxist and German educational thinking. In order to understand the changes which have taken place since 1945 we must look briefly at education in pre-war Germany.

Before 1933 the administration of education was fairly decentralized, being the responsibility of the regional governments of the *Länder*. Germany's schools and universities at that time reflected the social, religious, and even political divisions which kept Germans apart. Class or social differences were reflected in the structure of the school system—the free elementary school (*Volksschule*) for the masses; the fee-paying intermediate school (*Mittelschule*) for the lower middle-class; and the secondary school (*Höhere Schule*), with fees double those of the *Mittelschule,* for the upper middle class. They were also shown by the relative infrequency of transfer from one type of school to another, and by the low proportion of university students (6 per cent in 1930) from the 'lower class' (manual workers, shop assistants, etc.). Religious division was expressed chiefly at the level of primary education, in the prevalence of the confessional school (*Bekenntnisschule*), in which the teachers were Catholics or Protestants. It was their acute differences on this subject which prevented the moderate parties of the Weimar republic—the Catholic Centre Party, the Democrats, and the Social Democrats—from ever being able to formulate a national education policy.

There was also the tension between the two ideals of state service and general culture which chiefly affected the higher levels of education in the secondary schools and in the universities. The elementary schools were dominated by the idea of preparing children to be useful servants of the state, the intermediate schools took on a sharply vocational character. But in the secondary schools and in the universities the idea of general culture as the aim of education received more than lip service. Yet, even in the secondary schools, the other idea—that of the Prussian spirit of service—had its effects. Discipline was often harsh, teaching was along authoritarian lines and left little room for the pupil to exercise imagination and initiative. With the growth of social democracy before 1914 and with the coming of the Weimar republic this state of affairs came under attack, and in some areas of Weimar Germany, those under Social Democratic governments, certain limited changes were made.

Even in nineteenth-century Germany technical and vocational training was relatively important. In an effort no doubt to catch up with her rivals many technical colleges of a high level were established—Aachen (1870), Berlin-Charlottenburg (1879), Breslau (1910), Brunswick (1877), Darmstadt (1877), Dresden (1890), Hanover (1879), etc. Even before this certain states had established special technical institutions—the Mining Academy of Freiberg in Saxony, for instance, established in 1765. At a lower level there were the continuation schools (*Fortbildungsschulen*), trade schools (*Berufsschulen*), and technical schools (*Fachschulen*). The emphasis in all three was strongly vocational.

As for the universities attendance grew from 13,000 in 1871 and 21,000 in 1880, to just under 34,000 in 1900. In 1895 out of a population of about 52 million there was an academic enrolment of 28,500. Very often the students were the sons of those who had academic qualifications—high officials, judges and lawyers, university professors, secondary school-teachers, higher army officers, clergymen, and medical practitioners. In addition, about a third were the sons of 'merchants' and 'industrialists'. Of the students at Prussian universities between 1887 and 1890 little more than one in a thousand were the sons of workers.

Before 1933 there were 23 universities in Germany with something like 95,000 students (about 17,000 women). Students got there by passing their matriculation exam or *Abitur* and having enough money to pay their fees, usually paid by their parents. Students had a great deal of freedom to do as much or as little work as they liked. They also were free to move from one university to another during their undergraduate days. The regional or state governments of Germany seem to have had far greater control over their universities than pre-war British governments. This control was exercised chiefly over their finance and over the appointment to professorial chairs. In addition, the senior members of the teaching staff were civil servants, and appointments to professorships, though three names were usually submitted by the faculty concerned, were made by the Education Ministry. The professors thus appointed were required to take the oath of allegiance to the state. Although academics were supposed to enjoy *Lehrfreiheit* (freedom in teaching), a Prussian law of 1899 laid down that 'the deliberate promotion of Social Democratic aims is inconsistent with holding a position in a royal university'. There were also many cases where the state authorities refused to make an appointment and there was a general prejudice against Jews. Obviously this situation helped to produce a largely conformist academic profession. Many members of this profession were totally opposed to the Weimar republic but nothing was done to remove them. There were many incidents of open hostility to the republic. In 1922, for example, the Heidelberg physicist Lenard flew the Kaiser's colours above his institute unrebuked, while a socialist student who removed them was given a year's imprisonment; and a Marburg professor could store illegal arms for the Nazis to the knowledge, and with the silent connivance, of most of the university. Not all the university staff held these views. The fact, however, that the Nazis in their attempts to 'clean up' the universities removed relatively few academics—between 1933 and 1938 about one-third of university posts changed hands for *all* reasons including normal retirement—shows that many had much in common with National Socialism. What of the students? They too tended

12 * *

to be conformist and rightist organized, as many of them were in the duelling *Verbindungen*. Apart from these influential bodies which operated under the Weimar republic no less than under the *Kaiserreich* before 1918, there were the Nazis. Their influence increased with that of the Nazi Party in general. In 1931, for instance, they made great headway in capturing the representative organs of student opinion, the 'Asta' committees. The results of the elections to these committees for nine of the 23 universities of the Weimar republic are available and in all nine cases the Nazis won. The majority of students, it must be pointed out, did not bother to vote.

When the Nazis seized power, therefore, they found widespread support among the teaching profession at all levels as well as among the students. Having noted this fact we need not detail all the measures brought about by Hitler to make education serve his purpose, save to say that it became highly centralized, anti-intellectual, subservient to war preparations, and more vocational than ever; and that the numbers of university students were drastically reduced from 118,556 in 1931 to 49,543 in 1939. Only those whose racial descent, physical fitness, and record of service in the Hitler Youth were regarded as satisfactory were admitted to the universities.[1]

The School System

Remarkably perhaps, almost all schools in the Soviet Zone were opened for teaching on 1 October 1945. This must have represented a considerable achievement on the part of the Soviet administration and their German helpers. Approximately a fourth of all school buildings had been either totally destroyed or needed extensive repairs. Many schools had hardly any teaching materials, furniture, or heating facilities. Most school textbooks could not be used because of their Nazi orientation. Owing to lack of food, clothing, and shelter, and to the break in their education, it was not easy to get all the children back into the schools merely by opening their doors. The biggest single problem, however, was providing enough teachers to go round. It was decided that many of the existing staff were not fitted, because of their activities under the Nazis, to carry on shaping the minds of the young. Accordingly, 78 per cent of the teachers in the area of the present Democratic

---

[1] The whole of this section is based on *Germany II*, British Naval Intelligence (March 1944), B.R. 529 A (Rest.). The figures for student and social composition 1871–1900 are taken from Fritz K. Ringer, 'Higher Education in Germany in the Nineteenth Century', *Journal of Contemporary History*, Vol. 2, Number 3, 1967.

Republic were removed. Attempts were made to replace them by emergency-trained teachers chosen from among those persecuted by the Nazis, former emigrants, members of the pre-1933 working-class parties, and others against whom there was nothing on record. Naturally such an experiment could not be wholly successful. Some of the would-be teachers had only a very sketchy education themselves and because of the great demand for teachers the courses they took must of necessity have been short and rudimentary. In some cases too, the appropriate authorities were probably over-zealous in weeding out former 'brown' teachers. But this was preferable to exposing the children to further doses of Nazi ideology. In the school year 1945–6 a total of 15,000 'new teachers'—as those emergency-trained were called—were put into the schools. They were joined the following year by another 25,000. By 1949, when the East German state was set up, there were 65,207 teachers, 45,244 of them 'new teachers'. In 1966 the DDR had 128,877 fully qualified school-teachers; 93 per cent of them trained since the end of the war.[2]

The Soviets set up a German Administration for Education in the summer of 1945 to reorganize the educational system. The individual *Länder* or regions of the Soviet Zone adopted a model 'Law for the Democratisation of the German School' in 1946, which was to be the basis of the new school system. The Law sought to educate the young 'to be capable of thinking for themselves and acting responsibly, able and willing to serve the community.' The Law also determined that the new education should be free of militarist, imperialist, or racialist ideology. In addition it set the educational authorities three other basic tasks : to break the educational privileges of the old propertied classes; to bridge the gap between the schools in urban areas and those in the villages; to raise the academic content of the schools above the pre-war level. It is one thing to legislate and another to put things into operation, especially in the difficult conditions of post-war Germany. But over the years the first and third of those objects have been achieved and great progress has been made on the second. The Law also abolished fees for secondary schools.

Under the 1946 Law all children had to attend an eight-year elementary school or *Grundschule*. This replaced the pre-war *Volksschule*. After eight years in the elementary school children went on to the four-year secondary school or received vocational training. A special effort was made to improve conditions in the

[2] *Democratic German Report* (24 June 1966).

rural areas where the number of one-room, one-teacher, schools fell from over 4,000 in 1946 to 668 in 1949.[3]

The German Administration for Education was made responsible for all rules and regulations governing the schools of the Soviet Zone. All teaching materials and curricula had also to be agreed by the German Administration. Thus, from the start, Communist ideology could make its way into the classroom, for the German Administration was under Soviet/SED control. At this stage, however, such ideology was not paraded brazenly or aggressively. The regional governments were empowered to appoint teachers and run the schools, but in most, if not in all, cases, the Ministers of Education in these governments were SED members.

At university level various methods were used to eliminate old influences and reorientate higher education in the SED's sense. The rules for the admission of students issued by the German Administration in 1947 severely regulated the type of student who could be admitted. The children of the urban and rural working class, providing they had not been Nazi Party members, together with those persecuted by the Nazis, were to be given first preference. These were followed by those non-proletarians who had not been members of the Nazi Party or its auxiliary organizations. Third in order of preference came those who had only been in the Hitler Youth. Nominal Nazis and former officers could only be admitted after careful study of each case. Former active Nazis and 'enemies of democracy' were not to be granted admission. Another tool of change in higher education was the *Vorstudienanstalten* which offered matriculation courses for mature students who had not had the chance to gain their university entrance qualifications in the normal way. These were started in 1947 and were of particular help to those of working-class origin, ex-servicemen, and some ex-political prisoners. In 1949 they were transformed into *Arbeiter und Bauern Fakultäten* or Workers' and Peasants' Faculties. Under the new title they became more directly political and were used even more eagerly to change the social composition of the universities. In the years before the death of Stalin in 1953 there was also direct discrimination against potential students of middle-class background. But this policy has been gradually abandoned.[4]

In May 1949 the German Administration was given more influence over university teaching, research, admissions, and staff

---

[3] Dr Karl-Heinz Günther and others, *Education In The German Democratic Republic*, Leipzig, 1962, pp. 11–12; see also Helmut Klein, *Polytechnische Bildung und Erziehung in der DDR*, Rowohlt, Hamburg, 1962.

[4] Ernst Richert, *Das zweite Deutschland. Ein Staat der nicht sein darf*, Fischer Bücherei, Frankfurt/M, 1966, p. 151.

appointments at the expense of the regional governments. At the same time the university rectors were given more power on the campuses, the rectors by this time being individuals the SED thought it could trust. A new office of *Studentendekan* was created, the holder of which was responsible for admissions, discipline, grants, and welfare. He was appointed on the proposal of the regional Education Minister with the agreement of the German Administration and was enjoined to work with the 'democratic organizations' on the campus. Another move to bring the universities in line with the SED was to make the Marxist version of social science a compulsory subject for all students. This was announced in August 1950. The universities were formally brought under central control by a decree of 22 February 1951. This set up the *Staatssekretariat für Hochschulwesen,* in effect a Ministry of Higher Education. The decree spoke quite clearly about the centralization of higher education and, among other things, laid down that the needs of the economy had to be considered when planning courses. In the same year the German two-term academic year was abolished in favour of the Soviet ten-month academic year.

Apart from laws and decrees the SED gradually increased its control over education, and over the universities in particular, by getting its own members strategically placed or through its control of the Free German Youth. Sometimes it has relied on the more direct method of using the secret police to deal with obstructors. This was particularly the case in the early post-war period and again in the years 1956–8 when there was unrest in connection with the 'de-Stalinization' and the Hungarian revolution. However, as the East German frontier was open, at least in Berlin, until 1961 the SED often felt the need for caution lest it lose too many of its future intelligentsia. The open frontier also meant that those who opposed Unity Party control of education often went West.[5] In the period 1954–61 Western sources estimate that nearly 18,000 school-teachers left the DDR as well as about 770 university teachers.[6]

In 1952 Stalin revived the traditional Marxist idea of polytechnical instruction in schools, but in the years immediately following his death his heirs were concerned with other problems. In 1956 Khrushchev called for its implementation. Shortly after it was introduced in the USSR, the DDR followed suit in 1958. So much for the formulative period in the development of the DDR's

[5] E. Richert, *Sozialistische Universität,* Colloquium Verlag, West Berlin, 1967.
[6] *SBZ von A–Z,* Bonn, 1966, p. 146.

system of education. How has it worked in recent years? Compulsory education in East Germany, which starts at six and continues to 16, takes place in a 'Ten-year Comprehensive Polytechnical High School' (*Die zehnklassige allgemeinbildende polytechnische Oberschule*). The tasks and responsibilities of this co-educational establishment, like those of all other educational institutions of the Democratic Republic, were set out in the Education Law of February 1965 : 'The High School gives a modern, socialist, general training (*Bildung*) as the basis for every further training and for professional activity. In the High School training and education are to be closely related to life, work and with the practice of socialist construction. The High School educates the young people to be conscious, socialist, citizens, who take an active part in the life of society.'[7] The work of this school is divided into three stages or *Stufen*. In the first stage, covering the classes 1 to 3, the emphasis is naturally on the three 'R's' plus sport, music, drawing, gardening, and 'a first look at the economy of the local area' in which the school is situated. In the second stage, classes 4 to 6, natural science, Russian, history, geography, and civics (Communist version) are added. The pupils are also given their first careers' orientation talks. Pupils in the third stage, classes 7 to 10, start what is regarded as being at the very core of the system, 'polytechnical instruction'. This involves practical work in the factories or on the farms for 4 hours a week out of a total of 34–6 hours in school. This practical work is designed to help pupils to see how the scientific theories they have learned—in physics for instance—can be related to life, and generally to bring pupils into contact with the world of the majority of adults. For many it will mean the start of their training for their future trade. Polytechnical instruction has its roots both in the ideas of Marx and Engels and as mentioned above in the discussions of educationalists on how to equip the young for life in the new industrial age.

In addition to the Ten-year Comprehensives, there are also the 'Twelve-class Extended Comprehensive Polytechnical High School' (*die twölfklassige erweiterte polytechnische Oberschule*), special schools (*Sonderschulen*) for children with physical or mental disabilities, and a handful of schools for specially talented children.

Pupils at the Extended Polytechnics are selected from those who have completed the 8th class of the ten-class schools. Selection is based on examination results in school subjects, interviews, etc. These children have a better chance than the others of proceeding

---

[7] *Unser Bildungssystem – wichtiger Schritt auf dem Wege zur gebildeten Nation*, Kanzlei des Staatsrates der DDR, 1965, p. 95.

to higher education. It is at such schools that pupils are prepared for the traditional German *Abitur* (which is roughly the equivalent of the British GCE 'A' Level). They too undergo polytechnical training. Indeed they are trained as skilled workers at the same time as they are undergoing academic training. For example, the writer met a young man in Dresden who had gained his *Abitur* and his certificate as a qualified bricklayer at the same time. He wanted to study medicine. Like other would-be students he had to complete a year's practical work before being accepted at a university. In theory young men are also liable to be called up for military training, in practice many are either not called up at all, are deferred, or do their service at the same time as they are studying. As far as the statistics of East German schools are concerned, in 1965 there were 2,273,587 pupils at 8,051 ten-class schools, 85,279 attending 303 twelve-class schools, and 66,706 attending special schools. The ratio of pupils to full-time staff in the DDR was 20.3 to 1 in 1964. In West Germany in the same year it was 30 to 1. In the Democratic Republic in 1965 this ratio had improved to 20 to 1. It has been getting steadily better throughout the 1960s. The average class in the ten-class schools comprised 27.6 pupils, as against 26.1 in the twelve-class schools, and 16.3 in the special schools. Classes in the twelve-class and special schools have tended to increase in the 1960s but those in the ten-class schools have been getting slightly smaller.[8] The number of schools has also been falling over the last decade, in the case of the ten-class schools by nearly 200, which seems to indicate a modernization of school buildings.

What do the East German educational authorities hope to get from the polytechnical, vocational side of the education they give to their young people? Well, they can claim they are getting back to Marxist fundamentals. Karl Marx explained the fundamental idea behind polytechnical education one hundred years ago in *Das Kapital*:

Modern Industry ... through its catastrophes imposes the necessity of recognising, as a fundamental law of production, variation of work, consequently fitness of the labourer for varied work, consequently the greatest possible development of his varied aptitudes ... Modern Industry ... compels society, under penalty of death, to replace the detail-worker of to-day, crippled by life-long repetition of one and the same trivial operation, and

[8] West Germany: *Germany Reports IV Science And Education*, Press & Information Office, Federal Government of Germany, 1964, p. 15. DDR: *SJB der DDR*, 1966, p. 463.

thus reduced to the mere fragment of a man, by the fully developed individual, fit for a variety of labours, ready to face any change of production, and to whom the different social functions he performs, are but so many modes of giving free scope to his own natural and acquired powers. One step already spontaneously taken towards effecting this revolution is the establishment of technical and agricultural schools, and of 'écoles d'enseignement professionnel', in which the children of the working-men receive some little instruction in technology and in the practical handling of the various implements of labour ... there can be no doubt that when the working class comes into power, as inevitably it must, technical instruction, both theoretical and practical, will take its proper place in the working-class schools. There is also no doubt that such revolutionary ferments, the final result of which is the abolition of the old division of labour, are diametrically opposed to the capitalistic form of production, and to the economic status of the worker corresponding to that form.[8a]

Marx and Engels, then, believed that part and parcel of the socialist society was the education of many-sided individuals who would not be restricted to spending their lives in one small part of the productive process. They also believed it was necessary to overcome the division between mental and manual labour and between the 'two cultures'. In the first post-war decade East German educationalists had had their hands full coping with the problems left by the war and had had little time to experiment in the direction of a completely new organizational and intellectual set-up in education. Though it is only fair to point out that some educationalists were having thoughts on the subject, it must be admitted that the really big influence was the educational changes being introduced in the USSR. At the 20th Congress of the Soviet Communist Party in 1956 the then Secretary of the Party, N. S. Khrushchev, supported the idea of polytechnical education by stating that :

A big shortcoming of our school system is that the instruction is divorced from life to some extent; those who finish school are insufficiently prepared for practical work. Although the directives of the 19th Party Congress ... called for measures to introduce polytechnical instruction in the schools, this matter is moving ahead very slowly. ... To strengthen their ties with life the schools must not only introduce new subjects which teach the

[8a] Karl Marx, *Das Kapital*, translated from 3rd German edition, Swan, Sonnenschein & Co. Ltd., London, 1908, pp. 493-4.

pupils the fundamentals of technology and production, but also systematically accustom them to working in factories, collective and state farms, experimental plots and school workshops.[9]

In turn the Soviets could claim they were carrying into effect a classic Marxist ideal: 'Out of the factory system . . . springs the germ of the education of the future which for *all* children over a certain age will be a combination of work, formal teaching and learning and sport, not only as a method of raising social production but as the only means of producing universally educated people.'[10] One East German publication put the theory in the following terms:

> Through polytechnical training and education the pupils gain a basic knowledge of modern production, i.e., of the construction, application and method of handling the most important tools, machines, instruments and measuring apparatus, the main features of socialist economic policy, the technology and economy of the main branches of production and socialist organisation of work. The pupils learn the elementary application of tools, apparatus and machines. An important part of polytechnical education and training is a fundamental knowledge of mathematics and natural sciences. They are an indispensable prerequisite for the grasping of natural laws and their application in socialist production. Through their own productive work the pupils learn the part played by work in the development of society, as well as the efforts of the workers and farmers, and experience at first hand the principles of socialist morals at work. Honour and respect for work and the working people is awakened in them. They become used to physical work and their need to work for socialist society is developed. It is, however, false to see polytechnical training as simply the acquisition of technical abilities.[11]

Some critics of this polytechnical instruction given in East Germany have claimed that it is merely a system of cheap juvenile labour in a country short of labour. This seems hardly likely. In many cases factory managers have been only lukewarm or even hostile to the scheme because they have found it difficult to integrate the young people into the work of the enterprises. In addition,

[9] N. S. Khrushchev, 'Report of the Central Committee, 20th Congress of the Communist Party of the Soviet Union', Soviet News Booklet, No. 4, London, 1956, pp. 63–4.
[10] Dr Karl-Heinz Günther, op. cit., p. 81.
[11] Ibid., pp. 82–3.

many do not relish the idea of taking on the responsibility for the welfare and safety of the pupils allocated to them. Often production workers have to be diverted to supervise them and this can be costly. It need not be doubted that at least in some instances pupils regard this instruction merely as a welcome relief from the classroom and that many learn little of future practical value. Pupils, particularly those intending to go on to higher education, and parents have complained that they have enough to do with their very extensive academic studies, including by this time a second foreign language which is usually English, with their Marxist-Leninist studies, and with their serious physical education, in which they must also take an examination, and, not least, their Free German Youth activities. Perhaps the East German education-alists and their East European colleagues with their elaborate theorizing promise themselves too much from the polytechnical experiment. And there are already signs that the original enthusiasm has abated. Nevertheless, there are points in its favour. One would expect that it does ease those who will later work in factories and on farms into their future work. Possibly it persuades some, especi-ally girls, that there is more to be gained from life in learning a production skill rather than taking up dead-end jobs or relatively unskilled work in the service trades. Above all, as the writer knows from personal experience, it can help those who will not later do manual work to understand something of the life and work of the majority of citizens in any industrial community. Such bridge-building could be an important factor in promoting social harmony.

What are the prospects for those who do not go to the Twelve-class Extended Comprehensives? In theory they can get their uni-versity entrance qualifications in a number of ways. They can attend a factory school (*Betriebsoberschule*), taking a matriculation course. They can attend a course for a special qualifying exam (*Sonderreifeprüfung*)—roughly 1,900 were taking such a course in 1963–4. These courses are organized at *Volkshochschulen* which are roughly similar to British Further Education colleges. They can attend the above-mentioned Workers' and Peasants' Faculties and they can attend evening classes. In 1961 there were 5,557 industrial employees taking courses of university level. This number rose to 9,333 in 1966.[12] The proportion of full-time university students who have not attended the Extended Polytechnics is probably small. There are no statistics on this so far as the writer is aware, but other statistics lead to this conclusion. In 1966 17,080 pupils took the *Abitur* at Extended Polytechnical High Schools.

[12] *SJB*, 1967, p. 471.

They would presumably be seeking admission, after their practical year, in 1967. In that year only 16,450 students gained admission to universities in the DDR on a full-time basis.[13]

Higher Education

Who are the lucky ones who gain admission to East Germany's universities and what do they study? In 1967 there were 74,660 full-time students at 44 universities and other institutions of higher education. This compared with 27,822 in 1951 and 78,405 in 1963.[14] The latest figure is, proportionate to population, a little lower than that of the Federal German Republic, and, owing to the expansion in the 1960s, lower than the British figure on the same basis. In addition to the full-time students there were also some 28,900 external students in the German Democratic Republic in 1967. These students doing university degree courses are effectively part-time and operate through a system of local tutors, correspondence with their universities, and visits to the universities for special tutoring, advice, and seminars. If one includes these students in the number of East Germans doing university courses, the DDR would have a higher proportion of students to total population than the Federal German Republic. As for the social composition of the universities of East Germany, 39.1 per cent of the full-time students in 1966 were from the working class as against 48.7 per cent in 1962. There were 23.5 per cent of students who came from white-collar backgrounds as against 20.5 per cent in 1962. The percentage from the intelligentsia rose in the same period from 15.9 to 19.7. Those whose parents were said to belong to 'production co-operatives', which could include craftsmen and certain other trades organized on co-operative lines as well as farmers, made up 7.2 per cent in 1967. The proportion of those unclassified went up from 3.1 per cent in 1962 to 10.5 per cent in 1967. The proportion of working-class students was at its height during the period 1950–5. Like most British students, the bulk—61,400 in 1967—of East German students receive grants.[15] This compares well with the situation in the Federal German Republic where, in the academic year 1963–4, for instance, 57.7 per cent of the total and 66 per cent of the female students studied either at the expense of their parents or of their spouses. Only 11.2 per cent of all students and 9.4 per cent of women were receiving grants under

[13] *SJB*, 1967, p. 466 for *Abitur*; *STB*, 1968, p. 145 for admissions.
[14] *STB*, 1968, p. 144; *SJB*, 1967, p. 476 for 1951.
[15] *SJB*, 1963, p. 425 for 1962; *STB*, 1968, p. 144 for 1967. For grants in 1967, *STB*, 1968, p. 144.

the *Honnefer Modell* scheme, which is the main means of dispensing scholarship funds in West Germany.[16] As for the social composition of the West German student body, only about 5 to 6 per cent of university students are from the working class.[17] As for the general situation of West German education, Professor Ralf Dahrendorf, a leading Free Democratic educationalist and sociologist, summed it up as follows :

> One of the much debated points about German schools has considerable relevance for German society as a whole, and touches on a most painful aspect of German history and German society today. This is the very general belief among Germans that when you get down to it, you can't do anything about the world, about the way it is, and that in schools, essentially, you have to take the children as they are; it is pointless to expect to change them. Some of them who come from working-class families simply have bad homes, and it is therefore hopeless to try to get them to the *Abitur* unless they are exceptionally gifted, in which case they will probably be able to manage despite their parents. This widespread fatalism, this general mood of disbelief in the possibility of bringing about any real change in the world . . . is true not only in regard to the school in Germany . . . Educational defeatism is part of a somewhat fatalistic attitude to human beings and to things in general, and is one of the reasons for the high drop-out from educational institutions, especially those which go beyond basic education. And it is equally pronounced in the universities. There again, we have a drop-out of about 50 per cent, and in some subjects, notably in the philosophical faculties, of 70 per cent. In other words, no particular attempt is made to take teaching seriously.

In Britain, where the number of students in higher education rose from 50,002 in 1938–9 to 337,000 in the academic year 1966–7, the percentage of working-class students is about 20–25 per cent.[18]

The East German Ministry responsible for Higher and Technical Education, *Ministerium für Hoch und Fachschulwesen*, regulates the flow of students into the various faculties to ensure that the different sectors of the economy and administration are fed

[16] Statistisches Jahrbuch für die Bundesrepublik Deutschland, 1967, Wiesbaden, p. 98.

[17] Richard Hiscocks, *Germany Revived*, Gollancz, London, 1966, p. 158. The quotation which follows is from Prof. R. Dahrendorf. 'The Crisis in German Education', *Journal of Contemporary History*, Vol. 2, Number 3, 1967, p. 143.

[18] Financial Times Survey of Britain's Universities, *Financial Times* (11 March 1968).

with the right number of recruits at the right time, and to ensure that new graduates have no difficulty in getting jobs. The SED newspaper *Neues Deutschland* of 22 June 1965 quoted the deputy State Secretary in charge of Higher Education as saying that the chances of getting a university place were good if the interests of the applicant were in line with those of society. However, those hoping to study biology, pharmacy, psychology, foreign trade, librarianship, medicine, veterinary science, journalism, and languages would have little chance. The Secretary informed those intending to study that in future a central agency in Magdeburg would be in charge of sorting out and selecting would-be students. He also stressed that the *Abitur* would be the decisive factor in deciding their future. All candidates now fill in a card which is processed by machine.

The Ministry sees to it that large numbers of pupils are enrolling for courses in natural science and technology. In 1962, with roughly 3,000 more full-time university students, there were some 8,856 students of mathematics and the natural sciences. In 1965, with roughly the same number of students as 1967, there were 7,599 taking courses in these subjects. The total had risen to over 9,000 in 1967. The numbers studying technology in these three years were 18,930, 19,524, and 19,579. The medical faculties declined in numbers from 13,801 in 1962 to 12,133 in 1967, while those studying agriculture, forestry, and veterinary science rose from 4,912 in 1962 to 5,908 in 1967. There was an almost universal decline in the numbers of those studying social science subjects and the arts though theology retained a relatively good place. In 1962 there were 456 theological students as against 613 in 1967. Those undergoing teacher-training increased from 18,899 in 1962 to 20,296 in 1967.[19] One sees how strong the emphasis on certain subjects in East Germany is, if one makes certain comparisons with developments in the United Kingdom. It is possible to do this for the academic year 1965–6. In that year there were some 158,000 students at higher educational establishments in the UK plus about another 7,000 at technical colleges doing degree courses. In the DDR there were 74,500 full-time students at the same level. Yet in the DDR over 27,000 students were studying technological subjects as against about 31,000 in the UK. And East Germany, a highly industrial country, had many more students of agriculture, forestry, and veterinary science than the UK—over 8,000 as against about 3,700. In medical studies the DDR had proportionately more

[19] *STB*, 1968, p. 146.

students though in absolute terms the UK had a larger number.[20]

It is the intention of the East German authorities further to increase the proportion of students doing science and vocation-orientated courses. In October 1968 the DDR State Council decided on still more changes in higher education. The Minister for Higher and Technical Education, Professor Dr Giessmann, explained in *Der Morgen* (6 October 1968 and again on 4 January 1969) that these involved greater emphasis on co-operation between the universities and industry in research, planning courses, and so on, more emphasis on economics, management studies, cybernetics and—so the *Democratic German Report* (30 October 1968)—'a compulsory course in electronic data processing for all students'. The reform also meant the concentration of research in fewer and more specialized centres. About 900 institutes were transformed into 190 *Sektionen*. The traditional university senates were abolished and replaced by social councils (*Gesellschaftliche Räte*) consisting of professors, representatives of industry, students, and others from the mass organizations. The reform also called for the introduction of a scheme by which university teachers would spend a period in industry to improve the practical side of their qualifications.

These reforms will greatly interest university teachers in other countries. In Britain in particular, in the last few years, there has been increasing debate about the role of higher education in the age of technical revolution, worry about the growing cost of the universities, concern to concentrate research capacities more economically and get them geared to the needs of industry. There has also been a rapid extension of management courses and attempts to persuade students to read socially desirable subjects such as maths, technology, and physics. This would seem to be necessary. But there are dangers. Too much emphasis on the vocational side could lead to a destruction of the universities' traditional function, a function which is still valid, that of producing broadly educated, intellectually disciplined, thinking people. It could lead to a serious decline of pure research which often produces great practical changes in the long run. In East Germany universities have long ceased to be independent, but the latest reform with outside control exercised through the social councils could mean one further step in the direction of the elimination of the intellectually unorthodox.

Behind the university-trained scientists and technologists of the

[20] UK: Statistics of Education 1965, Part III, HMSO, pp. 129, 132; DDR: *SJB*, 1966, pp. 474–5.

DDR stand a growing army of technologists and other skilled personnel who are the product of the technical colleges or *Fachschulen*. There were 52,600 of these students undergoing full-time instruction in 1966. The number has been rising throughout the sixties.[21] The range of subjects is wide but once again the bias is towards science and technology. It is difficult to be exact about the level reached by these students. Entrance requirements are very roughly those of GCE 'O' Level, plus completion of a skilled trade training. But these students are on a higher level than skilled workers who are trained elsewhere. Another important group studying in the *Fachschulen* are teacher-trainees. There were 14,579 of them in 1966 and they were mainly destined for nursery schools, technical colleges of various kinds, and children's homes. Another large group not included in the university students are medical technicians taking courses at fifty-odd medical schools in East Germany. Officially, these medical schools belong to the network of *Berufsschulen* or vocational schools. There were 1,145 of these in 1966 with a total of 446,170 students on their books.[22] It is at these schools that the skilled workers are trained as well as some of those in the less academic professions. The high figure for enrolments probably covers most East Germans between the ages of 16 and 18, for all are required to continue some form of part-time education up to the age of eighteen. All these figures exclude those doing various courses including university degrees at evening institutes.

Teacher Training

What about those who keep this highly complex educational system in operation, the teachers and lecturers? What sort of training do they get? At present the arrangements are roughly as follows : nursery-school teachers qualify at pedagogic schools (*Pädagogische Schulen*) after a two-year training. Entrance requirements to this course are successful completion of the Ten-class High School followed by several years' work in production, combined with attendance at a part-time continuation school. The number of these teachers rose from about 21,000 in 1954 to over 30,000 in 1964 and over 34,500 in 1966. In the same period the number of children in their care rose from over 290,000 to over 533,000. The number increased again in 1967 when about 45 per cent of all children between the ages of three and six were in some form of nursery school or other.[23] Teachers for the first stage of

---

[21] *SJB,* 1967, p. 473. [22] Ibid., p. 467.
[23] Ibid., p. 461 for 1954–66; *STB,* 1968, p. 141 for 1967.

the Ten-class High School attend a three-year course at a teacher-training establishment. Entry requirements are similar to those for the nursery teacher course. On paper these trainee teachers pursue a course of study similar to those attending English teacher-training colleges : theory of education, psychology, methodology, social science, further general education, a special study of the subject they intend to teach, sport, etc. During their third year they work in schools as part of their practical training. In West Germany teacher training for this level is also three years. Teachers for the fifth to tenth classes of the DDR's ten-class schools qualify in the faculties of philosophy, mathematics, and natural sciences of universities, in the faculty of pedagogy of East Berlin's Humboldt University, and in various other pedagogic institutions. The prerequisite for admission to their four-year course is the *Abitur*. Some institutions run special one-year preliminary courses to enable mature students to prepare for the *Abitur*. Would-be teachers in the twelve-class schools require a five-year training. It can be seen from this brief outline of teacher training in the German Democratic Republic that for the East German equivalent of the British Grammar School and for the higher levels of the ordinary schools a higher standard of training is required than in the United Kingdom. The supply of teachers in East Germany's schools has more than kept pace with the number of pupils. In 1955 there were 75,572 teachers to educate 1,883,400 children. Ten years later there were 2,425,582 pupils and 121,580 teachers.[24] The position would have been even better but for the loss of teachers to West Germany before 1961.

One feature of East German propaganda over the years has been the emphasis given to claiming that equality of the sexes has been established. The writer does not doubt the sincerity of the intention, for equality of women with men has always been a feature of Marxist and German socialist thought. One of the greatest leaders of the movement, August Bebel, wrote a best-selling book on the subject. However, it is one thing to pass legislation to establish equality and another to realize it in practice. Women do get equal pay for equal work, though often they are doing different types of work anyway. In education traditional patterns have not been completely changed. Of East Germany's full-time university students over one-third were women in 1967 as against about one quarter in 1951. In the Federal Republic in 1963 25 per cent of the students were women as compared with about 32 per cent in East

[24] *SJB,* 1966, p. 463.

Germany.[25] What are the Democratic Republic's lady students reading? Well, exact statistics are not available but certain general information for 1964 is available. As might be expected, the numbers of women at teacher-training establishments and art academies were relatively high—43.3 per cent and 40.3 per cent respectively. At technical universities, again as one would expect, the numbers of women were correspondingly small—7.7 per cent. The number of women—56 per cent in 1963, 51 per cent in 1964—at the three medical academies of Dresden, Erfurt, and Magdeburg (there are other medical schools) was higher than is usual in Western countries. There were also sizeable numbers of women studying chemistry and architecture and even at the special mining academy at Freiberg the number of female students reached 7.4 per cent in 1964.[26] The number of women at the *Fachschulen* in 1966 was also high—23,000 out of 52,000 full-time students—but this is partly explained by the presence there of thousands of teacher-trainees many of whom were presumably women.[27]

As is normal in Communist countries the educational system of the German Democratic Republic is highly centralized. The system of higher education is closer in certain respects to Britain than to West Germany. As already mentioned, establishments of higher education are subject to the control of the Ministry for Higher and Technical Education in Berlin. The Ministry was formerly a state Secretariat. As in Britain would-be students apply to a central agency for university entrance. Again as in Britain degree courses are much more rigidly planned than in West Germany. Unlike West German universities, universities in the DDR and Britain do not tolerate 'eternal' students. Nor are students in these two countries free to move from one university to another as they are in the Federal Republic. In East Germany and the United Kingdom there are relatively fewer students than in West Germany, but the wastage rate is much lower than in the Federal Republic. East German university education is much more attuned to the needs of society than is higher education in West Germany or Britain, with correspondingly greater thought being given in the DDR to what students will do when they graduate.

Administration and Ideology

The East German school system is under the direction of the Ministry of People's Education, or *Ministerium für Volksbildung,*

---

[25] W. Germany: Statistisches Jahrbuch für die Bundesrepublik Deutschland, 1966, p. 101; E. Germany: *SJB*, 1966, p. 474.
[26] *SJB*, 1965, p. 460.   [27] *SJB*, 1967, p. 473.

13 * *

which is also in Berlin. It is quite different from the West German or British systems both of which are decentralized. All textbooks, curricula, and examinations in the DDR are centrally directed. All teaching appointments are made by the central authorities in Berlin. But the recruitment system is more flexible than this would suggest, for teachers at all levels are usually selected locally and their appointments are then confirmed by the appropriate Ministry.

The objections to a centrally directed and administered educational system like that of the German Democratic Republic are well-known and need not be spelled out again here, but there are also certain advantages. In West Germany, according to a British professor and authority on German affairs, the lack of a central authority has made it difficult to plan the Federal Republic's educational needs as a whole. It has also led, so says the same source, to a duplication of research which West Germany cannot afford.[28] Another British expert on German affairs has listed the problems of higher education in the Federal Republic as follows: 'One is that the channels of entry to higher education are too restricted. The second is the excessive wastage at almost all levels. The third is the out-of-date view taken by the universities of their function. The fourth is the lack of qualified teachers'.[29] The DDR has gone a very long way to solving all four of these problems. Some fundamental problems exist in the school system. As a British educational expert has written:

> Much effort is concentrated in completing the standard and uniform curriculum for each year of the school course. Pupils who fail to reach the standard stay down at the annual promotion or 'sit again'. They become 'repeaters'. It is a feature of socialist emulation in the DDR for schools to compete to reduce the numbers and proportion of 'repeaters'. This arrangement of the curriculum is rather like the English pre-Hadow 'standards'. It affects methods of teaching: it leads, for example, to an emphasis on sheer rote-learning. It would. however, be a great and unfair disservice to teachers in the DDR to character-ize their work as excessively formal or limited. Within the entirely acceptable and justifiable unstreamed class, even using a common textbook and following approved methods, teachers reveal both professional commitment and pedagogical skill.[30]

[28] Hiscocks, op. cit., pp. 156 onwards.
[29] Michael Balfour, *West Germany*, Benn, London, 1968, p. 255.
[30] David J. Johnson, in *Profile of East Germany*, Harrap, London, 1966, p. 84.

He also paid tribute to the widespread use of audio-visual aids and their variety.

What influence, if any, do parents have on the education of the children of the DDR? The 1968 constitution sets out the rights of parents in education in Article 38 : ' It is the right and the supreme duty of parents to educate their children to become healthy, happy, competent, universally educated and patriotic citizens. Parents have the right to a close and trustful co-operation with the social and state education institutions'. This 'close and trustful co-opera-tion' is supposed to be secured through the *Elternbeiräte* or parents' councils which are elected bodies of parents, teachers, representa-tives of any industrial organizations where pupils of a particular school do vocational training, and representatives of the Free German Youth. Thousands of these committees are in existence throughout East Germany and the writer knows enough to believe that by any standards they do good work, but he also believes they could not for long consistently contradict official policy. They are, nevertheless, one of the bodies through which the SED's leaders have, in recent years, carried on a genuine discussion with the people of the DDR. As we saw above, religion was for long a divisive factor in German schools. The Social Democrats, in those states which they ruled, tried to initiate reforms during the Weimar period. For different ends the Nazis gradually destroyed the con-fessional schools. To the regret of many liberals these were re-established in West Germany but in the East religion has been kept out of the classroom—except for those who are prepared to stay after school for it when instruction is given by clergy of the appropriate denomination. The authorities certainly do not neglect to impart their own version of moral training to their wards. It would require a separate volume to cover all aspects of this moral training, but it is instructive to examine what young East Germans learn in school about religion, friendship, love, and happiness.

In the section of the official school civics textbook which deals with religion[31] the aim is to set out the Marxist view of religion without, however, causing offence to Christians. Indeed, a further aim of this section is to stress just how much Marxists and Chris-tians have in common. The second aim is if anything more im-portant than the first. It gets roughly two pages as against one for the first. In setting out the Marxist viewpoint the writers quote the famous lines from Marx, 'Religious misery is, on the one hand, the expression of actual misery, and, on the other, a protest against

---

[31] Dr Dieter Wittich (ed.), *Staatsbürgerkunde 3,* Volk und Wissen Volks-eigener Verlag, Berlin, 1966, pp. 143–7.

actual misery'. Marx went on to say, 'Religion is the sigh of the oppressed creature, the kindliness of a heartless world, the spirit of unspiritual conditions. It is the people's opium'. These two sentences are, however, omitted. East German pupils are told that:

> The decisive roots of religion lie in social reality. The social relations of class society are those in which human beings are reduced to miserable, impotent, oppressed, degraded, stunted, beings, causing them to seek a fantastic, illusionary endorsement of themselves. The social practice of class society denies the human being consolation, endorsement, freedom, worth, security, warmth and sincerity in human relations. To the extent that he cannot see through this social practice on the basis of the world view of the working-class, he seeks them in the great Beyond.

But religion is not, according to this textbook, just an attempt to get in heaven the humanity one cannot get on earth. It is also a protest against real misery. Engels pointed out that originally Christianity was a movement of the oppressed, of the slaves and of the freedmen, of the poor and of those without rights, of the peoples under Roman oppression. This has important consequences for the shaping of relations between Marxists and believers. The practical struggles against hunger, war, and oppression had gained the support of more and more religious people and brought Marxists and Christians together. Religious conviction had proved itself a driving force to co-operation in the building of socialism. Arrogance and superciliousness in dealings with believers, which hurt their religious feelings, were not only not an expression of revolutionary attitude but were completely against Marxist teaching. Freedom of religion and of conscience were guaranteed in the constitution of the DDR. The book, which was published in 1965, contains a picture of Ulbricht with Evangelical Bishop Moritz Mitzenheim exchanging views in the bishop's residence in 1964.

As an example of true friendship the textbook offers its young readers the association of Marx and Engels. It quotes the authoritative biography of Marx by Franz Mehring:

> Their friendship is without equal in history, which can show many cases of famous friendships: the friendships of men whose life's work was so closely connected that it can no longer be divided into thine and mine, and German history can show such cases also. But always there has remained some trace of wilfulness or obstinacy, or even no more than a secret objection to abandoning completely the individual personality . . . The friend-

ship which bound Marx and Engels knew nothing of this last remnant of human pettiness. The more their thought and their development became one, the more they each remained a separate entity and a man . . . Both men gave themselves completely to the common cause, and both of them made, not the same, but an equally great sacrifice in its interests without the faintest trace of discontented grumbling or boasting, and for these reasons their friendship was an incomparable alliance of which history can show no second example.[32]

So much for friendship between men. But what about friendship between those of the opposite sex? Well, to begin with, it appears that, officially at any rate, the age of chivalry is not yet dead in East Germany. The young man is enjoined to carry his companion's shopping and greet her with flowers. In sport and hiking he should not expect as much of her as he would of a male friend. As for love it 'is something great and beautiful, but also something very serious with which one cannot play. Playing fast and loose with love is just the thing which can destroy the friendship between a boy and a girl. It demands of both a sense of responsibility and mutual respect. . . . Superficial flirting or sexual advances not only reduce the value of a friendship, but destroy the basis—respect and trust—from which real love can grow'. Some young people asked when should they start having sexual relations. Now Marxists were not apostles of abstention but it was difficult to be precise. But one should only have intimate relations with a partner one liked, with whom one wanted to live, and when one was mature enough really to judge one's own feelings and mature enough to appreciate the beauty and genuine enrichment of life that such an intimate association gave. Otherwise one was squandering one's emotional resources. What if as a result of such relations a baby arrives? Should the parents marry? A 'child is not sufficient reason for marriage'. Statistics showed that many such marriages failed. In the DDR a child born out of wedlock suffered no drawbacks and therefore love was the decisive factor in deciding whether or not to marry.[33]

'Man is born for happiness as a bird is made for flight', but, the East German textbook continues, a bird can only fly when nothing prevents it from moving freely. Man can only be truly happy when he has freed himself from the fetters of capitalist exploitation.

[32] *Staatsbürgerkunde 3* quotes this on p. 241. The author has used the translation in Franz Mehring, *Karl Marx*, Allen & Unwin, London, 1951, pp. 231–7.
[33] *Staatsbürgerkunde 3*, pp. 238–48.

Only in a socialist society can he develop all his talents and reach his full stature. Happiness is not something abstract, not something independent of the individual's class, people, or nation. Naturally a cosy home and love fulfilled are part of happiness. But when such things lack the safety of a community and the protection of a state they are like land without dikes which can be flooded in every storm. Happiness has many faces; it is not just love and it is not just struggle, but life teaches that 'the happiest person is the person who does most to make others happy, to make his people happy'.[34]

The Free German Youth

One final aspect of East German education needs to be outlined —the position of the Free German Youth. Since the fall of Nazism in 1945 there has been, apart from scattered religious groups, only one youth organization in East Germany—the *Freie Deutsche Jugend*, or Free German Youth, and the junior version, the *Junge Pioniere*, or Young Pioneers. The FDJ was officially founded in March 1946, about the same time as the Socialist Unity Party, as a non-party anti-fascist, 'democratic' body. Even in those days Communists and socialists of the SED played the decisive role in the youth movement, but the Free German Youth could claim to represent a wide range of opinion and political awareness. Like the other mass organizations, however, the FDJ soon fell into line behind the SED and has been in line ever since. In the early postwar years first the Soviets, and then the East German authorities, did all they could to boost the youth movement. A number of spectacular rallies were held at which all the theatrical effects associated with the Nazi régime to influence youth were used—mass marches with lavishly equipped bands, patriotic and other stirring music, uniforms, folk costumes, banners, flags, and symbols, mass releases of peace doves and balloons, etc. The two most noted of these rallies of the early years were the 1950 'German Meeting' and the World Youth Festival of Youth and Students of 1951. The latter attracted great attention around the world, the more so because the Americans tried very hard to prevent people attending it by closing their zones of Austria and Germany to trains taking young people to the Festival, and by persuading Western governments to do likewise. According to the *Manchester Guardian* (17 August 1951) the West tried to counteract this rally by various means. 'Leaflets were fired into the Soviet sector in rockets or dropped from a single helicopter. A television broadcasting station

[34] *Staatsbürgerkunde 3*, pp. 248–9.

was opened in the American sector, and the Ford Foundation publicly donated a large sum of money to the Free University of Berlin'. But these and other Western measures were not very successful: 'These Western diversions were supremely unco-ordinated and attracted about as much attention as a few minor fireworks would if let off in the immediate neighbourhood of a blast furnace'. According to the same reporter ninety-odd foreign delegations 'contributed a gaily clothed and enthusiastic concourse which was gradually swelled by fresh arrivals to a total of around 25,000 guests. . . . East German youth has been sadly cut off from the world, and this was a chance to meet British, French, Italians, as well as the peoples of the Eastern bloc'. The *Manchester Guardian* correspondent also mentioned that 'new sports stadiums, swimming baths, and parks had been created for this occasion', and called the Festival a masterpiece of organization attended by 'over two million Blue-shirts'. From personal experience of the Festival the writer can endorse these remarks. It is hardly surprising that never again was the FDJ able to achieve such a spectacular gathering.

In 1957 the Free German Youth officially declared itself to be 'the socialist youth organization of the DDR'. And this was enshrined in its statute of 1963 which also recognized the leading role of the Unity Party and obliged each member to 'master the scientific teaching of Socialism, of Marxism-Leninism'. Nevertheless, the FDJ also declared that this did not mean that only atheists could be members. Members also have the duty to foster their progressive national cultural inheritance and to help to develop a socialist national culture. The organization of the Free German Youth is similar to that of the SED, with groups in schools, places of work, in the armed forces, and anywhere else where young people are together. Officially its highest organ is the Central Council (*Zentralrat*), an elected body, which in turn elects a *Büro* and a *Sekretariat*. Its Youth parliaments, which are held every four years and which elect the Central Council, are similar to the *Parteitage* of the Unity Party. No details have been given recently of the numbers of East Germans in the Free German Youth but given the advantages of membership it seems likely to be high. The Young Pioneers, which cater for children from six to fourteen, had 1,829,733 members in 1965.[35] In 1960, when the organization had 1.3 million members, it claimed to embrace 74.83 per cent of all children in the relevant age groups.[36] This is hardly surprising in view of the facilities available to this organization, its

[35] *SJB*, 1966, p. 591.
[36] Karl-Heinz Günther, op. cit., p. 113.

access to the classroom, the pressures to conform and, no doubt, the good work it does, much of the latter being the normal kind of activity one expects in any youth movement—camping, hiking, hobbies, sport, and generally helping the young to make constructive use of their free time. But the Free German Youth is not just any youth organization. Its conscious aim is to win the young for the SED and to help to carry through the policy of that party wherever it has the possibility and responsibility for so doing.

Another organization which has important responsibilities in the field of youth is the Society for Sport and Technology, or *Gesellschaft für Sport und Technik* (GST), which was set up in 1952. In that year the SED decided in principle that the time had come to set up armed forces in the DDR and the GST was seen as a vehicle through which young people could be given pre-military training. Modelled on a similar organization in the Soviet Union and well provided for, the society offers a wide variety of courses in sports which could be of military value. Since the introduction of conscription in East Germany in 1962 the GST's activities have been intensified. In March 1963 the Ministry of People's Education issued a directive making the GST's activities an integral part of secondary school life.[37] Towards the end of 1968 renewed emphasis was placed on the GST. In connection with the 20th anniversary of the DDR in 1969 a recruitment campaign was launched under the title 'Signal DDR 20'. It is impossible to say just how successful the GST is in its work, but it seems doubtful that it has been completely successful in the schools. As in other countries, the majority of teachers in East Germany are women and it seems likely that they are not in any position to give instruction in, say, shooting or motor cycling or signalling. It is also likely, and one gains this impression from talking to young people in East Germany, that many of the younger citizens of the DDR regard military training both in the GST and in the armed forces as a waste of time. Occasionally official publications admit the same sort of thing.[38] The writer has no recent figures of the society's membership but one Western estimate, made before the 1968-9 campaign, put it at around 430,000.[39]

[37] *Zur Lage der Jugend im anderen Teil Deutschlands,* Herausgegeben vom Bundesministerium für Gesamtdeutsche Fragen, Bonn and Berlin, 1968, p. 44.
[38] Ibid., p. 33.
[39] Ibid., p. 39. A useful collection of official documents on East German education is contained in Siegfried Baske and Martha Engelbert, edd., *Dokumente Zur Bildungspolitik In Der Sowjetischen Besatzungzone,* Bundesministerium für Gesamtdeutsche Fragen, Bonn and Berlin, 1966.

Those who took over the running of the educational system in East Germany after the collapse of the Third Reich in 1945 were faced with enormous problems owing not only to material shortage but also to the need to overcome the evil legacy of the past. They also set themselves the noble task of giving every child the chance, denied in the past, to develop his abilities to the full. They sought to equip the rising generation for a new technology and, finally, for a new socialist society. Unfortunately, the last mentioned task was interpreted as inculcating the latest version of SED ideology on all possible occasions. Western educationalists will reject this aspect of East German education, but they will admire the progress made in other aspects of education, progress which may well, in the long run, help to remove some of the less desirable features of East German society today.

Chapter 9

East Germany Looks at Us:
Dickens is Dead

THE BRITISH AND AMERICAN people get little chance through the normal means of communication open to them, to learn much about East Germany. On television news programmes the only impression one gets of the DDR is limited to the Wall, escapes across it, and the occasional military parade. At another level Perry Mason or 'Danger Man' or Callan now and then have to foil dastardly attempts at blackmail or kidnapping by some stone-faced East German functionary. The East Germans in these series sometimes turn out to be old favourites from those wonderful Hollywood productions of the forties such as *Confessions of a Nazi Spy, Hangmen Also Die,* and so on. Books on East Germany are almost as few and far between as television programmes and are usually brief impressions of partisans of one side or the other. As for press coverage of the DDR, though it has improved in recent years, it is still sketchy and exhibits greater hostility to the DDR than to most other Communist states.

The East Germans, for their part, have not always helped matters. The DDR has produced relatively few outstanding films, fewer still about life in its part of Germany, such films are rarely seen in Britain or North America, and then only in film clubs or cinemas off the main circuits. In the 1960s the East German authorities have frequently granted facilities to non-Communist journalists and their 'image' has improved somewhat as a result. But for years they made it very difficult for journalists whose reporting they feared would be hostile. Finally, more than most Communist states, the DDR has suffered discrimination against its political spokesmen, cultural and other representatives. Thus it has been deprived of an important means of image-building open to most other states.

What of the other side? How do the mass media of East Germany deal with life in Britain and America? Of the USA the East German people learn little. From the East German media they

see riots in American cities, the Vietnam war, and hear commen-
taries on the 'global strategy of US imperialism'. The assassinated
Kennedys and Martin Luther King were treated sympathetically
by the East German press, being regarded as victims of a right-
wing plot. And after the historic moon probe of Colonel Borman
and his colleagues the East German media, following the Soviet
example, praised the courage, daring, and skill of the three. For
the average person, though, knowledge of life in America is con-
fined to a few novels by Germans, Stefan Heym for example, who
spent the Hitler years in the United States; fewer still translated
novels; and to American films. However, it should be stressed that
Cary Grant, Gregory Peck, James Stewart, Spencer Tracy, and
other Hollywood stars are better known than one would expect. In
April 1968 *Some Like it Hot,* with Marilyn Monroe, was being
widely shown in the DDR. Other films from America screened in
the 1960s include *12 Angry Men, High Noon, The Man With The
Golden Arm, Round The World In 80 Days,* and *Love With The
Proper Stranger.* The importing of films from the West is a problem of finance as well as politics.

In the schools of East Germany much more time is given over
to Britain than to America. And the standard of the content of
school-books devoted to the USA can be gauged from the following extract taken from the introduction to one of them :

> We consciously orient our pupils to solidarity with the most
> progressive part of the American working class and its van-
> guard, the Communist Party, with the negroes struggling for
> equality, with the small farmers, we refer to the progressive
> traditions of the American people. The description and explana-
> tion of this side of social life in classes is more important than,
> for example, an account of the level of production of the USA, as
> large circles of working people do not share in its possible benefits.[1]

Even so, East German children are at least acquainted in school
with the following American authors, among others : Mark Twain,
John Steinbeck, Richard Wright, Jack London, Walt Whitman,
Herman Melville, Stephen Crane, Theodore Dreiser, and Sinclair
Lewis. They also get on nodding terms with Tom Paine and
Thomas Jefferson.

What is the position regarding information about Britain? Does
the East German conception of Britain resemble the land we

---

[1] As quoted by Alfons Rothmund in his *Der englische und französische
Unterricht in den Schulen der sowjetischen Besatzungszone Deutschlands,*
Bonn, 1965, p. 39.

know or is it, as we are so often told about the Russian image of
Britain, the land of Dickens still or at best that of Keir Hardie?
First of all, let it be said that there is far more information on
Britain than on America. Politics, trade, and geography ensure
that there are far more contacts with the United Kingdom than
with the United States. As mentioned above, more time is devoted
to Britain in the schoolroom and in English-language evening
classes. More written and other material is available about Britain
and for this reason the writer is able to give a more comprehensive
picture of East Germany's view of Britain than he is of their view
of America.

As far as British films are concerned it is sufficient to say that
most of the best British films of the 'new wave'—*Saturday Night
And Sunday Morning, A Kind Of Loving, Look Back In Anger,
A Taste Of Honey, Room At The Top*—have been shown in the
DDR. As for modern British novels, the writer conducted a survey
in the main bookshops of eight out of fifteen provincial capitals
of the DDR in April 1968. He found in every case that there were
translations of post-war British novels available. The most recent
translated book available then everywhere was C. P. Snow's *Cor-
ridors of Power*. Other British authors whose works were available
included Monica Dickens, Alan Sillitoe, and Colin MacInnes.
The Irish writer Sean O'Casey also seemed to be very popular with
East German publishing houses. There was also the usual assortment of the classics.

Partly owing to pressure from below, developing trade, and internal relaxation, English is now the second foreign language in
the DDR, and in 1966 East Germans got their first chance to
learn English by television. Obviously, of all East German teaching
of English these TV programmes reach the widest audience. They
are also used in some schools. The writer was able to obtain from a
bookshop in Magdeburg the written material for lessons 32 to 57
inclusive. About five of the scripts could be called directly political
and politics came into about another five. The majority of the
scripts, the non-political ones, dealt with such normal language lesson
topics as the football match, a youth camp, an accident, at
the theatre, Christmas, a travel agency, at a hotel, in an office,
sight-seeing, and famous inventors. The ones which could be
regarded as political were concerned with Karl Marx in London,
looking for work, the South Wales miners, the friendship between
the twin towns of Dresden and Coventry, and the eleven-plus
examination. Most British people would not object to most of the
contents of these five programmes. The one dealing with Karl

Marx was just a straight account of Marx's life in London. Lesson 43 briefly attacks, by implication, the eleven-plus examination. The Dresden-Coventry programme pays tribute to the rebuilding of both cities. Of Coventry we learn that it has a 'beautiful new cathedral' and 'many other new buildings' including a 'famous shopping centre without any traffic' and 'the Lanchester College of Technology'. Much of this programme was shot in Coventry. We also hear about the delegations from Coventry to Dresden. Again, lesson 42, 'Looking For Work', is not really inaccurate or objectionable : 'The two factories where Tom and Peggy worked have closed down. Like many other people they are now looking for new jobs. At the Labour Exchange they get the address of Smith's Radio Factory, where they want workers—men and women. Tom and Peggy get jobs there'. When Tom gets his first wage packet there is not all that much in it : 'There are thirteen pounds in it. He needs nine pounds for rent, for food and for his mother. So there are only four pounds left over. That is not much, and Tom is not very happy. But he will get training and he will be a skilled worker. Then he can get a better job with more pay'. Peggy is even less happy. She likes the work but although she does the same work as Tom she has only got nine pounds pay. She has no prospects of becoming a skilled operative. The National Coal Board would certainly object to lesson 57 : 'There are many coal mines in South Wales. The miners' work is very hard because many mines are old and the working conditions in them are bad. More and more coal mines are closing down. It is difficult to sell enough coal. Oil is cheaper. But what about the miners? Many of them lose their jobs and it is not easy for them to find new ones. There is no plan to help them'. In this programme an older miner, Dave, tells his young colleague, Tom, that the Communist Party 'has always shown us the right way'.

A number of these programmes touch on living standards in Britain. In 'A Merry Christmas' we are told : 'The parents have bought everything : the Christmas presents, a fine Christmas tree and electric lights for it, holly and mistletoe, the Christmas pudding, a big turkey and something to drink. There is not much money left over now in their purses'. In 'The Kitchen Sink' Mrs White complains to the plumber who comes to mend her sink that she has been living in this flat for fifteen years and the landlord 'hasn't put a penny into it in all these years'. She pays three pounds a week for one room and the kitchen. The plumber advises her to see the 'rent officer and ask him to have a look at your flat and reduce the rent'. There is a comment on the conditions of the

London dockers in lesson 36 : 'I don't think their wages are good. I talked to one of them a few weeks ago. He's been a docker for twenty years. He has four children, and his wages are too small for such a big family'. However, we are told that in the East End of London 'there are many new houses there now' but 'a lot of people still have to live in old flats and have to pay a lot of rent'. In another programme, lesson 54, we hear about a problem which, in spite of the frustrations of shopping in Britain, is more likely to arise in the DDR than in England. Peggy wanted two small bookcases. 'She went to three or four shops, but they had only big cases there. So Peggy went to a joiner's shop and ordered two bookcases'. She had to wait so long that she eventually made one of them herself. Though one may have certain doubts about some of the comments in these programmes it must be admitted that they present the British as a friendly people living in a generally modern and pleasant land.

It is interesting to look at some books used at various levels of the educational system. Firstly, a book published in 1950 and used for several years, called *School Life In England,* was designed for the equivalent of fifth and sixth forms. This volume is made up of extracts from English texts, all of them in the original English, from British writers about the development of the educational system in England. The first of these was by Ernest Green, M.A., J.P., published in 1947 and tracing the development of education till then. This is a critical and sophisticated account of British education in the nineteenth and twentieth centuries. The reader is told by Mr Green that :

> the characteristic feature is the existence, side by side, of two quite different educational systems, one for the few and the other for the many. The two groups see as little of each other and can as little imagine the condition of each other's lives as can the dwellers in the East and the West End. As will be stressed later, all this would matter much less were it not for the fact that the influence of the schools for the few in the government of the many *is* and always *has been* out of all proportion to their numbers.

Green also tells us that 'though many students from working-class homes now reach the universities and distinguish themselves there, the road is steep and admission is highly competitive—but only for those who are not well off. And, in spite of all the difference that the scholarship system has made in the last generation, recent research has shown that, for seven fee-paying students who receive a higher education, only one free pupil of equal ability is so favoured'. Of the 1944 Act Green says :

Comment on the Education Act, 1944, has to be short, deliberately so because the Act itself is so complicated and is clothed in such legal formality that the reader would have been bored and confused by descriptive detail. The administrator will read and interpret the Act, but the ordinary man is only concerned with general principles. His main concern is to discover how far the Act really abolishes the defects and disabilities. He wants to know whether it will lay the foundation for a new Society. Will it make the dry bones of democracy live and clothe it in something more attractive than the threadbare garb of nineteenth century slogans? Will it strengthen democracy at its base, making government of the people, by the people, for the people a reality? Will it provide genuine equality of opportunity at every stage of educational development? These are only a few of the questions which come to one's mind as an effective test of what has been described as 'the greatest landmark of our educational history'.

Ernest Green's piece is followed by extracts from Charles Dickens's *David Copperfield*; Thomas Hughes's *Tom Brown's Schooldays*; Horace Annesley's *The Hill,* published in 1905 and telling about life at Harrow School; H. G. Wells's *Joan and Peter,* published in 1918 and describing life in a private school before the First World War; and Bernard Shaw's *Treatise on Parents and Children* (1910). These extracts were obviously designed to give the reader some idea of the development of Britain's educational system, and to introduce him to some of the classics of the literature of that country at the same time. *The New School Tie* written by G. C. T. Giles, the President of the National Union of Teachers in 1946, took a more contemporary look at the problems facing Britain's educationalists. Giles was brutally frank about the British educational system of his day : 'Up to now, we have never had in this country even the pretence of a national or democratic system of education. Equality of opportunity, the broad highway from nursery school to university, a career open to the talents—these have been and still are largely fine phrases. Our system as it exists now is a caste system reflecting the class division of our society'. Nevertheless, there are opportunities within this system for the very bright and lucky few from the working class. For instance, John Green, son of an engineer living in Middlesex, after starting in an elementary school and struggling through grammar school, in 1933 John's efforts and the sacrifice of his parents were rewarded. He was brilliantly successful in the Higher School Certificate examination, and was awarded a State Scholarship—one of the 360 open to all in that year. So John was launched on a university career. He went to Cambridge University, and after three years secured a good research post where he made rapid progress. He became one of the team of backroom boys who made such a tremendous contribution to victory. This story of a gifted working-class boy illustrates both the opportunities available, and the limits of those opportunities. Educational opportunity, except for the children of the well-to-do, depends almost entirely on success in passing a highly competitive test at the age of ten or eleven.

Karl-Heinz Wirzberger, the East German who was responsible for compiling this volume, gave his readers the chance to acquaint themselves with the 1944 Education Act by quoting substantial parts of the original.

The final article in *School Life In England* is taken from the *Daily Worker*. Written in 1948 by Communist teacher Max Morris, who in 1967 became the head of a London comprehensive school, it is headed 'Guns Before Butter Now'. Morris claimed that the 1944 Act was being shelved to divert the funds to rearmament, which was in turn necessary to support an imperialistic foreign policy.

> One great reform has been achieved: the raising of the leaving age to 15. No others are likely to be fulfilled without a complete reversal of present trends. The Ministry of Education puts an effective ban on Nursery Schools, Community Centres and Youth Clubs. The high hopes that were raised by the expansion of Technical Education are not to be fulfilled. In 1948 the target for Further Education is a mere £3½ millions, a figure totally inadequate in view of the abysmally low level of the existing facilities. Compare this figure with the hundreds of millions being spent on the armed forces!

Mr Morris also rightly pointed out: 'the operation of a universal free meals service, once priority No. 1, is no longer so'.

In *School Life In England* the East German authorities could claim to be giving their wards a fairly comprehensive and authoritative picture of education in England. After all, the extracts were all written by distinguished or expert opinion. Only one of the writers is Communist and there is virtually no East German commentary. If the views recorded are critical they only reflect the critical approach of British educationalists and many writers. This volume did at least tell its readers that, despite the lack of complete equality of opportunity in Britain, there was a chance for bright working-class children to get to university. This is a fact which is still not generally realized in many West European countries which, wrongly, regard Britain as more class-ridden than themselves. This was a volume produced at one of the bitterest phases of the Cold War and in use certainly until after 1953, until after the worst of that 'war' was over. All in all, one cannot be too critical of this East German presentation of Britain's educational institutions.

Our second East German volume on Britain was published in 1957, that is when East-West relations looked like turning sour again as the result of events in Suez and Hungary in the previous autumn. The title of this book is *England Between Yesterday and Tomorrow* and it was written for a general adult audience by 'the well-known English publicist Derek Kartun'. It presents the British as a sport-loving, fun-loving, widely reading, hard-working people. For instance:

> One cannot speak of Britain without mentioning sport, for it is a land of sport enthusiasts. At least one quarter of the adult population either take part in sport themselves or at least watch it. King of this sport is Football. Britain taught the world how to play football, even if today some of the pupils have grown to be better than the teacher. In England alone there are about 32,000 football clubs, and about 750,000 men and boys take part during the winter months . . . In summer cricket has a following only a little smaller, and tennis, hockey, sailing, swimming, light athletics, golf and riding are also very popular.

To show that British people are gay and fun-loving Mr Kartun mentions Blackpool. After giving a lengthy list of the attractions of that resort which would make its publicity office delighted, he comments: 'Blackpool exposes the falsity of the idea that Britishers are boring, reserved and inhibited'. Britain is also presented as a land of high living standards: 'Britain has in comparison to its West European neighbours a high standard of living'. This includes the British working class, millions of whom 'have radios or television, bicycles, motor cycles or cars. Certainly most of them have reasonable homes and are better dressed than the workers of West Germany'. This is not, however, true of many of the old-age pensioners who face poverty and struggle to make ends meet, though the large numbers of pensioners, it is pointed out, are the result of improved living conditions. The latter were partly the result of Labour's term of office after the war.

> A really significant step forward took place under the Labour government after the war. To the positive achievements of this government number the introduction of family allowances, the improvement of the law relating to accidents at work, the extension of education, the improvement of welfare measures for children and the old, and the passing of the law introducing the National Health Service. . . . This law created one of the best and most comprehensive, free, health services of the capitalist countries. . . .

But not one new hospital had been built in Britain since the war and fees had again been introduced for spectacles and dentistry. And the school medical service was inadequate owing to the lack of money. Where was all the money going? Partly it was being plundered by the capitalist class. Partly it was being squandered on armaments used in Kenya, Malaya, and Cyprus, and on nuclear weapons. This was affecting the nation's economy and thus in turn Britain's position in the world. On the one hand, Britain was the land of the biggest building firms in the world, the biggest motor-car exporters of the world, and the biggest cable-making plants; the land of great banks, of ICI, and the land which in the field of nuclear research and the development of nuclear power-stations was first in the world. In Britain too there was 'perhaps the greatest concentration of craftsmanship, technical and intellectual ability in the world'. But, on the other hand, owing to the end of empire and the necessity for huge imports of raw materials her economy was in a precarious position.

'Democracy for whom?', asks Mr Kartun in a chapter setting out Britain's constitutional arrangements. The reader is informed that in Britain there is the right to vote at free, secret, universal, elections. But, owing to the electoral system, which penalizes the smaller parties, especially the Communist Party, the House of Commons is never a true reflection of the political mood of the people. (Mr Kartun failed to mention that close association with Moscow was probably much more important in keeping the Communist Party small than lack of TV time. For instance, he might have mentioned the mass of resignations which followed the party's support for the Soviet invasion of Hungary.) There are the two major political parties but the Conservatives are essentially a party of 'the bankers and directors'. And the Labour Party? Well, despite four periods of office they had, as the *New Statesman and Nation* put it, not destroyed capitalism but renovated it. Labour troubles, says Mr Kartun, stem from the fact that the party is dominated by its parliamentary wing which contains so many 'safe' men who are not prepared to swim against the tide because they fear they will spoil their chances of promotion to the Front Benches.

Derek Kartun's book ends with an account of the Suez campaign which, he says, showed that 'the days of cannon boat diplomacy are over. The British government did not take account of that fundamental fact and suffered a defeat'.

First published in 1960, *Our English Friends* was last re-issued in 1966. This is the book in general use in East German schools. Part III contains bright pictures of the Shakespeare Memorial Theatre, Anne Hathaway's cottage, a forge in Birmingham, the port of Manchester, Blackpool Tower and beach, the College of Technology in Manchester, Edinburgh Castle, the Forth Bridge, the Scott Monument, Cardiff Civic Centre, the Rhondda Valley, Belfast shipyards, the National Eisteddfod of Wales, an Irish country scene, and an aerial view of London Airport. We also find portraits of Darwin, Shakespeare, Paul Robeson as Othello and Mary Ure as Desdemona, Stephenson, Marx and Engels, Watt, and Burns. The young readers are given the chance to learn the words of the 'Internationale', 'Land of My Fathers', 'The Wearing of the Green', 'The Bonnie Banks of Loch Lomond' and 'She'll Be Coming Round The Mountain'. Sir Walter Scott and Robert Burns contribute one poem each and there are proverbs, limericks, an epitaph, jokes, puzzles, and tongue twisters. The thin story line is centred around the activities of a Communist family, the Joneses. We first meet them on their way from London to Manchester where they are to visit their relations. They have just bought a second-hand, four-seater Austin in which they are making their trip. They stop at Birmingham, where, Mr Jones tells his family, 'There are about 8,000 factories in Birmingham. You can find them everywhere. People have said that the English prefer quiet towns but Birmingham has the heavy industry which provides the bread and butter for us. They produce almost everything here, from a pen to a hydraulic press; buttons, locomotives, artificial limbs and steel girders—and armaments'. Of Birmingham we are also told : 'The Jones admired the many new houses they could see from the road and it seemed to them that most of the towns had been re-built'. In Manchester the Jones stayed with Mrs Jones' sister, Joan Fletcher, a cotton operative, who told her relatives from London, 'she was on short-time working'. As for her son Harry,

They'll close my mill soon, but I think I can still find a job at some other mill where they may need another cotton printer to run a night shift.—Yes, it is really a shame that we seem to come back to mass unemployment. There's a lot of competition from artificial textiles, like nylon and Terylene, and from colonial countries like Hongkong, where they make cheap goods by sweated labour. You see, science has produced artificial textiles and automation, but capitalism has produced no answer to its old problems.

Mr Kartun had told his readers a few years before that unemployment did not exist in Britain.

This book also contains a short section dealing with Ghana which gives some prominence to the Volta River project. Kofi Asare, a young engineer, explains its significance to an English friend, David Oates:

Up to now the imperialists didn't want us to industrialise, because they wanted our raw materials such as timber, manganese, bauxite, and gold. In this way, instead of helping, they were robbing us. Now that we are politically free we must industrialise to raise the living standard of our people and to become economically independent too. We need electrical energy and fuel for that, but as far as we know there's neither coal nor oil in the country. So, with the help of British and American firms, we're going to build the Volta Dam. By damming the river Volta we'll be able to generate about 610,000 KW of hydro-electric energy every year. . . .

Kofi later went on a study trip to Eastern Europe and 'He was filled with admiration for the real New World he had been visiting'. On the way home he stopped off in London to visit his friend Mr Oates. Unfortunately his friend, apparently in the Merchant Navy, was away on another trip when he arrived. Nevertheless, David had left a letter for Kofi telling him that his friends 'will be delighted to meet you'. Though disappointed, the young Ghanaian thought, 'Friends, friends everywhere!'

One of our more recent East German books on Britain was published in 1966 and is called *A Trip To England*. It was written by Kurt Hackenberg and, like *Our English Friends,* was produced with some help from a British person. It appears to be written for an adult audience but contains a wide variety of photographs—a typical street in the Highgate-Hampstead area, Parliament, Westminster Abbey, the Cenotaph, Downing Street, the Royal Festival

Hall, the City, Tower Bridge, the Tower, St Paul's, Trafalgar Square, Piccadilly Circus, the British Museum, the Senate House of London University, Buckingham Palace, Regent's Park, Hyde Park and Speakers' Corner, the East End and Petticoat Lane, the Marx Memorial, the New Towns, Hatfield Technical College, several shots of Oxford and Cambridge, cricket and camping scenes, East Anglia and Ely Cathedral, several photos of Coventry including the Cathedral and the Belgrade Theatre, and the usual pictures of Stratford-Upon-Avon.

In his introduction the author tells that the book deals with the visit of Rolf, a young teacher from the German Democratic Republic, to his friends in London who are also teachers. They met when the young Englishman Mike Brown and some of his colleagues visited the DDR to study the educational system there. Rolf's trip must have caused some raised eyebrows and envy among Herr Hackenberg's readers, considering the virtual impossibility of an East German making such a private visit. Rolf finds that he starts having to revise his views on the British even before he arrives in London. He admits to his friend on arrival : 'I think we continentals have many wrong notions about the English . . . One thing I have found out on my way to London is that the English are very sociable . . . On the boat I made friends with an elderly couple from Durham, and on the train I had a chat with two young ladies. I must say, the English are not at all formal.' Even the customs officers seem to have been friendly. 'Everything was well organised, and the checking of passports and luggage went off smoothly. The Customs officer warned me to be sure to bring my cameras back.'

What kind of living standards do Mr and Mrs Brown enjoy? Mike Brown had not mentioned that he had bought a car. 'I bought it only four months ago. It isn't one of the latest models. I bought it second-hand, and got it very cheap.' As for housing, this London teacher and his wife live in a large bay-windowed house converted into two flats. Their flat comprises two bedrooms, two living rooms, bathroom, and a 'very modern' kitchen. Mike and his wife have a television set, radiogram, new electric cooker, and a refrigerator. They are saving up for a washing machine. Rolf is quite intrigued by British eating habits, breakfast for instance. 'I was told that the English generally have porridge for breakfast'. Jane Brown corrects him, pointing out that cereals have replaced porridge. 'We generally have them with milk. This is often followed by an egg, boiled or fried, or poached, or scrambled. Sometimes we eat a rasher of bacon or two, mostly fried, and meat or fish or ham'

From the account of British eating habits that he got Rolf would certainly conclude that the British are at least substantial eaters. Inevitably the East German teacher was taken to see the sights of London and he was impressed by some of the newer buildings as well as the older ones, among the former the Royal Festival Hall and the Senate House of London University. He learned too how London had suffered as a result of bombing. Mike told him : 'The Second World War ... brought immense devastation. Many buildings of historic value were laid in ruins by German planes. German rockets also hit London, mainly the East End'. What of the East End, incidentally? 'How different this district looks from the one where you live and from those in the West'! Rolf says to Mike of Stepney. And 'I must say these grey streets are pretty dismal. The block dwellings look more like warehouses than homes.' Mike explains :

> During the last century, when the population of London began to grow rapidly, to give them somewhere to live many houses like these were run up for working-class people. . . . The houses were badly planned and badly built, and were cheap. But they brought an income for their owners, and that was all that mattered. . . . Staircases are often insecure, there are holes in the floors, and the plaster comes off the walls and ceilings. In many of the buildings there is only one tap. . . , In a slum area it is by no means exceptional to find a whole family living in a single room, and rooms are often small.

Is there any hope?

> Well, it is not so bad as it used to be. The London County Council has made improvements. A number of the former buildings were pulled down, and were replaced by more sanitary buildings. Muddy lanes were transformed into well-paved roads. All houses are regularly examined by sanitary inspectors to make sure that they are fit to live in. But the slum problem has by no means been solved as yet. It isn't easy to enforce the law on private property and thousands of families in London are homeless living in Council hostels with little hope of a house for years. . . . under the Council House Programme the slum districts are being abolished to make way for modern buildings. However, progress is slow.

As for the council houses they 'look most attractive and seem to have bright and sunny rooms'.

To give their German friend a balanced picture of the housing situation the two Britons take Rolf to see the New Towns. They remind Rolf that it was Ebenezer Howard 'who first put the idea into practice at Letchworth in 1903.... In fact, his ideas have profoundly influenced town planning throughout the world, especially in the United States. Don't forget that he was honoured in the Soviet Union'. At Welwyn Garden City, where 'There were just a few farm-houses on the site ... no railway station, no water supply, drainage, electricity or gas, when building started', Rolf now finds buildings which are in his opinion 'very modern'. What about sports facilities? 'The town has an open-air swimming pool and some playing-fields providing facilities for athletic games, rugby, hockey, cricket, tennis and association football'.

Hackenberg's book also contains a brief but accurate description of the British educational system, even mentioning such things as the introduction of the Diploma of Technology, sandwich-courses, and the activities of the extra-mural departments of universities. The eleven-plus is condemned :

> Based upon the bourgeois theory that intelligence is inborn, unchangeable and limited to a minority, it prevents many work-ing-class children from getting a better education. The Labour and the Communist Parties have always fought for an education system which gives all children equal opportunities. Without the official consent of the Ministry of Education, a number of Comprehensive Schools have been set up in recent years. They take all children living in the area around the schools, disregard-ing their supposed intelligence. The syllabus offers a wide variety of courses and the opportunity for all children to take external examinations.

Rolf is also told, correctly, that 'the majority of all British students come from middle-class families. The number of students coming from working-class families is rather low'. Herr Hackenberg might have added—perhaps he did not know—that British univer-sities are more representative of the nation they serve than those in most other countries.

Finally, the German reader is given a brief outline of British political institutions :

> today Parliament consists of two Houses, the House of Lords and the House of Commons, or, as the two parts are sometimes called, the Upper House and the Lower House. ... The Sovereign is the ruler, assisted by the Cabinet. Parliament is not a governing body; it is a legislative body, but it does exercise effective

control over the executive power, i.e. the Ministers. The House of Commons alone controls the state finances, and this power naturally makes it the most important element in state affairs.

Rolf went to see the Commons for himself but, Mike told him, 'I'm afraid we can't go inside now. We'll come here some other day; but we shall have to come early in the morning, because there are hundreds of visitors each day, waiting in a queue until they are admitted and taken round by guides who explain everything'. Perhaps Rolf was given food for thought.

The most ambitious of the East German books on Britain was also published in 1966. Called *Modern Britain* and written entirely in English, it is the collective work of twenty writers, most of whom are British. It is divided into a survey of the regions of Britain : an account of London, 'The Greatest City In The World'; 'Life And Leisure'; 'Education'; 'The State And Political Institutions'; 'Agriculture'; 'The Press'; 'The Commonwealth'; and 'The Labour Movement'. Unlike Hackenberg's book there is not much in *Modern Britain* to enable the reader to get much of an impression about British living standards, though there is quite a lot of useful information in the section on food, drink, and entertainment. About London housing we are told that 'Despite many fine houses and flats built by the Council there are still miles of dingy little dwellings and many slums'. But we are also lectured by 'the popular town-councillor, Solly Kaye, on the Communist platform at Hyde Park Corner. "A lot of folks think," Solly is saying, "that Charles Dickens' descriptions of London are right out of date. Let them come down to Stepney with me and I'll show them the legions of germs in our lavatories, some of which are used by four or five families in common, and I'll introduce them to the armies of bugs behind the wall-paper" '. Like Hackenberg's book this book debunks a number of myths that foreigners have about the supposedly aloof, retiring, and cold British. It also points out, 'the average Englishman often lives and dies without ever having possessed a tweed suit'. In the 'Life And Leisure' section there is a useful piece on the theatre by Richard Findlater. The article on the cinema opens with the words, 'If you want to go to the cinema in Britain today you will have to face two problems. The first is to find a cinema in your locality which is still showing films and which has not been turned into a bowling alley, a bingo hall or a ballroom. The second is to find a film worth seeing'. The rest of the article is a fairly straightforward account of the film industry and its problems, including the monopoly of the two big circuits, Rank and ABC, the technical innovations, and the 'new wave' films. Few East German readers would be convinced by Diana Loeser's remarks implying that East European film-makers had been more successful in standing up to competition from television than their British colleagues. John Peet, an ex-Reuters journalist, explains the importance of advertising revenue to the press and admits that the quality newspapers at least, 'do report fairly fully on political events, so that an intelligent reader can form some idea of what is going on in the world'. The section on television is wholly inadequate, saying virtually nothing about commercial television and greatly oversimplifying the political and social slant of the BBC. This section is taken from a book by two British Communist writers, which points out that: 'For political broadcasts the BBC allocates to the three main parties in accordance with their polls at the last general election ... The claims of minority parties are only considered after Nomination Day. A minority party is entitled to one shorter broadcast if it has more than 50 candidates in the field'. The writers then go on rather naïvely to claim: 'This virtual veto on broadcasting imposed on the minority parties is one of the main factors preventing their rise'. Almost the whole of the section devoted to the British state and politics is taken from the book by the same two writers, Harvey and Hood, *The British State* published by Lawrence and Wishart. Two articles are devoted to education. The first outlines the school system in Britain, making the kind of criticism most reforming spirits in Britain make. Its summing-up is:

> Education in England is class-divided and selective. But it is free, universal (to fifteen) and far in advance of what is provided in many other countries. Books are lent to the pupils free. Free milk is provided daily to all pupils. But the vast majority leave school only half-educated and fit only for semi-skilled or unskilled occupations. That this situation is changing is due to the constant struggle of progressive educationalists, the political left and the organised working class, as well as to enlightened administrators.

The piece on British universities is less accurate. For instance, the authors rightly say that there have been demands for expansion of higher education and then tell us 'Some expansion has already occurred.' They mean since 1945. In fact in the twenty years between 1938 and 1958 the number of full-time university students in Great Britain more than doubled! This was before the post-Robbins expansion got under way.

Though this book contains some accurate information and useful facts about Britain and the occasional thoughtful comment about British problems, much of it is too narrowly party political to give its readers a really convincing picture of the country.

Two other East German books on Britain should be mentioned, *Let's Speak English 2* and *Englisch,* a textbook for university and technical students. *Let's Speak English* is issued to the equivalent of grammar schools, the extended high schools. Both books were published in 1967 and both cover the same kind of ground as *Our English Friends* (Part III), mentioned above—trips to the industrial centres of the Midlands, visits to Scotland and Wales, a note on British inventors, a piece on some aspect of education in England, and a brief article on trade unions or the Communist Party. The first of these two books distinguishes itself by a chapter on Alexander Fleming, the doctor who discovered Penicillin, and another on the radio-telescope at Jodrell Bank. When we consider that it is for university students, the second book is not very distinguished and does not rise above the other school textbooks. It also contains one fairly serious political distortion in a chapter on 'The British Peace Movement', inviting the conclusion that the Communist-dominated British Peace Committee is as important as, or more important than, the non-Communist Campaign for Nuclear Disarmament.

Finally, one other book, on English Literature, deserves not only a mention but also some praise. It is *Englische Literatur* by H. Findeisen and G. Seehase and was published in 1964. It consists of brief notes on English, Australian, Irish, Canadian, and South African literature, and biographical notes on writers from these countries. It covers everyone in the 'As' from Matthew Arnold and Jane Austen to James Aldridge and Kingsley Amis, and in the 'Ws' Waugh, Wesker, Wodehouse, and Wordsworth.

All of these books and others on Britain contain many of the expected clichés—'The people of Dresden . . . are doing everything to keep the peace in the world', says the TV series; or 'The Communist Party's influence grows steadily', Ernst Bartsch assures us in *Grossbritannien*—and they greatly exaggerate the importance of the British Communist Party. Yet despite the words attributed to Mr Solly Kaye, they recognize that Dickens is dead. They deal with the Britain we know, not the Britain of our grandfathers. Even at the height of the Cold War East German publications on Britain seemed more realistic, from all accounts, than those of certain other Communist countries. Why should this be so? Perhaps because East Germans were exposed, via West Germany, to much information about Britain, thus forcing them to moderate their tone or even influencing them to some extent. Yet this cannot be the only reason. East Germans can watch West German television and listen to West German radio to keep up with life in the Federal Republic. This has not caused East German media to soften their line on West Germany. Perhaps the relative realism on Britain is in part due to the fact that large numbers of East Germans knew Britain before the war, or during or after the war as prisoners. A relatively large number of 'top' persons in East Germany got to know Britain when they were emigrants. Many of them subsequently took up journalistic or literary posts in East Germany through which they, often friendly disposed towards the UK, would influence the official view of Britain. Another very important reason—proved by the relatively good press for France, Italy, Holland, Belgium, and Scandinavia—is that Britain is not seen as the main enemy; that position is occupied by West Germany and shared by it with the USA and the régimes of Spain and Portugal.

The improvement in the quality and quantity of information available on Britain in the DDR is further a reflection of the relaxing of Cold War postures, improving living standards, and the recognition that sound judgements can only be made on sound information. If, for instance, those East Germans who care are going to find out anyway that, say, living standards are in many respects higher in Britain than in the DDR, it is better that they find out from official East German sources rather than from Western ones. And if East German businessmen and technical experts are to visit Britain it is as well to give them a fairly realistic picture of what they will find there. Otherwise they will lose faith in their own official organs of communications.

Chapter 10

Women behind the Wall

THERE WERE IN 1967 153 women members of the 500-strong *Volkskammer*.[1] The East German parliament has more women both absolutely and relatively than the West German *Bundestag*,[2] the British House of Commons, or most other parliaments. And the number of women in the East German People's Chamber is increasing. In the parliament elected in 1963 there were 137 women members out of a total of 500. Admittedly, the People's Chamber has not got the same authority as the British Parliament, playing as it does a largely formal role. Still, the election of so many women to the *Volkskammer* is symptomatic of the efforts being made in all spheres of East German life to give women real as well as formal equality with men. Certain other figures illustrate the progress made so far. In the 15 regional parliaments of the German Democratic Republic there were in 1965 1,943 men and 886[3] women. In Law, traditionally very much a man's world, over 30 per cent of all judges are women.[4] The same sort of thing is happening in the medical profession. In 1964 51 per cent of all medical students in East Germany were women.[5] And even in technical spheres women are breaking in, or, in many cases, being persuaded to break in. In 1964 7.7 per cent of students at higher technical institutions were women.[6] In the electrical industry the number of female apprentices rose from 5 per cent of the total in 1961 to 9.6 per cent in 1965. The percentage of female apprentices in the metal-working industry rose from 4.6 to 9.0 in the same period.[7]

[1] There are 34 women in the *Bundestag* out of 518 members. *Amtliches Handbuch des Bundestages, 5 Wahlperiode,* Neue Darmstädter Verlagsanstalt.
[2] *Die Volkskammer Der Deutschen Demokratischen Republik, 4 Wahlperiode,* Staatsverlag Der Deutschen Demokratischen Republik, Berlin, 1964.
[3] Statistisches Jahrbuch der Deutschen Demokratischen Republik, Staatsverlag, 1966, p. 582 (henceforth *SJB*).
[4] Inge Hieblinger, *Frauen In Unserem Staat,* Staatsverlag, Berlin, 1967, p. 24.   [5] *SJB*, 1965, p. 460.
[6] *SJB*, 1965, p. 460.   [7] Hieblinger, op. cit., p. 90.

New Laws . . .

The East German constitution of 1968, like the earlier one and that of the Federal German Republic, grants women full equality with men. Article 20 of the DDR constitution states: 'Men and women have equal rights and have the same legal status in all spheres of social, state and personal life. The promotion of women, particularly with regard to vocational qualification, is a task of society and the state'. And Article 24 declares: 'Men and women . . . have the right to equal pay for equal work output'. Under Article 38 women have equality in married life with their husbands.[8]

More significant than these general formulations laid down in the constitution are the provisions of the Family Law which came into force on 1 April 1966. One need not doubt the official claim that this was the product of much discussion in over 34,000 meetings attended by 750,000 people. The authorities, above all the Ministry of Justice, went to a great deal of trouble to find out what people thought on the matter and also the kinds of relationships which already exist within marriage. The author has seen, for instance, a very carefully constructed questionnaire sent out by the Ministry to a representative sample of people. This questionnaire was designed to throw light on how married couples dispose of their incomes, what differences exist between 'mere' housewives and working wives, the differences between social groups in these respects, the extent of durable consumer goods, and so on.

The Law is divided into six parts.[9] Part one is concerned with general principles similar to those in the constitution emphasizing the equality of the spouses. Part two deals with marriage and starts with the traditional statement that it is a union 'for life founded on mutual love, respect and fidelity, and unselfish help for each other'. Paragraph three of this first chapter of part two, calls on those intending to marry seriously to examine whether they are suitable partners for each other. It then lays down that 'The will to this examination can be given expression in an engagement'. The legal age of marriage for both man and woman is set at 18 which conforms to other East German regulations concerning majority. The Law puts the emphasis on marriage in a registry office, but it does state that the marriage ceremony can be

[8] *Constitution of The German Democratic Republic,* VEB Staatsverlag, 1968.
[9] *Ein glückliches Familienleben—Anliegen des Familiengesetzbuches der DDR,* Kanzlei des Staatsrates, Heft 7 (4 Wahlperiode), Staatsverlag, 1966

performed outside of this office providing the responsible official is present. Part two also allows the spouses to choose which of their surnames they will use after their marriage. The Family Law obliges both partners to do their share of educating the children and of the housework. Both have the duty to contribute towards the maintenance of the family, though 'a spouse who has no income or means contributes through housework towards the upbringing of the children'. In theory this could be either partner. The Family Law breaks new ground in connection with property. The property of each partner which each has on marriage remains their own, as does any gift acquired during the marriage. Property of any kind acquired during the marriage by work becomes the joint property of both. This implicitly rewards women who spend their lives as housewives bringing up children. Another new feature of the Family Law in the DDR is that it does not give the wife the automatic right to be kept by the husband. In most cases she will have that right; if she is bringing up the children of the marriage, if she is old or sick, if she wishes to learn a trade or profession, but not if she merely wants to be a housewife, without children; and if able to work, she has no such right. On the other hand, the husband cannot prevent his wife from training for a profession; indeed he has the duty to help her in every way he can. Nor can he ask her to take on unskilled work instead of taking up professional studies.

The East German Family Law does not deal fully with divorce, which is subject to separate legislation. It does, however, state that in deciding divorce applications the court should weigh carefully the interests of any children involved.

One political aspect of the Family Law is that, according to section 42, paragraphs 2 and 4 of part three, parents are obliged to educate their children to 'a socialist outlook towards learning and work, to respect of the working people, to keeping the rules of socialist community life, to solidarity, to socialist patriotism and internationalism'. The parents are further required to cooperate not only with the school authorities but also with the Young Pioneer movement and with the Free German Youth. Let it be said that this is not supposed to contradict the right of parents to bring up their children in the spirit of religion or to acquaint their children with religion. Official spokesmen of the East German CDU have welcomed the Law, saying that it 'conforms to Christian principles'.[10]

---

[10] See *Ein glückliches Familienleben*, statement of Friedrich Kind, Member of the Praesidium of the *Vorstand* of the CDU, p. 51.

Some interesting comments on the Family Law were made in the West German newspaper *Die Welt* (24 December 1966), a newspaper not noted for its friendliness towards the DDR.

The new legal principles laid down have really given the woman a chance to be an independent and responsible partner of the man. The woman is given more duties, but also more rights, than she has in West Germany. This starts with the fact that there is no longer a division of duties in household and profession. In West Germany the Family Law lays down that the woman alone is responsible for the household. She may only pursue a profession 'insofar as this may be reconciled with her duties inside the marriage and the family'. The Federal Supreme Court specifically ruled on 10 March 1959 that professional ties could not free a woman from her duty of sole responsibility for running the household. This means that the West German husband can force his wife to the washing-up sink, even if she is ready and able to pay herself for domestic help.... The West German legislators simply did not take into consideration the fact that a married woman might have a legitimate interest in continuing her professional qualification.... When it comes to the question of divorce, the principle of 'guilt', the ruling principle in the Federal Republic, has been replaced by the principle of 'breakdown'. A marriage should be dissolved when it has ceased to be of value to the spouses, to the children, and to society. The Eastern legislators have also been completely consistent in settling maintenance payments after divorce. The divorced spouse, whether man or woman, is only entitled to maintenance if he or she is unable to support himself or herself.

The article closed, rightly so, on a cautious note : 'it remains to be seen whether women agree with the new role given them by the law makers'.

... Old Attitudes

How then do East German women view their role in practice, and perhaps equally important, where do their menfolk stand on this issue? Undoubtedly, owing to ideas from abroad, owing to the war, and owing to socialist propaganda, East German women are moving away from the view that their domain embraces the three Ks of *Kinder, Kirche, Küche* (children, church, and kitchen), and nothing else. But there is some evidence that, at least so far as careers are concerned, many young women, to say nothing of the older ones, still seek the traditional outlets rather than trying for

something still dominated by men. For example, in Halle the Office
of Labour and Careers Advice reported in 1964 that they had 26
girls trying for careers in Art although there were only six places
vacant. There were 25 vacancies for apprentice hairdressers sought
after by 52 girls. And although ten girls expressed the wish to
become beauticians there were no vacancies available. In the metal
and electrical industries the plan foresaw 179 apprenticeships for
girls, but only 54 girls expressed an interest. Even in factories with
a good 'image', well-known places, where the work is clean and
interesting, such as the VEB Film Factory Wolfen, only 89.8 per
cent of the vacancies for girl apprentices could be filled in 1964.
In 1965 roughly half the girls employed as apprentices were in
such traditional women's spheres as the catering trade, secretarial
work, nursing, shops and the like.[11] An East German lady writer
who has investigated the cause of this has put down this state of
affairs to the attitudes of so many parents who still think that it is
a waste of time for a girl to enter a trade or profession which
involves a long training or exacting study. They still think of their
daughters primarily as future housewives who will need to pick up
extra money for the family but not work at a serious career.[12] On
the positive side, opinion surveys show that as far as East German
women are concerned, few see marriage as an end in itself. Few
would seem to regard marriage as the gaining of the right to a
permanent 'meal ticket'. A survey was carried through among non-
employed housewives to find out why they were not gainfully employed. Nearly half, 44.6 per cent, said it was because of their
children, 29.2 per cent claimed bad health, 11.7 per cent were
invalids or too old, 0.4 per cent were full-time students. There
were only 7.6 per cent who gave their marriage as the reason.
The remainder gave a variety of reasons.[13] Less than 30 per cent
of East German women between the ages of 18 and 60 do not
work. And there is little reason to believe that there are many
bored graduate housewives. In the DDR 84 per cent of them are
employed, as are 75.8 per cent of those with a technical training.[14]

Now something should be said about the attitude of East German
men to the changing place of women in the DDR. The leading East
German economic journal, *Die Wirtschaft* (9 June 1966), published
the results of a survey conducted by a market research institute in

11 Hieblinger, op. cit., p. 91.
12 Ibid., pp. 92–3.
13 *Neue Justiz Zeitschrift Für Recht Und Rechtswissenschaft*, 2. Aprilheft,
Number 8, 1965, p. 233. This magazine is the organ of the East German
Supreme Court.
14 Ibid.

Leipzig. Ostensibly the survey was concerned with the burden of housework and with which members of the family carry that burden. The results showed that the normal East German household spent just under two hours per day on cleaning in 1966. Most revealing about the attitude of East German men to their wives' place in life were the survey's findings about who actually did the work. In households where the wife did not go out to work she did 75.3 minutes' cleaning per day. Her husband did 2.7 minutes' cleaning. The remaining 2.1 minutes of cleaning was done by the children, relatives, or hired help. This is what one would normally expect. But what about the households where the wife was gainfully employed? In such households the wife still spent 60.6 minutes cleaning as against the husband's 5.8 and 7.2 done by other persons. In all families, 87 per cent of the cleaning (102 minutes) was done by the wife, 5.7 per cent (6 minutes) by the husband, and 7.3 per cent (9 minutes) by others. On a more recent occasion (9 February 1967) *Die Wirtschaft* published the results of certain international investigations into the use of time. These showed that among the men of 11 nations East Germans did more housework, including looking after children, than Americans, Yugoslavs, West Germans, and Belgians, in that order. Poles did the most housework, followed by Czechs, Bulgarians, Russians, Hungarians, and Frenchmen (the latter two groups being on a par). In the same 11 countries Hungarian women spent the most time doing housework, including looking after children, followed in order by Yugoslavs, French and West Germans, East Germans, Czechs and Americans, Poles, Belgians, Bulgarians, and finally, Russians. In all countries the main burden of housework fell on the women. On the face of it these figures would seem to imply that East German women did less housework than some others, got more help from their spouses, and were therefore better off. This is not entirely true. The figures for net free time indicate this. Remarkably, East German men had more net free time in autumn 1965 than had the men in the other ten countries mentioned. East German women, however, were much worse off. Although they were better off in this respect than Soviet, Czech, Hungarian, Bulgarian, and even French women, they were worse off than those of Yugoslavia, Belgium, West Germany, and the USA. Whereas women in the Federal Republic had 31.5 hours per week to themselves, their sisters and cousins in the DDR had only 26.6 hours. East German men, though, had 37.1 hours per week free as against 30.3 hours for West Germans. East German women work harder than most women in the advanced countries. Their husbands, with more free time than the

15 * *

men in the other ten countries, would appear to work less. Moreover, East German women have not in the past had all the
gadgets and conveniences of life in the affluent society like those in
the West. They have had to suffer thousands of headaches owing
to the erratic supply of certain foodstuffs, poor shopping facilities,
the neglect of the service industries—launderettes, dry-cleaning
establishments, repair facilities, and the shortage of consumer durables. Though a great deal more needs to be done, there has been
a great improvement in all these things in the sixties, and the fact
that a considerable amount of effort is being used by official bodies
to carry out and discuss the implications of such surveys shows
that they recognize the problem. For them it is both a problem of
ideology and economics—dissatisfied and harassed women work less
well. It is also no doubt the case that East German men in influential positions are themselves harassed—by their wives. The writer
has always found the wives of professional men a very vocal and
critical group in the DDR.

Apart from these limited findings of surveys indicating that East
German men still have a long way to go before their views on the
equality of women, or at least their practice, would satisfy a
Friedrich Engels or an August Bebel, there are statements made
by the East German leaders expressing dissatisfaction with the
complacency of their colleagues. At the VII Congress of the SED
Herr Ulbricht admitted :

> Some people in leading posts are taking matters too lightly.
> They excuse all shortcomings in the promotion of women with
> their being burdened by children and the family. Apparently
> these people do not understand that this is precisely the reason
> why we work for the promotion of women, so as to counter these
> difficulties and permit them to participate in the development of
> socialist society on a basis of equality. The Central Committee
> of the Party is of the opinion that new forces will be won for
> social progress if we can more purposefully develop the ability
> and capabilities of women.[15]

Certainly in industry Ulbricht's words need to be heeded. In
1965 just over 40 per cent of the labour force were women, yet
only about 5 per cent of the 'masters', that is the highly skilled
operatives, were females.[16] Much has already been said in the
appropriate chapter about the position of women in higher education in the DDR, it is certainly better than in most European

15 *Neues Deutschland* (18 April 1967).
16 Hieblinger, op. cit., p. 133.

countries, though still not up to the standards East Germany has set itself. The number of full-time women students in higher educational institutes rose from 6,510 in 1951 to 24,900 in 1963. In percentages this means that in 1951 women represented 23 per cent of the full-time student body, in 1963 they represented 31.7 per cent.[17] Apart from the break-through in medicine, law and, to some extent, technology, the tendency among female students was still to choose the 'traditional' women's faculties. What about politics? As in other countries, East German women tend to be less interested in politics than men. However, the proportion of women members of the SED, to use one simple index, has gone up from 14 per cent in 1948 to 26 per cent in 1966. This increase could be simply a reflection of the increase of qualified women seeking responsible jobs for which membership of the SED is virtually essential, rather than any keen interest in politics as such. Women are still under-represented in the higher echelons of the Party. In the Central Committee elected in 1967 about 12 per cent of the 181 members and candidate members were women. In the *Politbüro* one woman, Margarete Müller, aged 36, a former tractor driver who later studied agricultural economics, advanced in 1967 to candidate membership. The number of women in the Council of Ministers has actually fallen as a result of the reshuffle after the 1967 elections. As we have seen, women are fairly well represented in the *Volkskammer,* though not in proportion to their voting strength, but there is some evidence to suggest that some have had to give up the prospect of marriage in order to concentrate on their careers : 86 lady members of the People's Chamber elected in 1963 were married, 51 were not; 36 of those not married were over 30 and many of them were in the professions. Many of their married colleagues were industrial or agricultural workers. This pattern does, however, appear to be changing and there are many examples of younger professional women who are also wives and mothers in the 1967 People's Chamber.

Sex and Marriage

Having set out the position of East German women today, it is useful to look at the situation of youth in the DDR and see what changes are taking place in the relations between the sexes. Fortunately a comprehensive survey has been done on this, the details

[17] 'Probleme Der Konsequenten Weiterentwicklung Des Frauenstudiums', *Schriftenreiche Der Gewerkschaft Wissenschaft, Forschung lehre Praxis,* Heft 2, 1966, (East) Berlin, p. 51.

of which were published in 1966.[18] The survey was planned and executed by Rolf Borrmann and in the course of it he interviewed 900 young people, 150 parents, 100 teachers in secondary schools, 50 teachers in trade schools—in all 1,200 people. Afterwards he discussed the survey with numerous people in the same categories as well as with lawyers, doctors, and others concerned with youth work. The survey did not reveal that East German youth was very much different from youth anywhere. The same tendencies were exposed. One important finding, which can be regarded as a sign of progress in that it means the end of the double standard of men towards women, concerned attitudes towards the premarital activities of future spouses. Most East German young men interviewed had rid themselves of the old-fashioned idea that it is all right for them to have sex before marriage but not for their future wives. 82.9 per cent of the young men interviewed did not lay down virginity as a requirement of their future partner, only 13.3 per cent did so. Of the girls interviewed, 80.4 per cent were prepared to marry men with previous sexual experience, only 14.3 per cent claimed they would not. It is as well that young East Germans have these broad-minded views because their partners are likely to have had premarital intercourse. Herr Borrmann's researches could none the less lead him to some optimistic conclusions. The great majority of girls did not enter into sexual relations lightly. They had to be convinced of the sincerity and love of their partner before having intercourse. Only 3.9 per cent of girls in the survey admitted to having relations with someone they had not known for at least a month. And a further 38.4 per cent of girls had known their first partner between three and six months. Another 19.2 per cent of girls had been friendly with their first partner for a year, and 19.9 per cent up to two years. East German youths were not quite so particular. Borrmann was also pleased to find that the majority of the youth of both sexes have their first intercourse believing either that they are in love or that they like the other person. Of the girls, only 3.2 per cent claimed to have been seduced (1.3 per cent of the young men), only 5.1 per cent because they were curious (22.2 per cent of men). This East German researcher was further gratified to discover that 87.1 per cent of the girls and 74.3 per cent of the young men changed their sexual partners either not at all or only occasionally—that is they had firm friendships. The East German government would be pleased that the survey revealed that the wish to found a family is strong

18 Rolf Borrmann, *Jugend und Liebe*, Urania-Verlag, Leipzig, Jena, Berlin, 1966.

among East German youth. Among the young men 72.5 per cent expressed the wish to father two children, 67.4 per cent of the girls wanted two. An additional 6.7 per cent of boys and 12.3 per cent of girls wanted three children. Only 2.5 per cent of the boys and 1.6 per cent of the girls were against having any children at all. The survey also showed that family life in the DDR is fairly satisfactory in that the majority of young people claimed to have been influenced to some extent by the example of their parents' relations to each other. Reading this survey one is struck by the apparently small influence of official persons or organizations on these young people. For instance, most met their friends of the opposite sex in dance halls or similar places, few in the Free German Youth. Only 24.6 per cent had learned most of their sexual knowledge from their teachers and only 30 per cent said they looked to any person as an example (other than their parents). The survey did not investigate the influence of religion, but indirectly one gains the impression that it had had little influence on the young persons concerned.

In East Germany as in other countries the age at marriage is dropping. In 1952 men were marrying on average at 25.6 years old. Women at that time were getting married when they were 23.8 years old. By 1962 the average age of men at marriage was 23.8 years old while that of women was 22.5.[19] As elsewhere there is also an increase in the number of babies conceived before marriage. Official figures show that 85 per cent of babies born in the first year of marriage belong to this category.[20] On the other hand, the number of children born out of wedlock is declining. This is somewhat surprising when one considers the increase in premarital intercourse and that there is no discrimination against the offspring of unmarried mothers. It is also surprising when one remembers that pregnancy is often given as the reason for having got married by young couples seeking divorce.[21] Clearly this points to the continued influence of the traditional view that to be an unmarried mother is a social stigma. Probably owing to the conservative influence of Stalin, and to try to counter low birth-rates, the East German abortion law of 1950 only allowed operations in certain narrowly defined cases. Although this law still applies, a circular was sent out by the Ministry of Health in 1965 widening its scope.

It is notoriously dangerous and difficult to compare divorce statistics, depending as they do on the type of divorce laws in force,

19 *Neue Justiz*, Number 8, 1965, p. 231.
20 Ibid., p. 232.
21 Ibid., p. 232.

religious and educational factors. Bearing this in mind we find that so far as the incidence of divorce is concerned, East Germany is in a fairly middle position in the international divorce league tables. In 1961, for instance, there were 21.8 divorces per 10,000 inhabitants in the USA, 18 in Romania, 17.4 in Hungary, 14.6 in Denmark, and 14.4 in the DDR. On the other hand, there were fewer divorces in the Soviet Union (13), Czechoslovakia (11.9), Yugoslavia (11.6), Sweden (11.4), Austria (11.4), Finland (8), West Germany (8.8), and Poland (5.5).[22] It is clear that particularly in Romania, Hungary, Czechoslovakia, Yugoslavia, Austria, West Germany, and Poland, religion is an important factor. The authorities in the DDR are not happy about the frequency of divorce. As a Ministry of Justice publication puts it: 'The number of divorces in the DDR is relatively high. ... Social security of the families does not automatically lead to stability in family relations.'[23] Its research showed that better-off families are frequently among those seeking divorce, as are the members of the intelligentsia. The agricultural and Catholic areas figured less prominently in divorce statistics than did industrial and Protestant areas. One positive phenomenon in recent years, positive that is from the point of view of female emancipation, is the growing proportion of divorce applications entered by women: 54.4 per cent of the total in 1958, 57 per cent in 1963. Finally, the most frequent reasons for seeking divorce in the DDR are the adultery of the man, hasty marriage, drunkenness on the part of the man, adultery of the wife, and sexual difficulties.

The German Social Democratic leader, August Bebel, who died in 1913, was the author of a highly successful book on the emancipation of women, *Die Frau und der Sozialismus,* which ran into 50 editions by 1909. In it he expressed many advanced ideas, including some, such as communal kitchens to help free women from the drudgery of the old-fashioned kitchen,[24] which the East German authorities and people would be hesitant about introducing. Most of the ideas expressed by Bebel are widely held in the advanced countries by Marxists and non-Marxists alike. East German writers on the subject often refer to this book and, broadly speaking, one can say that the DDR has made a great deal of progress in the direction of realizing Bebel's ideals. As we have seen, they still have a long way to go.

[22] *Neue Justiz,* Number 8, 1965, p. 234.
[23] Ibid., p. 234.
[24] August Bebel, *Die Frau und der Sozialismus,* Verlag von J. H. W. Dietz Nachf. GmbH, Stuttgart, 1911, p. 470.

Chapter 11

The NVA: the Red Prussians or the Proletarian Guard?

Merely a Police Force?

THE GOOSE-STEPPING guards in 'stone grey' uniforms, the rumbling heavy *Panzerwagen*, and the martial strains of Beethoven's Yorck March on Berlin's Marx-Engels-Platz celebrating the end of the war or May Day could lead a modern Rip Van Winkle to believe that Germany had somehow turned the tide in 1945 and won the war after all. It could lead the cynical to suppose that the Soviets had simply re-activated their share of the Prussian military caste and set them marching again. Happily Rip Van Winkle would be wrong for, as usual, the truth is not as simple as it first appears.

It is difficult to say precisely when the East German armed forces were set up, for this partly depends on how one interprets the various para-military units which existed prior to 1956. A West German writer has commented :

> The decisive step was made by the Soviets in the summer of 1948. . . . The . . . order of 3 June 1948 introduced the decisive phase in the build-up of the regular military forces. The German Administration of Interior was ordered to establish training institutions and units for the creation of military cadre formations.

According to the same writer :

> The management of the disguised military forces, now standing under the Chief Administration of Schooling, was taken over in September 1949 by Wilhelm Zaisser, a specialist in civil war who was trained in the USSR and who made his reputation as 'General Gomez' in the Spanish Civil War. . . . His deputy became Heinz Hoffmann, also trained in the USSR, at the Frunze Academy. He, too, was an officer of the *International Brigades* in Spain.[1]

[1] Thomas M. Forster, *The East German Army,* Allen & Unwin, London, 1967, pp. 19–21.

229

In 1949 the *Deutsche Volkspolizei*, or German People's Police, was officially set up as the national police of the then Soviet Zone with units similar to the para-military formations of the French and Italian police. Certainly in 1952, at the second *Parteikonferenz* of the Socialist Unity Party, two months after the signing of the European Defence Community Treaty by the West German Federal Republic, and a short time after the setting-up of the *Amt Blank* (the forerunner of the West German Defence Ministry), the decision was taken to set up armed forces (*bewaffnete Streitkräfte*) in East Germany. Such formations were still called police but in British eyes, at any rate, they looked more than merely police. The British government, in an attempt to mobilize opinion for West German rearmament, issued a White Paper in July 1954 dealing with the military wing of the East German People's Police which claimed that these forces consisted of between 80,000 and 85,000 men : 'There now exist two Soviet-type rifle corps, each of two infantry divisions and one mechanised division. There is also one independent mechanised division. It is estimated that altogether about 1,300 tanks and self-propelled guns and 1,300 field, anti-tank and anti-aircraft guns are held.'[2]

The White Paper also noted that the East Germans had a sea police, 'naval in character and about six thousand strong with thirty small minesweepers, patrol boats, and auxiliaries'. The air police, the White Paper continued, had a total strength of about 7,500 men equipped with 75 Soviet 'Yak' trainers. West Germany had at that time, according to the same source, the Federal Frontier Defence Force of 'rather more than ten thousand men equipped with pistols, rifles, light machine-guns, and about fifty armoured cars ... The force includes a marine detachment of about seven hundred men in guard and patrol boats armed with machine-guns'. In addition, each *Land* of the Federal Republic had its own mobile police force which taken together amounted to about 10,000 men, armed with pistols, rifles, and light machine-guns. West Germany had no units equipped with aircraft at that time.

On Frankfurt/Main station in August 1952 the writer was surprised to see numerous men in American military uniforms but with shoulder flashes bearing the word 'Germany' or 'Ukraine' or 'Latvia' or 'Poland'. These were members of the so-called 'Labour Units' and the 'Industrial Police' and were not mentioned in the British government's White Paper, although they had existed more or less since the end of the war. Already in November 1945 the Americans were using uniformed, armed, Germans, some in 'mobile' units,

[2] Germany No. 1 (1954) (12 July 1954), Cmd. 9213, HMSO.

officially to protect military supplies.³ On 23 October 1950 the West German newspaper *Nürnberger Nachrichten* reported the US Army Headquarters in Germany as denying rumours that these units were a camouflaged army. The Americans, it said then, had some 30,000 men in such units. The newspaper continued : 'The majority of the men are Germans, about 60 per cent former soldiers including former *Wehrmacht* generals. The former Lieutenant-General Gustav von Varst, who served under Rommel in Africa, is with the Labour Companies in Nuremberg. . . . In addition the former Generals von Schlieben, Paul Mahlmann, and former generals of the *Luftwaffe* hold the ranks of Majors in the Labour Companies.'

The British also maintained such units. In addition the Western Allies employed former German naval personnel on minesweepers.

As late as 22 November 1954 *The Times* did not take the military formations of the People's Police too seriously : 'Their equipment is known to be antiquated. A genuine Soviet desire to turn them into an effective striking force must inevitably show up first in the delivery of modern tanks, artillery and aircraft; and this evidence has so far been lacking.'

The build-up in the numbers of the *Kasernierte Volkspolizei* (KVP), as the para-military units of the People's Police were known before 1954, was the result of the stepping-up of military propaganda among the young and pressure of various kinds. The young were encouraged to learn skills, in the newly organized *Gesellschaft für Sport und Technik*, or Society for Sport and Technology, which could be regarded as of military value. These include shooting and field sports; gliding, training in sports aircraft, and parachuting; automobile and motorcycle sports; navigation, signals, diving, and swimming; radio and signalling; sports associated with horses, dogs, and pigeons.

In 1953 East Germany's armed forces got their first taste of action during the *Volksaufstand*, or People's Revolt (Western version), or *faschister Putsch* (Eastern version). This event, as the writer has heard from persons who were in the KVP at that time, shook East Germany's military formations to their very roots. Nevertheless, by the beginning of 1955 the West German Ministry for All-German Affairs reported that morale among the officers was high, with relatively few desertions. More than 65 per cent of the deserters were under twenty-one. Most of them had not completed one year's

³ Oliver J. Frederiksen, 'The American Military Occupation of Germany 1945–1953', Historical Division, US Army, Europe, Headquarters, 1953, p. 53; see also p. 70.

service. Only 2 per cent of them had spent over four years in the force.[4] This was possibly because 'in 1955 the training and equipment of units were generally improved. The training places of the troops were extended. In October of the same year the first large-scale autumn manoeuvres took place in which several divisions participated'.[5]

On 2 January 1956 the first recruits joined the West German *Bundeswehr*. A few days later, on 18 January, the DDR People's Chamber passed an Act setting up the *Nationale Volksarmee* (NVA), the People's Army. Thus the East German forces in their present, truly military, form were established.

Some Dilemmas

It is difficult to estimate the exact value of the People's Police in barracks in building up the *Volksarmee*; clearly they played their part. As two East German military historians have put it :

Although the cadre of the KVP were on no account scheduled from the start for involvement in an army, they represented, in the first phase of the build-up of the national armed forces [*Streitkräfte*], an appropriate reserve, which the leadership of the DDR could and must use when selecting the officer corps [of the NVA]. And, in any case, after the integration of West Germany into the aggressive NATO pact, there was every reason to prepare the KVP officers for such a possible use; accordingly, appropriate measures were introduced.[6]

Nevertheless, the same source tells us, a great many officers were recruited from civilian life, including many who were delegated from the Socialist Unity Party.

From the start of their campaign to build up something more than just ordinary police forces the East German leaders and their Soviet sponsors were faced with certain dilemmas. In the eyes of the world, and in the eyes of many of their own staunchest supporters both inside and beyond the frontiers of the Democratic Republic, the German armed forces of the past were an intrinsic part of the German authoritarian and aggressive state. How could a new East German fighting force effectively dissociate itself, and convince the world it was so doing, from the aggressive forces of the past, and at the same time remain German? What uniforms would its members wear? Who would lead it? How could its soldiers be

[4] *Manchester Guardian* (1 February 1955).
[5] Forster, op. cit., p. 27.
[6] *Zeitschrift für Militärgeschichte* (*ZMG*), No. 1, 1966, p. 33.

educated for the new society? And how could that society ensure that the new force would remain its servant, and not become its master?

The effectiveness and spirit of any army cannot be gauged from its uniforms alone, but they can be important psychologically, and any revolutionary régime has a difficulty with them. It wants to show it is carrying on the best of the past but also introducing something new. If it is to win the support of the people for the new force it must consider their likely response to various uniforms. Moreover, in countries where military propaganda has been widespread and most men have served in a national service army the old uniforms are likely to be popular if only because they have been worn by loved ones and are familiar. Of course, in this case, in the case of Germany, the leaders of the Federal Republic had exactly the same problem. They ignored the views of many of the older generation and decided on American uniforms to appease world public opinion. As this writer found out talking to *Bundeswehr* recruits, these uniforms were not popular. They have gradually acquired more of the cut and style of the old uniforms.

The first uniforms of the KVP were typically German without being exact replicas of anything prior to 1945. After October 1952 the KVP started to be issued with uniforms of a distinctly Slavonic style and at a distance its members could be mistaken for Russians. Perhaps these uniforms were meant to allay the fears of the Soviet people and the Soviet Union's allies or perhaps they were meant to show the Soviets' determination to build up a thoroughly pro-Soviet force in East Germany. Whatever the reasons, they were not very popular in the German Democratic Republic. The *Nationale Volksarmee*, in keeping with its name, got traditional German uniforms from the outset and has retained them since it was set up in 1956. A Western report[7] claimed shortly after their introduction, that they had 'broken the ice' in the relations between the People's Army and the population and had helped to improve these relations. These NVA uniforms are very similar to those of the *Wehrmacht* and the *Reichswehr* which existed before it. When they were first introduced in 1956 Willi Stoph, then Minister of Defence, attempted to justify them in the following terms:

There are important progressive traditions in the military history of our people which found expression in the uniform. German imperialism and fascism, however, degraded the uniform as a symbol of military and national honour ... In the National

[7] *Frankfurter Allgemeine Zeitung (FAZ)* (3 August 1957).

People's Army, the German uniform will have a true patriotic meaning as an expression of a resolute preparedness for the defence of our democratic achievements.

And :

In these uniforms, but with red armbands, the armed workers in 1918 chased out the Kaiser; the Hamburg workers, miners from the Ruhr, workers and peasants from Saxony and Thuringia fought against the nationalist Freikorps and the reactionary *Reichswehr*. In these uniforms, in the Second World War, many officers and soldiers came forward in the National Committee Free Germany against the Hitler fascist army.[8]

The East German leaders must remain uneasy about the uniforms of their troops. Their enemies label them the 'Red Prussians', yet had their soldiers worn Slavonic-type uniforms they would have given more force to the charge that they were merely 'Soviet puppets'. Although the People's Army got back traditional German military uniforms it did not get back the right to wear medals belonging to the old régimes. This contrasts with the situation in the West German armed forces whose members are allowed to wear belonging to the old régimes. This contrasts with the situation in medals worn by members of the NVA will be for activities after the setting-up of the DDR. However, three medals have been created to cover activities before 1945. In May 1965 there were six members of the NVA who had the right to wear the medal for taking part in the struggles of the German working class between 1918 and 1923. The Medal for Fighters against Fascism 1933 to 1945 was worn by 158 East German soldiers at that time. These would include both those who worked illegally in Germany and some who carried on propaganda for the USSR. The Hans Beimler Medal was awarded to those who had fought on the Republican side in the Spanish Civil War. In 1965 42 members of the East German armed forces had been granted this honour.[9] No doubt there were also members of the forces who had the right to wear Soviet and other suitable decorations mainly connected with the 1939–45 war.

Officers and Ideology

Four or five socio-political groups can be noticed among the officers of the National People's Army. As one would expect from the above-mentioned medals, there are those who were Communists

[8] Forster, op. cit., p. 142.
[9] *Taschenbuch für Wehrpflichtige,* Deutscher Militärverlag, 1965, pp. 14–15.

or socialists before 1933, who fought in Spain, who were emigrants, or who were imprisoned by the Nazis. Then there are the former *Wehrmacht* officers who, almost exclusively, were captured by or surrendered to the Soviets on the Eastern Front. Thirdly, there are former NCOs and soldiers who were also prisoners-of-war in Soviet hands. Fourthly, there are younger men with no military experience before 1945 who, although ill-equipped educationally, were from the right, that is proletarian, backgrounds. Finally, newer still, are the rising group of officers who are part of the post-war social and educational revolution which has been going on in the German Democratic Republic. The first group were and are important in determining the political orientation and tone of the NVA. Out of about 50 top officers up to 1962 at least 33 belonged to this group.[10] About 12 top officers belonged to the second category—four *Wehrmacht* generals, one colonel, four majors, one lieutenant, one second lieutenant, one rank unknown. In almost all cases the members of this group changed sides before the end of the war and carried on propaganda activities against the Nazis. They were taken on because at least a minimum number of officers with military knowledge were required. In 1957 a West German report estimated that only between one and 2 per cent of the officers of lower rank were taken over from the *Wehrmacht*.[11] The same report said that even at that time officers who served under Hitler were being removed to merely administrative posts. Several of the top officers in this category are, like Colonel Adam, Major-General von Lenski, and General Vincenz Müller, either retired or dead. The third and fourth groups are more and more giving way to the fifth group of young, highly trained, and highly educated professionals. The East German officer corps differs sharply from that of West Germany in that it is younger and, sociologically speaking, is more representative both of the various sections of the East German élite and of the population in its part of Germany. It also differs sharply from the old German officer class. As one West German academic put it: 'Whereas in the Federal Republic the old experts were used, who in their backgrounds differed little from the old German officer corps, the DDR has been apparently successful, with the help of former experts, in forming a new military élite, in no way connected with the traditional German officer corps'.[12]

Most armies today try to give their soldiers a certain basic

[10] Werner Baur, 'Deutsche Generale' in *Studien zur Soziologie: Beiträge zur Analyse der deutschen Oberschicht,* edited by Wolfgang Zapf, R. Piper & Co, Munich, 1965.

[11] *FAZ* (3 August 1957).

[12] Baur, op. cit., p. 122.

minimum of civic training in the norms and ideals of the society they are supposed to be serving. In Communist armies this is of the highest importance and in the NVA more important still, owing to Germany's recent past. Soldiers get a minimum of four hours' weekly political education, officers a basic eight hours a month.[13] There are also political lectures and discussions organized especially for members of the *SED* and the Free German Youth (*FDJ*). This political education may be given by a particular unit's NCOs or officers, or by the specially trained *Politoffiziere*, who do not, it must be noted, enjoy the power formerly held by the Political Commissars of the Soviet forces. Journals such as *Armee Rundschau* (monthly) and *Die Volksarmee* (weekly) also get the Party's message across to the troops.

The official *Taschenbuch für Wehrpflichtige* (literally 'pocket book' but, better, Handbook for National Servicemen) gives us some idea how history is dealt with in the *Volksarmee* and what themes are considered important. The starting point is the German peasant war of the sixteenth century which is presented as an anti-feudal, national revolutionary war, a war partly fought to bring about a national German state. The war produced notable peasant military leaders such as Jäcklein Rohrbach, Anton Eisenhut, and Michael Geismayer, who led ill-trained and ill-equipped armies to victory against the professional soldiery of the lords. By contrast, this period of German military and social history went unmentioned in Captain Gesterding's *Zwanzig Offizierthemen*, an official pamphlet produced for officers in 1935. Both volumes deal with the campaign against the French 300 years later. The *Taschenbuch* puts the emphasis on the people fighting against French invaders and feudal lords, the latter selfishly compromising the national interest. The leaders of this patriotic movement were, says the *Taschenbuch*, Scharnhorst, who said, 'Tradition in the army means to march at the head of progress'; and Gneisenau: 'Every nation must so honour itself that it does not tolerate any institution which lowers its standing in the eyes of other peoples.' The third national military hero at this time was, according to this Communist version of history, Field Marshal Blücher. The Communist version also emphasizes the military alliance of Germany and Russia, at that time both engaged in expelling the French. The Nazi version of Captain Gesterding puts the emphasis, when discussing this period, on the kings of Prussia and claims that the military contribution of the

[13] Thomas M. Forster, *NVA, Die Armee der Sowjetzone*, Markus-Verlag, Cologne, 1964; this is the German version of the book referred to above.

citizen volunteers, as opposed to the professional troops, has been overrated. It is interesting that in West Germany, as in East Germany, the very same quotations from the Prussian military reformers are being bandied about to prove that the *Bundeswehr* too is following in their footsteps. The first *de facto* West German Defence Minister, Theodor Blank, quoted the very same words of Scharnhorst in 1955 as he was propounding his 'citizen in uniform' conception.[14] Again in contrast to the Nazi pamphlet, the *Taschenbuch* gives appropriate praise to the national democratic revolution of 1848–9. The various left-wing armed risings from 1918 to 1923 are also of obvious importance to the historians of the NVA. The *Taschenbuch*, for instance, claims :

> In October 1923, in the last year of the revolutionary post-war crisis, Ernst Thälmann, the unforgettable leader of the German working class and later Chairman of the KPD, led the Hamburg proletariat in an armed revolt. With unequalled courage and military finesse 300 badly armed workers gave thousands of well-armed police and counter-revolutionary soldiers a good, heroic, class struggle.

This revolt is presented as a victory for the working class even though it was in fact put down by the authorities. The struggle of the International Brigades in Spain is another important lesson for the NVA. According to the *Zeitschrift für Militargeschichte* it

> can be rated as an outstanding example of unconditional loyalty to the working class and its Marxist–Leninist Party. Its correct evaluation can contribute to the development of such socialist military virtues as confidence in victory, the readiness to sacrifice and struggle, discipline, valour, and close allegiance to the working class and all toilers as well as hatred of the enemies of the peoples.[15]

In the same article the part played, on the Republican side, by Poles, Hungarians, Czechs, and Russians and, on the other side, by Hitler's 'Legion Condor', is stressed. It is pointed out that the East German Minister of Defence, Heinz Hoffmann, fought in the *Interbrigaden* : General Heinz Trettner, until July 1966 Inspector of the *Bundeswehr*, served in the 'Legion Condor'. This fact, and West Germany's close ties with Franco's Spain, help to convince East German writers that their leaders, the anti-fascists of the

---

[14] Norbert Tönnies, *Der Weg zu den Waffen*, Erich Pabel Verlag, Cologne, 1961, p. 18.
[15] *ZMG*, No. 2, 1966, p. 216.

1930s, are still waging the same struggle against the same people, now in the uniforms of the *Bundeswehr*.

Walter Ulbricht, East German Head of State and SED First Secretary, once admitted that neither the illegal activities of the KPD nor those of any other group had had much effect in the campaign against the Third Reich. Despite this, in recent years SED researchers have looked hard for any scrap of evidence of KPD underground fighters, Germans who changed sides to join partisan units, and all others who stood up to the Nazis. The aim is to show that there always was 'another Germany', and that the best representatives of that other Germany were more often than not in the Communist Party. A recent piece of research discovered that 'alone in the Belorussian and Baltic sectors of the Eastern Front there were 14 armed groups of German anti-fascists'[16] operating against the *Wehrmacht*. According to this Communist researcher the members of these groups were 'sincere anti-fascists deeply convinced of the rightness of their struggle. Time and again they risked their lives in order to help to shorten the war and to save as many as possible of their former comrades from ruin. Their number grew continuously'. One such group, we are told, was led by a certain Captain Peukert, a holder of the Nazi Knight's Cross and a battalion commander before being taken prisoner at Stalingrad. This group went into action barely one month before the end of hostilities and tapped the remaining telephones of the *Wehrmacht* and distributed leaflets urging German troops to surrender. Richard Sorge, the German Communist spy who passed Nazi secrets to the Soviet Union, is now recalled as a great hero.

The only war memoirs which are allowed to be published in East Germany are those which expose Nazi crimes and bring home the horror of death in the snow and mud of the Eastern Front. The reminiscences of Colonel Wilhelm Adam, former 1st Adjutant of the ill-fated 6th Army of Stalingrad, underline this:

> The German soldier achieved in the battle on the Volga an unutterably high effort. He fought with daring and bravery and readiness to make sacrifices ... 76 days and nights he sustained the worst privations, fighting against cold and hunger. Certainly, the personal sacrifice of the numbers of the *Wehrmacht* must not be denied. But that is not the point. The question is why the sacrifice was made. What law ordered them to the Volga to spread death, suffering and destruction? ... Painful and bitter it was for me, a professional soldier, to discover that I had served,

[16] *ZMG*, No. 1, 1966, p. 52.

THE NVA

in good faith, a bad cause and been involved with guilt and responsibility. Only after a long process of rethinking ... was the
reason for our defeat gradually clear. It was not the result of the
cold or mud or the 'largeness of Russia', or the military mistakes
of the generals or Hitler's alone, as so many West German
memoirs try to convince us. Nor was it the result of a 'stab in
the back'... It was the consequence of the ruinous policy of
conquest of German imperialism and militarism, to which the
army of the first socialist state answered with a steel 'Stop!'

Adam's admission of guilt is in contrast to his colleagues who
published their memoirs in the West. And, as Adam points out, they
try to throw the blame on Hitler or the weather or their allies. As
Field Marshal von Kleist put it, 'We did not underrate the Red
Army, as is commonly imagined. The last German military attaché
in Moscow, General Köstring—a very able man—had kept us well
informed about the state of the Russian Army. But Hitler refused
to credit his information'. Speaking about Stalingrad, General
Blumentritt claimed that an attack had been launched by 'only
one Russian battalion, but an entire Italian division had bolted'.[17]
He also spoke about the 'Slav-Asiatic character' of the Russians
which 'only understands the absolute, disobedience is non-existent'.[18]

Neither Colonel Adam nor any other East German writer deals
with the Russo–German military co-operation of the 1920s initiated
by General Hans von Seeckt, who was Chief of the German Army
Command from 1920 to 1926, and terminated by Hitler.[19] The East
Germans are probably embarrassed by this co-operation even
though, from the Marxist standpoint, it was entirely justified.

For Communist writers Colonel Graf Schenk von Stauffenberg,
the man who placed the bomb in Hitler's East Prussian headquarters, is a hero, but they distinguish two groups among the
plotters of 1944. The one group consisted of officers such as von
Stauffenberg, Henning von Tresckow, and Mertz von Quirnheim
and Social Democrats such as Professor Reichwein and Julius
Leber. These plotters, so we are told,[20] were prepared to take up
contact with the *Nationalkomittee Freies Deutschland,* the Communist-run anti-Nazi committee of German emigrants and German

[17] The quote from Adam is taken from Wilhelm Adam and Otto Rühle,
Der Schwere Entschluss, Verlag der Nation, Berlin, 1965, pp. 6–7; the
quote from Blumentritt is from B. H. Liddell Hart, *The Other Side of the
Hill,* Panther Books, London, 1956, pp. 225, 247.
[18] Hart, op. cit., p. 247.
[19] F. L. Carsten, in *Survey,* No. 44/45 (October 1962).
[20] Gerhard Förster and others, *Der preussisch-deutsche Generalstab 1640–
1965,* Dietz Verlag, Berlin, 1966, p. 291.

16 * *

prisoners-of-war operating from the Soviet Union. The others are presented as reactionaries, which so many of them undoubtedly were, who were for Hitler when he was riding high, but who turned on the Führer when the tide of war turned against him. They sought a separate peace with the Western Allies.

Nowadays East German publications deal much more than in Stalin's day with the war effort of the Western Allies in the 'Anti-Hitler Coalition'. A technically excellent book, *Der zweite Weltkrieg: eine Chronik in Bildern,* by Heinz Bergschicker, and published by the Deutscher Militärverlag, gives due attention to the Battle of Britain, the war in Africa, the war at sea starting with the sinking of the *Graf Spee,* the struggle against Japan, and the resistance movements in Western Europe. The British convoys to Russia are shown and British help is mentioned. There is criticism of the Narvik operation, the Dieppe landings, the slowness of the start of the Second Front. Allied bombing of Germany, it is correctly pointed out, did not stop war production from rising. As for the efforts of British troops in North Africa, we are told (p. 291) : 'In two years brave struggle they succeeded on a front, on which the German High Command, due to its increasing worries in the Soviet Union, did not put great value. Their success greatly influenced Italy. Germany's military position was hardly affected.'

The East German military press probably differs little in style and subject matter from most others. It is a mixture of pin-ups, sport, soldiers' jokes, soldiers' problems, and pictures designed to increase the troops' knowledge of, and interest in, weapons of friend and foe of yesterday and today. There are also occasional articles presenting short stories, telling how recruits are surprised to find that they can withstand even the hardest of training exercises such as marching, at night, kilometre after kilometre, over rough country in anti-radiation masks.[21] The East German military press also tries hard to make the soldier feel he is part of the strongest military alliance the world has ever seen, an alliance based on friendship and mutual respect. Pictures show *Volksarmee* soldiers smiling arm in arm with Soviet, Czech, or Polish servicemen even though in real life Soviet servicemen stationed in Germany rarely get the opportunity to mix with ordinary East Germans. One difference between East German and official Western soldiers' magazines is that the former are much more political. They try to give their readers basic orientation on happenings in various countries and concentrate much of their effort denouncing West Germany's rulers. Naturally they have made much of the 'Starfighter' crashes,

[21] *Armee Rundschau* (June 1965).

the 'U-4' submarine disaster, the inadequacies of Franz-Josef Strauss, and the crisis over Bonn's generals in the 1960s.

Officers and Men

What is life like for the soldiers of the NVA? What rights do they have? Living standards, though lower in certain respects than those of West Germany, are high in the DDR and the soldiers of the *Volksarmee* enjoy those high standards. As in all armies there is a good deal of drinking and boredom, but those in charge try to overcome this with cultural activities and sport. The *Taschenbuch* claims that soldier's libraries in the DDR contain over a million volumes, that there are nearly 350 places equipped to show films, that almost every company has its own television set, and that there are many literary, photographic, scientific, musical, and other clubs with appropriate facilities. One need not doubt this, nor the claims about opportunities for sport, which is a serious matter in all modern armies. The NVA has more proof than most armies that such opportunities exist in the form of the success of its members in international competitions. At the Olympic Games of 1960 East German servicemen won two silver and one bronze medals. In 1964 they won one gold, four silver, and five bronze medals.

East German soldiers get relatively more holidays than those of the pre-war *Wehrmacht*. Those doing their 18-months' national service have the right to 18 days' paid holiday and to see their families at least six times during their service. In addition to evening and weekend passes soldiers also have the right to two of the four recognized public holidays—Easter, Whitsun, Christmas, and New Year. They can also get time off for good work, illness, and on a wide variety of compassionate grounds. Soldiers, but not officers, who leave their quarters on short passes must normally wear their uniforms, though their superiors can give them permission to do otherwise. Those on longer holidays need not wear them. Living quarters are said to be more crowded than before the war, but professional soldiers, NCOs, and officers have the right to live outside military quarters. The average monthly industrial wage in East Germany is about 650 MDN per month. Conscripts get 80 MDN; a regular starts at 300 MDN as does a second lieutenant; a major receives 600 MDN.[22] Conscripts do not have to pay tax or social insurance out of this. Nor do those who get certain extra allowances—panzer soldiers, frontier troops, sailors, for example. On demobilization conscripts get a small allowance to help them in their return to civilian life. They also have the right to get

[22] Forster (German version), op. cit., pp. 218–19.

their old jobs back. Their families get allowances from the local authorities which vary according to the size of the family and the wife's ability to work. Such allowances in no way affect the normal children's allowances which are paid in the DDR for the first and all subsequent children. The wives of conscripts can also get rent and other allowances in certain cases. Conscripts who have signed hire-purchase agreements, taken out insurance policies, have to re-pay housing or other loans can either, where the money is owed to a public undertaking, have repayments suspended, or, if the money is owed to a private body, get an interest-free loan to cover re-payments. This applies when such obligations have been entered upon before call-up.

The relations between officers and men in the NVA are supposed to be determined by 'socialist norms'. The traditional *Burschen-dienst*, the use of soldiers as servants for officers, has, in accordance with these norms, been officially abolished. A former NVA officer, a deserter, has written[23] that although the officers at the Defence Ministry hold to this rule, their colleagues in provincial towns do not always do so. But he went on to admit that those soldiers who complained about this were usually successful. Relations between officers and men seem to be much more relaxed than those in, say, the British Army, or, for that matter, the Soviet forces. Even the casual observer notices this in East German garrison towns. No doubt this is partly the result of official ideology; it is certainly partly connected with the fact that there are many working-class officers in the East German armed forces, and many more from non-officer families.

The armies of Hitler and the Kaisers were well known for the *Kommisgeist*, that compound of blind obedience, clockwork reflexes, and corpse-like discipline. But the official training manual of 1938, *Der Rekrutenunteroffizier*, condemned this:

> The best educational medium is always the example. The NCO's way of life, both on and off duty, should therefore be exem-plary ... Whoever attempts to hide his own incompetence and ignorance by shouting and cursing runs the danger of becoming the laughing-stock of his men ... Strictness and severity must be coupled with benevolence. But strictness and severity have noth-ing to do with chicanery and ill-treatment, and benevolence has nothing to do with weakness ... The personal honour of sub-ordinates is just as important as that of superiors.[24]

[23] *Der Spiegel* (15 July 1959).
[24] Klaus Stock, *Der Rekrutenunteroffizier*, Verlag von E. S. Mittler & Sohn, Berlin, 1938, pp. 1–2.

Notwithstanding these high sentiments, the *Kommisgeist* triumphed in the *Wehrmacht*. Now both German armies claim to have abolished this spirit. There has been enough evidence from West Germany over the last few years to show that there the *Bundeswehr* has not entirely succeeded.[25] This is despite a carefully worked-out legal framework granting the West German soldier many more rights than the older generation of German soldiers enjoyed, as well as the abolition of military courts and the setting-up, following the Swedish model, of the institution of parliamentary commissioner, or *Wehrbeauftragter*, to protect the rights of servicemen. Despite all the constitutional devices, malpractices have taken place. This writer believes there would have been more had it not been for these constitutional devices. What is the situation in the *Volksarmee*? The East German authorities claim that the kind of brutalities which have soiled the honour of the West German armed forces could hardly happen in the National People's Army because by its nature it is a socialist force, both officers and other ranks having a socialist consciousness. They do admit, though, that owing to the 'remnants of views about military service from the past' and the personal weaknesses of individuals the power to command is sometimes misused. An example of this is given. A company is on a march. They are given the order to sing. They are not very successful. The officer then orders them to put their gas-masks on. They then march on wearing their masks.[26] The East German colonel giving this example points out that it is perfectly proper for a fellow officer to order his men to march in gas-masks in order to increase their military efficiency but not to degrade them. There is no special institution in East Germany which concerns itself exclusively, like the West German *Wehrbeauftrager*, with protecting the rights of the troops. However, the *Taschenbuch* (pp. 318–19) assures its readers:

> The provost-marshal's organs pay great attention to the maintenance of the rights of the individual members of the NVA. They see to it that the legally guaranteed rights of soldiers, NCOs, and officers are strictly observed, in that they investigate every infringement of individual rights and, when appropriate, initiate the punishment of those responsible. All soldiers, NCOs,

[25] See *Quick* (25 August 1963); *Der Spiegel* (21 August 1963 & 24 June 1964).
[26] *Militärische Erziehung und Bildung, Heft 10, Die Autorität des Offiziers von Oberst Dr. Werner Butter*, Deutscher Militärverlag, Berlin, 1967, p. 39.

and officers can turn privately and confidentially to the military
legal organs . . .

Unlike West Germany, East Germany re-introduced military
courts in April 1963. They are under the jurisdiction of a special
department of the Ministry of Justice and ultimately are responsible
to the *Staatsrat* and the *Volkskammer*. Normally soldiers must complain through their immediate superior who must, when and where
necessary, pass it on to higher authority. Complaints cannot be
made during daily training periods or when on duty, which seems
to limit the possibility of refusing to carry out an order. Unlike the
West German *Soldatengesetz* which reminds soldiers of their right
not to carry out an order which would 'wound human dignity' or
which would thereby result in a crime,[27] East German conscripts
are told to give their superior's 'unconditional obedience'.[28] Indeed, an official instructors' manual says that part of the object
of 'square-bashing' is to educate the soldier to 'complete obedience
vis à vis his superiors (*widerspruchlosen Gehorsam gegenüber
Vorgesetzten)*'.[29]

How does all this leadership and subordination square with the
Marxist ideology? Luckily for the SED, Engels, noted for his interest in things military, had something to say on the subject when
he was denouncing the anarchists in the working-class movement.
He wrote in 1872 : '. . . a certain authority, no matter how delegated,
and, on the other hand, a certain subordination, are things which,
independent of all social organization, are imposed upon us together
with the material conditions under which we produce and make
products circulate'.[30] This quote gets the appropriate mention in
East German military literature.

It may surprise some to learn that a form of alternative service
exists in the DDR. Such service is done in *Baueinheiten* of the
National People's Army and, as the *Taschenbuch* says, 'is carried
out without arms'. The members of such units, *Bausoldaten,* are not
required to swear the normal military oath and, as the name implies, they do various kinds of construction work, including work
on military establishments. Official publications have spoken with

[27] *Soldatengesetze,* Goldmann Verlag, Munich, 1961. This gives all the
laws relating to military service in West Germany. It is introduced by Gerd
Schmückle, Chief Press Officer, West German Ministry of Defence; p. 44.
[28] *100 Fragen 100 Antworten Zur Wehrpflicht,* Deutscher Militärverlag,
1966, p. 90. This is intended to give young East Germans some basic
knowledge of their rights and duties as national servicemen.
[29] *Exerzierausbildung, Methodische Anleitung für den Ausbilder,* Deutscher
Militärverlag, Berlin, 1963, p. 5.
[30] Karl Marx and Friedrich Engels, *Selected Works,* English edition,
Moscow, 1962, Vol. I, pp. 637-8.

the highest respect about these units and the writer has heard from anti-Communist sources that Christian pacifists who have served in them have no complaints. There is no provision for those who, on grounds of conscience, refuse to wear a military uniform or help projects of military value. This is in contrast with the situation in West Germany where conscientious objectors come under the Ministry of Labour and work mainly in hospitals and mental institutions, or act as relief workers in natural disasters. The position of objectors is, however, better than in many other countries. Official spokesmen argue that as the authorities never call up all those liable for service, they can afford to pass over the small number of extreme pacifists. However, a Western report claims : 'There have been several cases of prison sentences of up to eighteen months being served on conscientious objectors even after the introduction of this law' (concerning the *Bausoldaten* or 'building soldiers' and passed in 1964).[31]

The *Volksarmee* is subject to extensive political control designed to ensure doctrinal purity and to help prevent it becoming 'a state within a state'. Most officers are members of the SED, the only one of the republic's five parties allowed to organize in the East German armed forces, and are therefore subject to the decisions of that party. As one military publication puts it : 'To be an officer of the National People's Army means to be loyal and faithful to the Socialist Unity Party and our Workers' and Farmers' State. . . .'[32] There are very few officers in the highest organs of the SED and those who are are usually politicians who have become soldiers rather than the other way round. Through the *Politische Hauptverwaltung,* which operates from the Ministry of Defence but is responsible to the SED Central Committee, the Party exercises its control. Civilian district party organizations also have the right to exercise control functions over SED organizations in local NVA units. To a lesser extent the Free German Youth, which also organizes in the armed forces, may be seen as a party watchdog. Finally, there is the State Security Service (SSD) which is responsible for political as well as military security.

The East German armed forces are firmly anchored in the Warsaw Pact. And we have already noted in an earlier chapter that under Article 6 of the DDR constitution, 'The German Democratic Republic fosters and develops all-round co-operation and friendship with the Union of Soviet Socialist Republics and the other

[31] Amnesty International, *Prison Conditions in East Germany*, London, August 1966, p. 10.
[32] Butter, op. cit., p. 68.

socialist states on the basis of socialist internationalism'. Under Article 7 the armed forces of the DDR cultivate 'close comradeship-in-arms with the armies of the Soviet Union and other socialist states'. Its soldiers swear when joining the forces to defend socialism side by side with the Soviet Army and the armies of the other allied states. It is unthinkable therefore that the East German forces would be used independently, outside the Warsaw Pact organization. What is their value to that organization? As early as 1959 the deserter officer mentioned above remarked that when the new generation of officers then under training completed their courses the National People's Army would be a factor the West should not underestimate. About the same time Emanuel Shinwell, former British Defence Minister, and Colonel George Wigg, sometime member of the British Cabinet, visited units of the East German forces. Colonel Wigg had this to say about their general impressions :

> We were very impressed with the general standard of training, with the standard of discipline which I thought, was up to the kind of discipline that one finds in the British Army. We were also impressed by the friendly relations which exist between officers, NCOs, and men ... We were both convinced that here was a force that had been democratised. There was no trace of the old military tradition and we were also convinced that it was organised on a defensive basis.[33]

Soldier, the magazine published by the British Ministry of Defence, quoted, in its October 1966 edition, an expert as saying : 'the East German Army forms a large question mark ... Nevertheless, its modern equipment and combat-ready status make it a substantial addition to the total Soviet Bloc arsenal.' A West German expert has said that the NVA leadership 'can be satisfied with the level of equipment as well as with the level of weapon and tactical training'. He went on to say that it would be a fatal mistake to regard the NVA 'as unreliable and without any fighting value. In a total dictatorship like that of the SED the masses of soldiers will be, even in the future, decisively influenced by force, habit and political reality. In addition, the majority of officers and part of the NCOs are reliable supporters of the SED régime and they are exercising a firm control over the soldiers.'[34]

It seems likely that the NVA, whose strength in 1966–7 was estimated at 122,000 by the London Institute of Strategic Studies,

[33] *Democratic German Report* (22 May 1959).
[34] Forster (English version), op. cit., pp. 244–6.

suffered at least a temporary set-back in morale as a result of its use in Czechoslovakia.

The East German armed forces were set up to defend the part of Germany known as the German Democratic Republic, to maintain the existing order there, to show Soviet determination to uphold a friendly régime in its former occupation zone, and to form an integral part of Soviet defence strategy. These forces are not 'Red Prussians', being little like earlier German military formations except in certain superficial ways. Nor are they a 'Proletarian Guard' in any real sense, as they are very similar to other modern armies in most respects, though in the social structure of their officer corps they are more broadly based than most. If one believes that the Soviet Union has no interest in a third world war the NVA poses no threat to anyone—save possibly dissident Communists such as the Czechs. In its ideology the NVA has eliminated the old German imperialist and revanchist outlook and, in practical terms, it is both numerically weak and completely dependent for its weapons on the USSR.[35] The Socialist Unity Party's dominant position in the People's Army reduces still further the chance of either any independent initiative or of it attempting to become anything like a 'state within the state'.

[35] *Der Spiegel* (2 June 1965).

Chapter 12

East Germany's International Position: Ignored but not Isolated

I F ONE LOOKS at the DDR's international position merely in terms of the number of states according it full diplomatic recognition it is in a weak position, weaker than nationalist China, Nicaragua, and South Vietnam. Indeed, on this basis, East Germany has not improved its position in a fundamental way since its foundation in 1949. It still only has ambassadors in the Communist capitals of the world.[1] The chief reason for this is well known and need not be laboured unduly. It is that the Federal German Republic claims the sole right to represent the German people abroad, has been able to persuade its allies of this doctrine, has been able to threaten to invoke economic sanctions against lesser states considering recognition, and, until recently, has refused to have diplomatic relations with any state, the Soviet Union excepted, recognizing East Germany. In view of the power of West Germany's purse, it is a wonder that the DDR has made even the limited progress that it has. In the period 1956–64 the net outflow of resources from the Federal German Republic to the developing countries was below resources flowing from the USA, France, and the United Kingdom.[1a] Nevertheless it was still much larger than the DDR or most other countries could afford to offer.

The German Democratic Republic enjoys full diplomatic relations with all its allies in the Warsaw Pact—the Soviet Union, Bulgaria, Czechoslovakia, Poland, Hungary, Romania. It also enjoys full relations with the other Communist states, that is with Albania, Cuba, China, North Korea, North Vietnam, the Mongolian People's Republic, and Yugoslavia. It has managed to establish consulates or consulates-generals in the following countries : Burma, Ceylon, Iraq, United Arab Republic, Cambodia, Indonesia, Syria, Tanzania, Republic of Yemen. Finally, it also has trade representations at government level in Algeria, Colombia, Ghana,

[1] Though an exchange of ambassadors with Iraq was announced in 1969.
[1a] World Economic Survey, Part I, United Nations, New York, 1966, p. 48.

India, Lebanon, Morocco, Brazil, Finland, Guinea, Mali, Sudan, Tunisia, and Uruguay. The bland recital of the official level of these relations does not always convey the actual intensity of the ties between East Germany and certain other states. Nor does it indicate the grim diplomatic actions which have been fought in order to gain such relations.

Ups and Downs in Belgrade

Taking East Germany's relations with Yugoslavia first, they illustrate the tensions which have developed or which have been resolved in the Communist bloc. When the DDR was set up in 1949, for instance, the Stalinist anti-Yugoslav campaign was in full swing. The DDR, a creature of the Soviet Union, raised its voice as loudly as any in condemning the 'hangman of the Yugoslav people', Tito, and his clique.[2] The Federal Republic was able to benefit from this and established relations with Belgrade. These relations became very cordial and there were many cultural, parliamentary, and academic exchanges as well as the development of trading links on a considerable scale. By March 1956 Yugoslavia owed West Germany 200 million marks in post-war commercial debts. In that year, after about 18 months of negotiations, the two states agreed to settle outstanding claims made by Yugoslavia for pre-war and war time deliveries to Germany, war damage, etc. West Germany agreed to payments and credits worth 300 million DM, nearly $74.5 million.[3] However, after Soviet leaders Khrushchev and Bulganin had visited Tito in 1955 to seek a reconciliation, and especially after the 20th Congress of the CPSU in 1956, East German-Yugoslav relations started to develop. Some Western observers of Eastern European affairs believe that Tito, impressed by Gomulka's national and 'liberal' posture at that time, was persuaded by the Polish leader to recognize the DDR. In October 1957 they agreed to exchange envoys which prompted Bonn to withdraw its ambassador from Belgrade. These new relations were threatened by renewed attacks on Yugoslavia by the Sino-Soviet bloc parties in 1958 after the congress of the League of Yugoslav Communists of that year. The Yugoslavs were cautious in their handling of the East Germans and of the German question. At their congress in April 1958, held at Ljubljana, the Yugoslav Communists said little about Germany, mainly pointing out that : 'The Second World War left many problems unsettled and their

[2] Wolfgang Leonhard, *Die Revolution Entlässt Ihre Kinder*, Kiepenheuer & Witsch, Cologne, 1955, pp. 504–17.
[3] Keesing's Contemporary Archives, 28 April–5 May 1956, 14839.

solution is being constantly deferred. The populations of Germany, Korea and Vietnam, are living in partitioned states with different social systems, divided by artificial frontiers; these countries represent latent hotbeds of open conflict.'[4] Ulbricht and his colleagues could extract little of value from this rather ambiguous statement and at their V Party Congress of the same year they joined in the new onslaught against 'Yugoslav revisionism'. Broadly speaking, since then East German-Yugoslav relations have mirrored the improvement of relations between Moscow and Belgrade. Increasingly delegations of top people have been exchanged and increasingly President Tito has become committed to the East German cause. On the occasion of the visit in 1960 of a DDR parliamentary delegation headed by Professor Johannes Dieckmann, President of the East German parliament, Tito pronounced : 'It is fortunate that the DDR exists, otherwise there would be no knowing what would happen in Europe'. A similar statement followed in 1961. The President championed the DDR's cause at the meetings of the Third World heads of state. At the first meeting of the non-aligned states held in Belgrade in 1961 he emphasized : 'The existence of the two German states is a factor today that cannot be denied, for it represents a heritage of the war and the sixteen years of post-war development'.[5] Relations between the two states steadily got closer. Perhaps the really big turning point came in 1965. But this turning point was the culmination of earlier diplomatic activity between East Berlin and Belgrade. Three treaties agreed in 1964 brought the two states closer together and a Yugoslav delegation headed by veteran leader Edward Kardelj visited East Germany. Ulbricht and Tito met in the summer of that year when the German leader was returning from Bulgaria. A short non-committal communiqué was issued at the end of the meeting.[6] The developments of the following year must have come as a shock to the West Germans in view of this. Tito angered the West Germans on two occasions in 1965. Firstly, he greatly eased Ulbricht's visit to Cairo, a visit he no doubt had helped to arrange when he went to Egypt in October 1964, by allowing the East German party to use the airfield and port of Dubrovnik for going to, and returning from, the UAR. Tito's second slap in Bonn's face was his state visit to the DDR. This was undoubtedly a personal triumph for Ulbricht

4 'The Programme of the League of Yugoslav Communists', International Society For Socialist Studies, London, 1959, edited by Kurt Dowson, p. 52.
5 *A Journey of Friendship*, Verlag Zeit im Bild, Dresden, pp. 17, 26.
6 *Dokumente zur Aussenpolitik der DDR 1964*, Band XII, Staatsverlag Der Deutschen Demokratischen Republik, Berlin, 1966, pp. 820–1 (henceforth *Dokumente*).

which must have boosted his prestige in the Communist and non-committed world, and caused the West German government to lose face not only outside, but also inside, Germany. Whether or not the average East German cares about Tito is beside the point. The average German on both sides of the Elbe knew that the West German government had tried hard to prevent East German-Yugoslav relations in the first place, and had also tried hard to prevent Tito's visit. Germans in Hamburg and Munich, as well as in Leipzig and Dresden, could be forgiven for thinking that the visit once again underlined that the DDR was there to stay. *Der Spiegel* (16 June 1965) thought that the Yugoslav had chosen his words carefully in East Berlin, but Bonn reacted sharply that Tito 'had completely lost his entitlement to describe the Yugoslav Government as uncommitted'. In their communiqué the two Communist leaders had said that the 'increasing activity of the militarist and revanchist powers in West Germany is the main obstacle to the peaceful development and the security of the peoples of Europe'.[7] They avoided any statement about the differences in the world Communist movement.

That relations between the DDR and the Socialist Federal Republic of Yugoslavia have become closer is shown by the development of trade between them. Taking 1958 as 100, the official index of trade stood at 346.5 in 1965. The DDR had become Yugoslavia's second largest trading partner, coming next to the Soviet Union.[8] Here a factor on the Yugoslav side could have been increasing difficulty with exports to the Common Market countries. In 1960 East Germany exported 408 million marks-worth of goods to Communist China against 143.8 million to Yugoslavia. By 1965 the respective figures were 110.6 and 255.8 million.[9] Even so, from the Yugoslav point of view, West Germany and Western Europe remain important as trading partners: in 1964 the Yugoslavs still did more trade with the countries of Western Europe than they did with the Communist states.[10] The Czech crisis of 1968 imposed new strains on East German-Yugoslav relations, marking a turning for the worse, with East Berlin providing the Soviet Union with troops in Czechoslovakia and Yugoslavia opposing such actions. In the same year Bonn and Belgrade re-established diplomatic relations, though the Yugoslavs continued to maintain relations with the DDR.

[7] *Guardian* (16 June 1965).
[8] *A Journey of Friendship*, p. 12.
[9] Statistisches Jahrbuch der Deutschen Demokratischen Republik, 1966, Staatsverlag, p. 388 (henceforth, *SJB*)
[10] 'Yugoslavia', an OEEC Report, Paris, 1965, p. 11.

Courtship on the Nile

Easily as sensational as Tito's visit to East Germany, sensational for it did represent a break-through made more important by West German efforts to prevent it, was Ulbricht's above-mentioned trip up the Nile. The success of the East Germans with the Arabs has been made possible by Bonn's Middle East policy rather than because of any natural affinity between Arab nationalists and German Communists—though one need not doubt that if the Arabs continue in a socialist direction they will gain increasing interest in the DDR. Throughout its history the Federal Republic has failed to make up its mind completely as to whether it wants friendship with the Arabs or Israel. Officially it wanted both. Such a situation it might conceivably have engineered had it stuck to a relationship based entirely on trading in non-military goods. As it was, it appeared to be exporting its military technicians to Egypt, which angered the Israelis, and it provided substantial military equipment for Israel, which angered the Arabs still more. Even before the Egyptian revolution of 1952 former German officers and technicians found their way to Cairo. Some went because they were anti-Semites, others because there they had the chance of carrying on the jobs they had been trained to do. Despite Israeli protests to Bonn, attempts to get their passports withdrawn, and even, on occasion, bomb attempts, by 1965 there were some 20,000 West Germans living in the UAR, 4,000 of these German women married to Egyptians. Thus the West Germans formed the largest group of foreigners in that country.[11] The German experts worked on aviation and rocket projects, but it seems likely that their effective contribution to Nasser's military capacities was small. The West German parliament had agreed in 1953 to pay large reparations to Israel. By 1956 the Federal Republic was helping Israel to build up its armed forces.[12] Rumours about this started to be heard at the end of 1957, but these were categorically denied and it was only in October 1964 that the veil was partly lifted.

It was the revelation of the extent of these deliveries, which included planes, tanks, trucks, artillery, two submarines, and other equipment, that led Nasser to invite Ulbricht. The Egyptian President has explicitly stated this.[13] However, Egyptian relations with East Germany go back to 1953, the year when West Germany finally decided on reparations to Israel. In that year the two

[11] *Der Spiegel* (24 February 1965).
[12] Ibid.
[13] Ibid

states agreed a trade and payments treaty, the first such agreement the East Germans concluded on the African continent. In 1955 the DDR Minister for Foreign Trade, Heinrich Rau, took home a consular agreement after his visit to Cairo. This was the time of the Bandoeng Conference of non-aligned states which, it has been said,[14] greatly influenced Nasser, causing him to take 'several defiant initiatives'. By 1959 it was the turn of the East German Prime Minister, the late Otto Grotewohl, to journey to Cairo where he received the 'Order of the Nile' and gave the Egyptians 87.5 million marks credit. Neither Grotewohl nor later Ulbricht managed to persuade the Egyptian President to grant the DDR the much coveted prize of full diplomatic recognition. Fear of Ulbricht's visit led to West Germany agreeing to stop arms deliveries to Israel. When the visit nevertheless took place, the West Germans carried out their threat to give Israel full diplomatic recognition and block further loans to the UAR. Ten Arab states then responded by breaking off relations with Bonn. In Baghdad the Bonn embassy was set alight. Nasser retained the 'ultimate' sanction of recognizing East Berlin as a reserve weapon. From the East German point of view, the success of the visit is shown by the following account of it given in the *Guardian* (25 February 1965):

> The East German Communist leader, Herr Ulbricht, arrived here today to a five-star reception. If Bonn still entertained faint hopes that his visit might be downgraded in style as a sign that the door was not quite shut in its face they were completely dashed by the warmth of President Nasser's welcome for his guest. As Herr Ulbricht's train drew into Cairo station from Alexandria, bringing him on his first official visit to any country outside the Communist block, the first boom of a 21-gun salute startled the waiting parade to attention.... Besides President Nasser and his wife, the platform party included the entire Cabinet of the United Arab Republic, members of the diplomatic Corps with the Soviet Ambassador to the fore, and most of the East German colony in Cairo. There was not just one red carpet. The platform was covered with them from end to end.

However, despite all the glitter, pomp, and back-scratching, there was no agreement to establish diplomatic relations.

The theme of the joint communiqué which ended Ulbricht's visit to the UAR was anti-imperialism. It included the following passage: 'Both sides condemn the apartheid policy of the South African government and every other form of racial discrimination

[14] Peter Mansfield, *Nasser's Egypt*, Penguin African Library, 1965, p. 85.

as a denial of human rights and the equality of peoples and nations'.[15] In other words, Ulbricht, who has numerous Jewish colleagues, was not prepared to mount an anti-Jewish platform. He stressed this on his return to the DDR in a television interview : 'I would like to point out that the German Democratic Republic has always had a clear standpoint towards the role of the imperialist military base of Israel. We have never confused the problem of atonement and restitution for the suffering and injustice imposed by the criminal Nazi régime on the Jewish citizens of Germany and other European states.'[16]

Another diplomatic dog-fight of 1965 from which the DDR emerged with heightened status was the row over representation in Tanzania. Just one month after it gained independence Zanzibar's Arab-dominated government was overthrown by a revolutionary régime. The Chinese and the East Germans, among others, rushed to aid the new republic. East Germany succeeded in exchanging ambassadors with Zanzibar. Zanzibar soon announced its intention of merging with Tanganyika, and in April 1964 an act of union was signed. In addition to all its other problems the new union of Tanganyika and Zanzibar had to decide with which German state it was to have relations. Tanganyika, the senior partner in the union, already had full relations with Bonn. Another difficulty was that West Germany was providing military aid to Tanganyika. In January 1965 13 West German *Luftwaffe* officers and NCOs, nine officers and men of the West German navy, and numerous aviation technicians arrived in Dar-es-Salaam.[17] President Nyerere of Tanzania felt he was neither able nor willing to expel the East Germans from Zanzibar. Bonn had to accept a compromise. They kept their ambassador in Dar-es-Salaam, the East Germans lost theirs in Zanzibar. But the DDR was awarded a consulate-general in Dar-es-Salaam and a consul in Zanzibar. Tanzania lost its West German military aid, though Zanzibar gained useful East German help. After reviewing the progress made by Zanzibar in two years of independence a Western correspondent pointed out : 'Much of Zanzibar's achievement has been made possible by the lavish aid programmes of China and East Germany. . . . East German aid pretty well runs the whole gamut—planning, financial and banking advisers, teachers, nurses and help with housing, radio, newspaper, fishing and fruit canning projects. Each East German project has a built-in training scheme, and the establishment of

15 *Neues Deutschland* (2 March 1965).
16 *Neues Deutschland* (8 March 1965).
17 *Die Welt* (15 January 1965).

the canning industry includes a guaranteed market. In contrast, western aid has been limited.'[18]

The relations of the two Germanys with the other non-aligned, developing countries have tended to follow the same pattern. Aid has been a weapon of diplomacy. The Federal Republic has obviously had greater resources at its disposal than the Democratic Republic. This competition has often been to the advantage of the recipient nations. Take, for example, the case of Algeria. In June 1964 West Germany agreed to provide the Algerian republic with credits and technical aid worth 54 million marks. However, difficulties arose when it came to the signing of the agreement. Algeria refused to meet Bonn's wish that the agreement should contain a clause which would, in effect, recognize West Berlin as part of the Federal Republic. East Berlin immediately responded with an offer of 55 million marks credit on more favourable terms. In the end Algeria accepted the so-called Berlin clause and got for its trouble not 54, but 74, million from West Germany.[19] West Germany has not always managed to be consistent in using economic aid as a political weapon against East Germany. For instance, West German economic aid to Ceylon amounting to 13 million marks was suspended because the DDR had been granted the right to establish a consulate-general in Colombo, whereas similar aid to Syria totalling 350 million marks was not interrupted despite the setting-up of an East German consulate-general in that country.[20]

Apart from its aid to other Communist countries East Germany handed out $179 million to development countries between 1955 and 1964. Just what kind of sacrifice this was is difficult to say. In relation to the other Communist states its position between these dates has been about fifth. The largest amount of aid naturally was provided by the Soviet Union, with over 60 per cent of the Communist total, followed by the Chinese People's Republic, which accounted for about 13 per cent. Czechoslovakia and Poland followed with shares of 10 per cent and 6 per cent respectively. The participation of East Germany, Hungary, and Romania amounted to about 3 per cent each of the total, and that of Bulgaria to less than one-half of one per cent.[21] It is difficult to draw any hard conclusions from these figures, though perhaps one can say cautiously that, although East Germany has used aid to seek recognition, this has not been seen as priority number one. In any

[18] *The Economist* (12 March 1966); see 'With Ulbricht's Aid'.
[19] *Der Spiegel* (17 March 1965).
[20] Hans Speier, 'The Hallstein Doctrine', *Survey* (October 1966), p. 100.
[21] World Economic Survey, Part I, p. 100.

case, the DDR has been able to carry on trade and even a kind of diplomatic relations with the Third World and certain other states without official recognition. A measure of this 'kind of diplomatic relations' is the number of official 'Herzliche Grüsse' telegrams which are received by Head of State Ulbricht and his governmental colleagues from their counterparts around the world. In 1965, apart from Communist statesmen, there were such New Year greetings telegrams from the President of Mexico, the President of the UN General Assembly, the Presidents of Finland, a nation which accords both German states equality, Iraq, and the Congo (Brazzaville), the King of Morocco, the Prime Ministers of Sierra Leone, Kuwait, and the Sudan, the President of the Belgian Chamber of Deputies, the Presidents of the National Assemblies of Ghana, Cambodia, and Algeria. Even Pope Paul sent such a telegram to Ulbricht.[22] And as one Western expert put it :

> Nor does the list of countries in which the DDR is represented in some form reveal the full extent of East German influence abroad. For example, in Algeria, Tanzania, Ghana, and the UAR, more persons are assigned to the DDR missions than to the respective embassies of the Federal Republic. In Africa the DDR exerts influence also through foreign correspondents, all of them members of the East German communist party; they are permanently assigned to Accra, Algiers, Bomaco, Dar-es-Salaam, Zanzibar, Cairo and Alexandria. Furthermore, the DDR operates abroad through its labour unions and youth organisations, through invitations and stipends, at scientific and cultural conferences, and through printed materials sent to Africa in Spanish, French, English and Arabic.[23]

The Federal Republic, it should be noted, uses most of these channels too.

Help from the Lords

Among West Germany's allies the DDR has had very limited success to date. There have been parliamentary and trade union delegations over the years from France, Italy, and Belgium, and lesser ones from Britain. From East Germany there have been cultural, sport, and academic exchanges, though not without difficulties. The situation was put in a letter to *The Times* (2 November 1966) by a member of the Organizing Committee of an International Conference on Gravitation which was held in London :

22 *Neues Deutschland* (4, 10, & 14 January 1965).
23 Hans Speier, *Survey*, p. 100.

Four physicists from East Germany attended but three others were not allowed by their Government to come ... Recently, during a visit to the Friedrich Schiller University of Jena, I made inquiries about the reason for this ... Basically, of course, difficulties arise because the British Government does not recognize the German Democratic Republic. However, I was told that in spite of this the East German authorities would ease travel restrictions to Britain if the procedure for applying for a British visa could be altered. At present an East German citizen wishing to visit Britain must first go to the Allied Travel Office in West Berlin to obtain a 'temporary travel document' which takes the place of a passport. Until this document has been obtained the British Visa Office will not consider an application for a visa. The temporary travel document is very strongly resented by the East German authorities. I was told many times that more East Germans would be allowed to seek British visas if applications could be made direct to the Visa Office. To the diplomatic mind, of course, the temporary travel document may seem an essential corollary to the non-recognition of the German Democratic Republic. However, to those of us who wish to ease the scientific exchange between the two countries it seems an unnecessary formality.

As another letter two days later pointed out, Sweden, Switzerland, Austria, and other non-NATO states do not recognize the DDR, yet they do permit East Germans to apply directly to them for visas. For their part the East German authorities recognize a British passport and it is now relatively easy to get a visa.

A number of members of the British House of Lords raised the question of visitors from East Germany, in April 1963. Lord Kennet (Wayland Young) asked the government whether they would rescind their decision, a retaliation against the building of the Berlin Wall, to refuse visas to scientists and artists from East Germany while permitting them to merchants. He claimed it could be against Britain's interest because organizations would start to hold their conferences in other countries. An example, he said, in sport was the International Yacht Racing Union which had 30 members and its permanent seat in London. In the past three years there had been no East Germans at the annual conference in London, though there were Russians, Poles, and Czechs, who were beginning to think that the conference should be moved to a place where all members could be represented. There had also been the case of the *Berliner Ensemble*. He was supported by Lord Boothby, the Earl of Lucan, the Labour chief whip, Lord Kilbracken (Liberal), and the Labour Lord Shackleton. Their Lordships got little encouragement from the government.[24]

Apart from sportsmen, those interested in Brechtian theatre or historical German towns, academics, and a tiny handful of genuine tourists, those Britons going to East Germany have been mainly motivated by interest in trade or in the DDR as a buffer against an all-powerful new Reich. On the DDR's trading position *The Times* (1 March 1965) believed: 'However limited may be the success of East Germany in acquiring diplomatic respectability among the western or uncommitted nations, its status as a leading industrial power and as an economic go-between for east and west is more striking with every year that passes, and finds palpable expression in the Leipzig Spring Fair'. On Britain's trade with East Germany a group of British businessmen have written that it 'rose from £1.79 million in 1953 to £16.22 million in 1962. There is undoubtedly a market in the DDR for the more sophisticated and advanced British equipment. In return the DDR can offer plenty of specialised products suitable for the British market.' This trade has continued to increase; even so, it is still less than one per cent of British trade.[25] Although not recognized by Britain East Germany can console itself that there have always been advocates of recognition in the British Parliament. These have been mainly, though not exclusively, on the Labour side of the two Houses. Apart from the late Konni Zilliacus, Frank Allaun, and others on the far left associated with them on the backbenches, there have been others, higher up in the party hierarchy, who have called for recognition. In characteristic style, Emanuel Shinwell, ex-Defence Minister and later Chairman of the Parliamentary Labour Party, told the House of Commons: 'The British Government should face the fact that the German Democratic Republic exists, and should recognise it. What would be the consequence? Dr Adenauer would be furious. The Americans might be too. But why can't we take a line of our own occasionally? We should tell West Germany that they must come to some sort of agreement with East Germany.'[26] Mr Shinwell found himself in unusual company. Viscount Hinchingbrooke, the right-wing Conservative, said he 'heartily agreed'.[27] Richard Crossman told *New Statesman*

[24] *Democratic German Report* (5 April 1963).

[25] 'East–West Trade', a report of PEP, May 1965, p. 176. The quotation is from 'Expansion of East-West Trade' (July 1963), published by a group of British businessmen headed by R. W. Asquith, Chairman and Managing Director, Asquith Machine Tool Corporation Ltd, p. 33.

[26] Hansard (11 February 1960), col. 735.   [27] Ibid., col. 772.

readers on 6 February 1960 in an article which praised the progress made in the DDR, that he too favoured recognition. Both Mr Crossman and later Lord Boothby coupled recognition with guarantees about the West's position in Berlin.[28] When Harold Wilson became the Leader of the Labour Party in 1963 he made a series of confusing statements about recognizing East Germany which angered Bonn. He talked about 'some measure' of recognition and at least seemed to mean that East Germans ought to be able to get visas directly with their passports rather than the temporary travel document :

> Some time ago, because of a problem of movement of East German businessmen, we had to forbid their coming through to Britain. We lost a lot of orders which the West German industries were not slow to pick up for themselves. And on questions like cultural contact, sporting contacts, and above all, trade contacts, we believe that it is possible to have a measure of de facto recognition, which, as I say, other countries have already got. If the discussions mean some further recognition in a political sense, I do not think we ought to be afraid of that.[29]

Needless to say, since Mr Wilson became the Prime Minister there has been no 'measure of recognition' let alone 'further recognition in a political sense', though the Lords have handed down a judgment in favour of the Carl Zeiss firm of East Germany, recognizing East German courts whilst emphasizing their view that the DDR was a creature of the Soviet Union.[30] This judgment is said to have been a 'bitter pill' for Bonn by the Hamburg weekly *Die Zeit* (15 July 1966).

As reported in the *Morning Star* (18 March 1967), William Wilson, Labour MP for Coventry South, said that forty MPs were members of the British-German Democratic Republic Parliamentary Group and that they would 'continue to press the Government to give the GDR diplomatic recognition. It is an uphill fight, but we are so satisfied that it is the right fight that we shall continue to press it.' Mr Wilson believed, 'It was the only way to securing real peace in Europe and by any normal standards of diplomacy this recognition would have been given 15 years ago'. The same source named Arnold Gregory, Labour MP for Stockport North, as secretary of the group. In June 1968 East German organizations successfully organized a conference in Helsinki to gather support

[28] *Survey* (October 1966), p. 126.
[29] *Democratic German Report* (5 April 1963).
[30] *The Times* (20 May 1966).

for recognition of the DDR. Among those present, according to the East German newspaper *Der Morgen* (16 June 1968), were Liberal MP Eric Lubbock and Conservative MP George Drayson. The same newspaper reported on 19 September 1968 that the 18th Pugwash conference meeting at Nice had also called for recognition of the DDR. This meeting was attended by scientists, journalists, and academics from Britain, the USA, and other NATO countries, as well as their colleagues from the USSR and Eastern Europe.

Influential American advocates of the recognition of East Germany have been few. Walter Lippmann has called upon the West German government to conduct an 'agonizing reappraisal' and accept that 'The living reality is that, as a result of the defeat of Germany, there are now two German states'.[31] Similar statements have been made by Senator Wayne Morse. One improbable American advocate of East German recognition is Brigadier General Hugh B. Hester (retired) who served with the American occupation forces in Germany. In a letter to the *New York Herald Tribune* (22 November 1963) he said that the DDR signified a peaceful government ruling a peace-loving people. Charles W. Thayer, formerly an American diplomat in Germany, shared the view of his military colleague that it was high time to recognize the reality of two German states (*Harper's Magazine*, New York, 30 May 1962).

The East German participation in the occupation of Czechoslovakia must be counted as a set-back for attempts to win over Western and neutral opinion to the view that the DDR should be recognized.

'Revisionism' in Prague

There was a time when the DDR's relations with its allies were simple and straightforward, being governed by the 'monolithic unity' of the socialist camp. De-Stalinization, economic progress, the reappearance of nationalism, and the Sino-Soviet differences have changed all that. Broadly speaking, one can say that, the Soviet Union apart, up to August 1968, East Germany's relations were closest with its immediate neighbours, Poland and Czechoslovakia. Obviously geography and economics are partly responsible for this, but political factors have been more important still. These two nations, which suffered so much from Nazi aggression, fear that

[31] *New York Herald Tribune* (26 March 1965); Wayne Morse, *Democratic German Report* (4 October 1963).

one day the Federal Republic may still try to regain the former Reich territories now within their borders. The DDR officially accepted the Oder-Neisse frontier as long ago as 1950 and since then has given these nations no cause for complaint on this score. The DDR represents for them a bulwark against revived German nationalism. Even the Federal Republic's 'peace note' of 24 March 1966 did nothing to still their fears, for it made no clear and categorical renunciation of German claims. West Germany has no territorial claims on Bulgaria, Hungary, or Romania and thus there is one less impediment to relations with Bonn. Until the 'Grand Coalition' of Christian Democrats and Social Democrats was formed to govern the Federal Republic at the end of 1966, Bonn had refused to contemplate diplomatic relations with these states because of the Hallstein Doctrine, defined in 1955, which stated that, except for the Soviet Union, West Germany would have no diplomatic relations with any state which recognized the DDR. This has not stopped West Germany from trading with the East and, although this trade forms only a small part of West Germany's trade, it does more trade with Eastern Europe than any of its NATO allies.[32] Nor has it prevented the establishment of trade missions in Poland, Hungary, Bulgaria, and Romania. (These countries have similar missions in West Germany.) It has also not impeded the flood of West German tourists to these countries in recent years and increasing cultural exchanges have also taken place. Obviously East Berlin has kept a close watch on such developments, fearing that they could be the first steps on the, admittedly, long road to a sell-out. The arrival of the Grand Coalition with Willy Brandt as its Foreign Minister has brought greater flexibility in Bonn and efforts have been made to establish relations with the states of Eastern Europe. Not surprisingly, in view of Bonn's refusal to recognize the Oder-Neisse frontier or the DDR, or sign the non-proliferation treaty, or clearly renounce a nuclear role, these efforts have only been fully successful in the case of Romania. On 31 January 1967 the two countries announced that they would establish full diplomatic relations.

This was in a sense somewhat surprising in view of a speech made by Nicolae Ceausescu, General Secretary of the Romanian Communist Party, on 7 May 1966 on the occasion of the 45th anniversary of his party's foundation. He promised that Romania would make every effort 'to contribute to the strengthening of the true unity of the socialist countries' and, later on, referred to relations with Bonn : 'It should be mentioned that progress has been

[32] 'East–West Trade', PEP, May 1965, p. 176.

made in the economic relations with the German Federal Republic; these could develop in other fields as well, if West Germany would give proof of a more realistic assessment of the present international political situation'.[33] In July the Warsaw Pact states met in Bucharest and issued a statement declaring that in the interests of European peace and security, the West German government should recognize the existence of two German states; abandon claims to a revision of European frontiers; abandon claims to be the 'sole representative' of Germany; and cease exerting pressure on states which recognize the DDR. As it turned out, the Romanian leader was easily satisfied, for the West German Chancellor, Kurt Kiesinger, stressed that in establishing relations with Bucharest the Federal Republic was not giving up its claim to be the sole representative of the German people. What was the official East German attitude to this new situation? Commenting on the Bonn-Bucharest agreement, an official DDR spokesman stated :

> The establishment of diplomatic relations between two states is in principle to be welcomed, if it is really in accordance with the principles of respect for sovereignty, equal rights and non-intervention in internal affairs. The claim of the Bonn Government to be the 'sole representative' of Germany, and other revanchist Bonn claims, are the main obstacle to the efforts being made by the socialist states, the neutral states, and some capitalist states, for the establishment of European security. It is regrettable that the Rumanian Foreign Minister was not ready, during the negotiations, to insist on rejecting the 'sole representation' claim, and to declare that conditions for diplomatic relations were not ripe so long as the Bonn Government insisted on its 'sole representation' claim and other revanchist demands.[34]

The Polish premier, Josef Cyrankiewicz, called the new relations between Bonn and Bucharest 'a diplomatic manoeuvre meant to camouflage the basic motives of Bonn's foreign policy'. He emphasized that West Germany must recognize the unchangeability of the existing status of Europe and of its frontiers.[35] *The Times* (1 February 1967) in an editorial also criticized the West German move. It asked whether this was really so clever. 'To start with Rumania is to invite the suspicion that Dr Kiesinger is less inter-

[33] Nicolae Ceausescu, *The Romanian Communist Party—Continuer Of The Romanian People's Revolutionary And Democratic Struggle, Of The Traditions Of The Working-Class And Socialist Movement In Romania,* Meridiane Publishing House, Bucharest, 1966, pp. 89, 97.
[34] *Democratic German Report* (10 February 1967).
[35] *Guardian* (27 February 1967).

ested in reconciliation than in driving wedges between members of the Warsaw Pact'. Referring to the position of East Germany it said : 'A powerful school of thought believes that East Germany must be isolated until she becomes a burden on her neighbours . . . In the long run this road leads to a dead end. Any progress in healing the division of Europe must start with mutual respect for existing alliances. East Germany, as an important member of the eastern alliance, cannot be left out of the progress without inviting trouble from her allies'. The editorial ended by calling for a relaxation of the conditions imposed by the NATO powers on East German journalists, sportsmen, and other travellers.

Apart from arguments with Romania and skirmishes with Poland and Hungary over 'revisionist tendencies' in 1956 and relations with Bonn in the early sixties, the DDR severely strained its relations with Czechoslovakia in 1968 owing to its participation in the Warsaw Pact occupation of that country.

Even before the removal of the Czechoslovak Communist Party boss, Antonin Novotny, in January 1968, the SED had had its reservations about the comrades in Prague. These doubts seem to date from 1963 when the Czechoslovaks embarked on economic and—unlike the East Germans—political reforms as well. For their part, by the end of 1965 the Czechs and the Slovaks were getting less enthusiastic about East Berlin, for, in line with their economic reforms, they wanted to develop wider trade links with West Germany. This worried the East Germans. However, after the Soviet bloc summit in Karlovy Vary in 1967, the Czechoslovaks were officially in line again with their allies. A treaty of friendship, co-operation, and mutual assistance was signed by the DDR and Czechoslovakia on 17 March, two days after the signing of a similar treaty between the DDR and Poland. Later similar treaties were signed with Hungary and Bulgaria. The treaties were valid for 20 years : all recognized the finality and inviolability of the existing frontiers of the countries concerned, and all pledged mutual assistance in the event of aggression against any of the three by Bonn or any state or group of states allied to Bonn. The only substantial difference between the DDR-Czechoslovak treaty and that concluded with Poland was that the former proclaimed the Munich agreement of 1938 invalid. Just as the East Germans were feeling pleased with themselves, Prague slapped them in the face by signing a trade and payments agreement with Bonn in August of the same year. The two states agreed to set up trade missions in Prague and Frankfurt. The question of the agreement's applicability to West Berlin—so important because the DDR claims West Berlin is a separate entity, not part of the Federal Republic—was settled in an exchange of letters which were not published. Bonn already had similar agreements with most of the other states of Eastern Europe.

It was after Alexander Dubček took over from Novotny that East Germany became seriously critical of Czechoslovak 'revisionism'. True, Ulbricht congratulated Secretary Dubček on his appointment, but his telegram was cool by usual Communist standards. In the early months of 1968 the East German press showed its unease at events in Prague by highly selective coverage of Czech developments. DDR papers, though, continued to hope for the best and emphasized any statements made in Prague expressing solidarity with the Warsaw Pact. This happened after the Dresden summit of Communist leaders in March. By May Prague and East Berlin hissed at each other over the DDR's refusal to allow West Berlin's mayor, Klaus Schütz, to drive through East Germany to Czechoslovakia. This led to an angry article in the Czech Communist Party organ *Rude Pravo* which heretically referred to the 'four-power status of Berlin', no longer recognized by the DDR. This in turn brought a protest from the East German ambassador in Prague. Relations between the two states continued to deteriorate in the following months. The East Germans joined the parties of the USSR, Bulgaria, Hungary, and Poland in sending a joint letter criticizing 'revisionism' in Prague. A SED *PB* resolution of 25 July regretted that the Czechs still underestimated the anti-socialist forces at work in their country and the dangers of interference from Bonn. The meetings between the Soviet and Czechoslovak Communist parties at Cierna in July/August and the meeting of the six parties at Bratislava in early August brought largely non-committal reporting in the press of the DDR. However, after the encounter by Ulbricht and Dubček at Karlovy Vary on 12 August there was a little more optimism. On 14 August *Der Morgen* published a photo of Ulbricht and Dubček smiling broadly and shaking hands, and on the same day the London *Times* believed that Ulbricht's visit had ended on a friendly note.

After the occupation of Czechoslovakia in August the DDR faithfully followed the Soviet interpretation of events, claiming, in the words of a Central Committee, government, and Council of State joint statement, published in *Der Morgen* on 22 August : 'a group of personalities of the Party and State in Czechoslovakia, truly devoted to socialism, took up the public fight on 20 August for the defence of the socialist state order against counter-revolutionary plots. This had become necessary owing to an acute political crisis caused by the sharpened rightist course of a group in the leadership

of the Communist Party of Czechoslovakia and the increased
activity of anti-socialist forces.' These personalities, the statement
claimed, had called on Czechoslovakia's Warsaw Pact allies to give
them every assistance, including military help, and the allies had
complied with that request. The statement further accused 'a group
in the Presidium of the Central Committee of the Communist
Party of Czechoslovakia, headed by A. Dubček of failing to fulfil
the pledges given by the Czechoslovak CP to its allies at earlier
negotiations at Cierna and Bratislava. These were to ensure the
'political control' of the mass media 'in the spirit of socialism', to
enact without delay a law banning the activities of 'anti-socialist
parties, clubs and organizations' and, 'to create in the leadership of
the party and state the necessary guarantees for a consistent course
guaranteeing the vital interests of the Czechoslovak Socialist
Republic'.

At no point did this, or other, East German statements make
clear that Party Secretary Dubček' had the confidence of the great
majority of the Central Committee, the Czechoslovak National
Assembly, and all other recognized popular bodies in Czechoslovakia. Nor did it strike the East Germans as odd that the 'group'
appealing to them were acting against the cherished principle of
Democratic Centralism by opposing majority decisions and forming
a faction. They later tried to justify the action of the Warsaw Pact
states by claiming that developments in Czechoslovakia endangered
not only that country's security but also that of the other socialist
states, and that therefore these states had a right to intervene under
the terms of the defence alliance.

To the genuine Marxist-Leninists in the SED this argument was
no doubt less than satisfying. Some of them would ponder Lenin's
words : ' "No nation can be free if it oppresses other nations," said
the greatest representatives of consistent democracy of the nineteenth century, Marx and Engels, who became the teachers of the
revolutionary proletariat. And we Great-Russian workers, filled with
a sense of national pride, want at all costs a free and independent,
democratic, republican, proud Great Russia, which shall base its
relations with its neighbours on the human principle of equality,
and not on the feudal principle of privilege, which is degrading to
a great nation.'[36]

The situation was certainly embarrassing for the East German
leaders, particularly, as they were later forced to admit, in the
words of *Der Morgen* (4 September 1968), that 'at most only a few'

36 V. I. Lenin, *The National Pride of the Great Russians*, Foreign Languages Publishing House, Moscow, 1951, English edition, p. 9.

Czechoslovaks understood the situation. It was difficult to conceal the truth from the East German people because, apart from Western broadcasts, about half a million East Germans visited Czechoslovakia in 1968. This was reason enough for the more cautious and conservative East German leaders to be scared. They feared that the Czechoslovak ideas would spread like an infectious disease into the DDR.

'*Adventurism*' *in Peking*

The DDR's other major dispute in the Communist bloc has been with China and Albania. Although there does not seem to have been any pro-Chinese wing in the SED the writer has gained the impression that Sino–Soviet differences have been a matter of deep regret, especially among the pre-1945 Communists and socialists. More than most of their allies the East Germans feel themselves to be under attack from the West. The unity of the 'socialist camp' is, they feel, the best guarantee of their safety. By projecting the image of the camp as a vast international community which is invincible they have tried to convince the more sceptical among their citizens. This was in a way similar to official West German efforts to 'sell' the Common Market and other forms of Western integration to West Germans.

For the veterans the idea of internationalism, summed up in the International Brigades, the 'Internationale', the 'Solidaritätslied', Paul Robeson, etc., exercises a powerful emotional pull. They were as enthusiastic as any about the setting-up of the Chinese People's Republic in 1949. Officially relations between the two states are regulated by the Treaty of Friendship and Co-operation signed by Chinese premier Chou En Lai and premier Otto Grotewohl in 1955. The eight-article treaty was drafted in very general terms—they pledged themselves to work together for world peace and security in line with the principles of the UN; in the spirit of fraternal alliance they would discuss all important international questions which affected them; they would observe the principle of non-interference in each other's affairs, co-operating as equal partners; they would use every opportunity to aid each other economically and develop economic co-operation; they would co-operate in scientific, technical, and cultural affairs, etc.[37] The treaty did not bind them to any kind of military co-operation. The promises of the treaty were not to be fully realized. The Sino–Soviet conflict, in which East Germany inevitably sided with the Soviet Union, saw

[37] *Handbuch Der Volkskammer Der Deutschen Demokratischen Republik*, Kongress Verlag, Berlin, 1957, pp. 101–3.

to that. It is difficult to say precisely when that collision became inevitable. Perhaps it was in 1955 as a result of Soviet aid to such non-socialist régimes as India, Egypt, and Indonesia, as well as to the Khrushchev–Bulganin pilgrimage to Belgrade.[38] However, at this stage such differences as existed did not interfere in relations between East Berlin and Peking. Trade between the two states increased year by year and there were cultural, academic, and even military exchanges. As mentioned in Chapter 1, at the V Congress of the SED in 1958 it was the Yugoslavs who were denounced, not the Chinese. Ulbricht recorded the progress made by the Chinese and seemed to be taking seriously their announcement that they would overtake Britain in gross industrial production within '15 years or less', and would overtake British coal production by 1959.[39]

By 1960 it was the Chinese who were under attack. In 1959 Khrushchev had gone to the USA and made many conciliatory remarks which greatly angered the Chinese. He went to China in the same year, but 'it was this visit . . . that brought final confirmation of the existence of a major quarrel'.[40] This major quarrel found reflection in Sino–East German trade. In 1960 East Germany exported 408 million marks-worth of goods to Communist China. This fell to 43.7 million in 1963 but, perhaps remarkably, rose again to 110.6 million in 1965.[41] This latter figure represented only about one per cent of East German exports. The year 1963 represented a low ebb in Sino–East German relations. This was because of the bitter attack against the Yugoslavs launched by the Chinese 'fraternal' delegate to the SED VI Congress. This time there was no sympathy for the anti-Yugoslav line but a slow handclap and the stamping of feet. Surprisingly, in view of this tragi-comedy, the SED leaders tried after 1963 to act as brokers between the warring factions in the world Communist camp. In 1964, for instance, they showed some independence of Moscow after the fall of Khrushchev. Speaking at a meeting at the 'Schwarze Pumpe' coal combine on 3 November Ulbricht said:

The Chinese People's Republic will naturally take decisions in the political and economic field in accordance with its conditions, but I must say quite frankly that our knowledge is not great enough to say anything in detail about such questions. We have enough to do dealing with our own tasks in the DDR. Without

[38] Edward Crankshaw, *The New Cold War: Moscow v. Pekin,* Penguin Books, 1963, p. 56.
[39] *Protokoll Der Verhandlungen Des V Parteitages Der Sozialistischen Einheitspartei Deutschlands,* Dietz Verlag, Berlin, 1959, Vol. I, p. 27.
[40] Crankshaw, op. cit., p. 86.
[41] *SJB,* 1966, p. 388.

intervening in the internal affairs of the Chinese People's Republic we are interested in the development of friendly relations between China, the Soviet Union, the DDR, and the other People's Democracies.

He then went on to back the Soviet scheme for a world Communist conference.[42] The 'Great Cultural Revolution' of 1966–7 has made it impossible for the East Germans to keep this relatively central position on Sino–Soviet differences. Red Guards did not make any distinction between imperialist and revisionist diplomats and East Germans were among those physically assaulted in Peking. Naturally enough, the East German government protested at this treatment and on 4 September 1967 the Central Committee of the SED issued a statement about the situation of the Chinese Communist Party. Under the circumstances it was a remarkably moderate document. It referred to the recently published communiqué of the Central Committee of the Chinese party, outlining the decisions of its eleventh plenum. It claimed that this document showed that the Chinese leaders were continuing their 'anti-Marxist' anti-Leninist policy which they have pursued for some years to the damage of the international communist movement'. It continued : 'This divisive policy has encouraged the aggressive forces of US imperialism. It has encouraged the ultra-left, adventurist elements and in such countries as Indonesia severely damaged the Communist Party and the entire national democratic movement.' It warned the Chinese that they were isolating themselves from the rest of the world movement. More serious still, it accused them of rejecting all proposals from the other parties to work together to defeat US aggression in Vietnam. Turning to the Great Proletarian Cultural Revolution the East German statement continued :

> With deep astonishment we see the effects of the so-called proletarian cultural revolution, during the course of which the great cultural heritage of the German people is being slandered, as the attacks against the great German composers Bach and Beethoven, who are esteemed by all peoples, show. This has nothing whatsoever to do with the teaching of Marx, Engels, and Lenin who confirmed the historical mission of the working class as the chosen heirs and continuers of the great achievements of world culture.

The attacks on DDR diplomats were against the elementary rules of international law. The situation in Vietnam and the attempts of the West German militarists and imperialists to get atomic

[42] *Democratic German Report* (13 November 1964).

weapons made the need for unity on the part of the Communist and working-class parties greater than ever. The statement ended by saying that the SED would continue to strive 'for joint action and understanding with the Chinese Communist Party on the basis of Marxism–Leninism and the declarations of 1957 and 1960, and for friendship between the DDR and the Chinese People's Republic'.[43]

Colony or Partner?

It only remains now to outline the relations between the Soviet Union and the DDR, certainly the most important relationship for East Germany. Very few people know the exact nuances in the relations between the Soviet Union and its protégé, few can say just how important East Germany is to the Soviet Union. Two points can be made with certainty. Firstly, the DDR is not absolutely indispensable to the economy of the Soviet Union and, despite East Germany's progress, in the long term it will be less and less important. However, the DDR *is* important in economic terms and to some extent in military terms. Secondly, one can say that, with the Soviet Union claiming to be the leading force in world socialism, the continued existence of the DDR is of the greatest importance. It is hard to see how the Soviet Union could go on claiming to be interested in the achievement of world socialism if it were to abandon the DDR. Before we try to evaluate these statements the development of relations should be traced at the formal level.

In the development of its relations with the DDR the Soviet Union has tried, at a formal level, to match the development of relations between West Germany and the Western powers. Both states were set up in 1949 within weeks of each other, both were officially granted their sovereignty in 1955 within weeks of each other. In the case of the Soviet Union, its changing relation with the DDR was presented as answering the changing situation in West Germany. For instance, the treaty of 1955 states that it was the result of the new situation created by the coming into operation of the Paris treaties, between Bonn and the Western powers, of 1954. The treaty, signed by Otto Grotewohl, the East German Prime Minister, and the Prime Minister of the Soviet Union, N. A. Bulganin, was seen as a contribution towards maintaining and strengthening world peace and towards the reunification of Germany. The first three articles of the treaty were very similar to those in the Sino–East German treaty signed in the same year : working together for peace in accordance with UN principles;

[43] *National-Zeitung* (4 September 1966).

developing economic, scientific, and technical contacts; non-interference in each other's internal affairs. Article 4 stated that the
Soviet forces in Germany would continue to be stationed there
with the agreement of the government of the DDR, but that the
actual terms under which they would remain there would be the
subject of a separate agreement. It did, however, lay down that
these Soviet forces would not interfere in the internal affairs of the
DDR. Article 5 stated that both parties were agreed that the aim
of their policy was to bring about a peaceful settlement for the
whole of Germany, and the reunification of Germany on a peaceful and democratic basis. The treaty was to remain in force, according to Article 6, either until this unity had been achieved or until
both parties were agreed on its modification. It was Article one
which recognized the sovereignty of the DDR.

The Soviet–East German treaty of 1955 was followed four months
later by the Warsaw Pact treaty signed in May. Like the previous
treaty the preamble to the Warsaw treaty claimed to be a response
to Western military treaties. The first four Articles of the eleven-
Article treaty put the emphasis on working together to solve international problems in the spirit of the United Nations. The following
three Articles would appear to be the key ones—the establishment
of a joint military command (Article 5); the establishment of a
political advisory committee with one member from each country
(Article 6); the obligation of member states not to join any coalition
or alliance, or sign any treaty which contradicts the treaty (Article
7). Article 8 pledged the members to strengthen their ties with each
other. Any other state, irrespective of its social or state system, was
given the right, in Article 9, to join the alliance providing all members agreed. Ratification of the treaty by member states was required by Article 10, and Article 11 laid down that the treaty was
in force for twenty years in the first instance. The serious nature
of the treaty was emphasized in that there was no provision for
withdrawal, though the treaty would become void immediately a
collective security treaty embracing the whole of Europe came into
force. One minor curiosity of the treaty is that its official texts are
in the German, Russian, Polish, and Czech languages only. Thus
it seems to imply closer ties between these states and, perhaps, to
emphasize that they have, over and above their other common ties,
a special link with each other—fear of West Germany.[44]

The most recent, now the most important, and equally as binding, treaty between the Soviet Union and the DDR is the eleven-
Article document signed in Moscow on 12 June 1964 by Nikita

[44] *Handbuch Der Volkskammer,* pp. 93–7.

Khrushchev and Walter Ulbricht. This treaty in its preamble once again emphasized that it was within the spirit of the United Nations, in accordance with the Warsaw treaty and the earlier Soviet–East German treaty. It also mentioned, though less forcibly than in 1955, that it was being entered into in the wish that it would ease the conclusion of a German peace treaty and the realization of German unity on a peaceful and democratic basis. The preamble also emphasized that both parties were determined to oppose the 'threat to international security and peace by revanchist and militarist forces seeking a revision of the results of the second world war'. It said that they were prepared to defend each other's territorial integrity and sovereignty. The first five Articles of the treaty largely restated these points; the last three dealt with the validity of the treaty, for twenty years in the first instance, its need for ratification, etc. Article 8 pledged the parties to develop further economic, scientific, technical, and cultural co-operation, especially in accordance with the principles of Eastern Europe's common market, the Council for Mutual Economic Aid. Articles 6 and 7 are the really important ones which give the treaty its distinctive character. Both parties, states Article 6, regard West Berlin as an independent political entity. Article 7 argues that owing to the existence of two German states, the creation of a peace-loving, democratic, united German state can only be achieved by negotiations and agreement of the two sovereign German states.[45] This treaty did not entirely fulfil East Berlin's earlier expectations about getting a separate peace treaty and despite its recognition of West Berlin as a separate entity, something in fact recognized in large measure by the Western powers, it marked the end of Moscow's and East Berlin's attempts to force the issue of setting up West Berlin as some kind of Free City—a course rejected by the West. Nevertheless, as one Western expert has written, the treaty

> has brought the SED leadership to the goal of its long courtship of the Soviet Union. The pact affords the DDR a lasting guarantee from the USSR which gives the East Berlin régime privileges in comparison with its east European partners, and secures it against the West to the extent that no bilateral agreements between Moscow and Bonn can pass it over. 'Goodbye to a sellout via Bonn' was the comment often heard in East Berlin following conclusion of the treaty.[46]

So much for the development of formal diplomatic relations

[45] *Dokumente*, pp. 1021–5.
[46] *Survey* (October 1966), p. 59.

18 * *

between Moscow and East Berlin. To what extent are all the formal protestations of 'socialist equality' in these treaties real? Is East Germany really a state or just a far-flung colonial province? Obviously, owing to the Second World War East Germany was, in all but name, a colonial province. Most Western observers do not believe this is the case today. Even Willy Brandt, who has to be extremely cautious in such matters, was prepared to say at the Social Democratic Party congress at Dortmund in 1966, that is, a few months before he became West German Foreign Minister, that East Germany could 'be called a colonial territory of the Soviet Union [but] its progress from the status of a satellite towards that of a partner is unmistakable'.[47] And a West German specialist on East German affairs summed up the situation in 1966 as follows:

> The relationship between the DDR and the Soviet Union has changed slowly but steadily in recent years. The SED is no longer a vassal but a partner in a joint venture. It no longer copies blindly every change of Soviet policy but selects what it can use. It even exports its own experiences, particularly in the economic field. A political slogan of the Stalin period illustrates the change. Whereas once the catch phrase went: 'To learn from the Soviet Union is to learn how to be victorious', today it goes: 'To be allied with the Soviet Union is to belong to the victors'.[48]

What has brought about this change in relations between East Germany and the Soviet Union? Undoubtedly the development of the economic power of the DDR has been a major factor, together with de-Stalinization and the Sino–Soviet disagreement. Apart from the Soviet Union itself, East Germany is the most important industrial power in the Communist camp. It is the Soviet Union's biggest trading partner, being responsible for roughly one-quarter of Soviet imports and 75 per cent of its imports of machine tools.[49] It exports not only large quantities of machines and machine tools but also clothes and consumer goods of all kinds. In addition, as mentioned in our earlier survey of the East German economy, the DDR has the largest reserves of uranium in Europe, apart from those in the Soviet Union itself. Although a blanket of security surrounds the joint Soviet–East German exploitation of these reserves, an East German publication has claimed: 'The miners of this enterprise make an important contribution to the strength of

[47] *Die Welt* (2 June 1966).
[48] *Survey* (October 1966), p. 165.
[49] *Der Spiegel*, No. 47/1965.

the world peace camp. It is also due to them that Soviet nuclear technology leads the world'.[50] Undoubtedly the knowledge of all this has given the East German leaders, especially the younger ones, a feeling of self-respect when dealing with the Soviets. From the military point of view also the DDR has something to offer the Soviet Union. Obviously the stationing of Soviet troops in East Germany means that potentially unfriendly forces are just that much farther away from Soviet territory. The DDR is part of the Soviet Union's outer defensive perimeter. The coastline of the DDR is also of interest for Soviet naval squadrons which are badly off for ports open all year round. Then there are the East German armed forces themselves. Although an unknown factor, they are probably, technically speaking, on a higher level of efficiency than most of the other Soviet allies. The *Volksarmee* gained recognition from the Soviets when in autumn 1965, in the biggest Warsaw Pact manoeuvres ever staged, a Soviet division was placed under East German command. These hard economic and military facts together with de-Stalinization and the troubles with China have meant that the Soviets must woo the East Germans a little more than in the past.

From time to time the East Germans have shown that they are aware of this 'coming of age'. For instance, when Khrushchev was forced to retire Ulbricht issued a cautious statement, claiming in effect that the DDR had not fallen for all Khrushchev's schemes and that they would therefore not be rushing to get into line with the latest Soviet shake-up : 'Details of the various mistakes, and how they should be corrected, is a matter for our Soviet comrades. I can only say one thing : we in the DDR did not carry out any of the proposals made by Comrade Khrushchev with regard to agriculture, and I am therefore not in a position to discuss this matter.'[51] On another occasion, when reviewing the progress made since 1946, Ulbricht pointed out : 'We had no pattern on which we could model ourselves. The task was to carry out socialist transformation in a highly industrialized country the economic basis of which had been mutilated by partition...'[52] This is very different indeed from the earlier emphasis on the great Soviet example gratefully imitated. Another example of this new maturity is found in the field of culture, where East Germany's cultural administrators now pick and choose from among the latest products of Soviet arts—some would

[50] Gerhard Schmidt-Renner, *Wirtschaftsterritorium Deutsche* Demokratische *Republik,* Verlag Die Wirtschaft, (East) Berlin, 1962, p. 89.
[51] *Democratic German Report* (13 November 1964).
[52] *Neues Deutschland* (28 April 1965).

say, not always to the advantage of the East German people.[53]
East Germany has also, reported the West German newspaper *Welt
am Sonntag* (13 October 1968), broken with Soviet methods of
training in sport, with the result that the DDR did relatively better
than the Soviet Union (or West Germany) at the Mexico Games
in 1968. Finally, East Germany has shown a modicum of independence by taking a more 'advanced' line on sex education than the
Soviet Union. Apparently an East German manual on sex is much
sought after by the young ladies of Moscow who cannot find any
Soviet guide to the problem.[54] These examples may sound trivial.
But they would have been unthinkable deviations in Stalin's day.

Despite these changes in the relations between East Germany and
the USSR it would be quite wrong not to emphasize that there are
severe restrictions on the DDR's freedom of action. There are of
course the formal limits imposed by East Germany's military alliance
with the 'socialist camp'. There are the practical limitations imposed by the large Soviet troop concentrations in East Germany.
As important, in the long run, as the troops are the economic ties
between the USSR and the DDR. In 1964 almost half of East
Germany's imports, including the greater part of its raw material
imports, came from the Soviet Union. In the same year over half
its exports went to the Soviets.[55] The position since then has probably changed in favour of even more trade with the USSR. It is
also significant that certain important sectors of the East German
economy have been developed on the assumption of long-standing
exports to the Soviet Union.

What Sort of Future?

The German Democratic Republic still has great problems, not
least of which is to convince both world opinion and a good many
of its own citizens that it is a legitimate state which is here to stay.
But who can doubt that it is any less of a state than so many other
internationally recognized states—Guatemala, Panama, and South
Korea, or Czechoslovakia, Hungary, and Mongolia, for instance?
And who can doubt that short of a nuclear war it is likely to last?
It is a state which could rapidly become as viable politically as it
is becoming viable economically. Whether it can do this will
depend, to some extent, on who eventually replaces the vigorous
yet ageing Ulbricht, whose 75th birthday was celebrated with some
pomp in 1968. To a much larger extent it will depend on the

[53] *Survey* (October 1966); see Ilse Spittmann's contribution.
[54] *Morning Star* (28 November 1968).
[55] *SJB*, 1965, p. 390.

Soviet Union and the changes which take place there. Not least it will depend on developments in West Germany. In the DDR, as in the USSR, the products of the new cultural and technological revolution will demand, with much more verve and with much more right, the intellectual and personal freedom, now so very limited, which their colleagues in certain other advanced nations enjoy. For a time in the sixties, there were signs that the East German leaders had become dimly aware of the problem and had come to believe that, backed by a sound economy, with sufficient international prestige to create an East German patriotism, they could make a start by introducing the necessary reforms. Up to August 1968 there had been a harvest, though a small one. Whatever happens in East Germany as a result of the Czechoslovak crisis, there, as in the USSR, the new, rising élite of able, thoughtful, flexible, and technically competent young people are slowly replacing the old guard. They are a group largely unburdened by the mistakes and animosities of the past, an élite better able to carry on a dialogue between the rulers and the ruled. In such circumstances an effective dialogue between the two parts of Germany could also become possible. But it would have to be conducted on the West German side too by politicians unburdened by the past, who have put their own house in order, who recognize East Germany as an equal discussion partner and not just as something to be outmanoeuvred and annexed. Whether such a dialogue, which seems far away at the moment, could produce reunification is impossible to say. It could at least produce the normal relations which should exist between any two states which still have so much in common.

Index

Warsaw Pact, 17, 35, 43, 245–6, 248, 262–5, 270–4
Wehner, Herbert, 49, 51
Weimar, 117, 120, 148
Weimar republic, 17, 19, 21–2, 58–9, 68, 87, 105, 114–15, 163, 174–6, 193
Weissbach Gebr., 132
Weiz, Herbert, 74
Wernigerode, 147
Western Germany, *see* Federal Republic
Wigg, Col. George, 246
Wilson, Harold, 259
Wilson, William, 259
Wirtschaft, Die, 150, 153, 163, 171, 222–3
Wirzberger, Karl-Heinz, 206
Wismut A.-G., 56, 145
Wittkowski, Grete, 114, 132
Witzleben, Job von, 120
Wolf, Christa, 51, 77
Wolf, Friedrich, 77
Wolf, Konrad, 117
Wolffheim, 118
Wolgast, 149
Wollweber, Ernst, 40
Women's League, Democratic (DFD), 123

World Council of Churches, 110, 112
World Peace Council, 112, 123

Yemen, 248
Youth, 50, 65, 81, 90–1, 96, 111, 171, 173–99, 225, 256; *see also* Education; FDJ
Yugoslavia, 16, 28, 37–8, 42, 45, 64, 76–7, 131, 136–7, 150, 152, 154–5, 171–2, 223, 228, 248–51, 267

Zaisser, Wilhelm, 34, 37, 40, 229
Zehlendorf Conference, 23
Zeiss, Carl, 131, 138, 148, 259
Zeit, Die, 48, 89
Zentralausschuss, Zentralkomitee (ZK), (Central Committee, SPD and SED), 23–4, 28, 40–1, 47, 50–1, 53–5, 65, 73–4, 114, 125, 224–5, 264
Zentralsekretariat (SED), 25–6, 47–8, 50, 55–6
Ziller, Gerhart, 40
Zilliacus, Konni, 258
Zweig, Arnold, 57, 63, 74, 77, 114
Zwickau, 144, 147–8

UNIVERSITY OF WOLVERHAMPTON
LIBRARY

Printed in Great Britain by the Garden City Press Limited, Letchworth, Hertfordshire SG6 1JS